CW00541711

Two Regimes of Madness

SEMIOTEXT(E) FOREIGN AGENTS SERIES

The publication of this book was supported by the French Ministry of Foreign Affairs through the Cultural Services of the French Embassy, New York.

Published by Semiotext(e)
501 Philosophy Hall, Columbia University, New York, NY 10027
2571 W. Fifth Street, Los Angeles, CA 90057
www.semiotexte.com

Special thanks to Giancarlo Ambrosino, Jon Brilliant, Justin Cavin, Ben Hodges.

Cover Art by Channa Horwitz
"8 part Fugue" Ink on Mylar, 42" x 80", 1980.

Back Cover Photography: Sacha Goldman
Design by Hedi El Kholti

ISBN: 1-58435-032-6
Distributed by The MIT Press, Cambridge, Mass. and London, England
Printed in the United States of America

Two Regimes of Madness

Gilles Deleuze

Texts and Interviews 1975–1995

Edited by David Lapoujade

Translated by Ames Hodges and Mike Taormina

<e>

Table of Contents

1

Two Regimes of Madness

1. Guattari talked about a formalism of power. As agreed, I now interrupt him, but in order to say much the same thing. Our question is not the same old question that was still being asked only a few years ago. Today, we're not asking what the nature of power is, but rather, along with Foucault, how power exerts itself, where it takes shape, and why it is everywhere.

Let's begin with an example: the puppeteer. He has a certain power, to work the puppets, but also the power he exerts over the children. Kleist wrote an admirable text on the subject.[1] One could say that there are three lines. The puppeteer does not operate according to movements that already represent the figures to be achieved. He makes his puppet move according to a vertical line, wherein the puppet's center of gravity, or rather, center of levity, is displaced. It is a perfectly *abstract* line, not in the least *figurative*, and no more symbolic than figurative. The line is mutant because it is made up of as many *singularities* as stopping points, and yet these do not break up the line. There is never any binary relationship or bi-univocal relations between this vertical, abstract line—which is for this reason all the more real—and the concrete movements of the puppet.

In the second place, there are movements of an entirely different kind: tangible, representative curves, an arm that rounds itself out, a head that tilts. This line is no longer made up of singularities but rather of very supple segments—one gesture, then another gesture. Finally, there is a third line, one of a much harder segmentarity which corresponds to the moments of the story represented by the play of the puppets. The binary relationships and bi-univocal relations that the Structuralists tell us about might form in and between segmentarizable lines. But the power of the puppeteer himself arises more at the point of conversion between the abstract, non-figurative line, on the one hand, and the two lines of segmentarity, on the other.

Or take the example of a banker, banking-power in capitalism, it's almost the same thing. It is well known that there are two forms of money, but they are sometimes improperly identified. There is money as financing structure, or even as monetary creation and destruction: a non-realizable quantity, an abstract or mutant line with its singularities. And then a second, completely different line, concrete, made of tangible curves: money as means of payment, capable of being segmented, allocated for salaries, profit, interest, etc. And this money as means of payment will carry in turn a third segmentarized line: all goods produced as a whole in a given period, all the equipment, and all the consumption (the work of Bernard Schmitt, Suzanne de Brunhoff,[2] etc.). Banking-power occurs at the level of conversion between the abstract line, the financing structure, and the concrete lines, means of payment-goods produced. The conversion occurs on the level of central banks, the gold standard, the current role of the dollar, etc.

Another example. Clausewitz speaks of a flow which he calls "absolute war," which would never have existed in a pure state, but which would nonetheless have crossed through history, irresolvable, singular, mutant, abstract.[3] Perhaps this war flow has, in fact, existed as the unique invention of nomads, a war machine independent of states. In fact, it's striking that the great states, the great despotic apparatuses don't seem to have based their power on a war machine, but rather on bureaucracy and the police. The war machine is always something that comes from the outside and is of nomadic origin: a great abstract line of mutations. But, for reasons easily understood, states will have to appropriate this machine for themselves. They will put together armies, conduct wars, wars serving their politics. War ceases to be absolute (abstract line), in order to become something that is no more amusing: limited war, total war, etc., (second line, this time segmentarizable). And these wars take this or that form depending on the political necessities and the nature of the States that conduct them, that impose their ends and their limits upon them (third segmentarized line). Again, what is called the power of war resides in the conversion of these lines.

Many more examples could be given. The three lines have neither the same pace, nor the same speeds, neither the same territories, nor the same *deterritorializations*. One of the principle goals of schizoanalysis would be to look in each one of us for the crossing lines that are those of desire itself: non-figurative abstract lines of escape, that is, deterritorialization; lines of segmentarities, whether supple or hard, in which one gets entangled, or which one evades, moving beneath the horizon of one's abstract line; and how conversions happen from one line to the others.

2. Guattari is in the process of plotting a chart of semiotic regimes; I would like to give an example, one that could just as easily be called pathological as historical. An important case of two regimes of signs was present in the psychiatry of the latter part of the 19th century, but this case also extends well beyond psychiatry to concern all of semiotics. One can conceive of a first regime of signs that functions in a very complex way, but in a way nonetheless easily understood: one sign defers to other signs, and these other signs to still other signs, to

infinity (irradiation, an ever extending circularity). Someone goes out to the street, he notices that his concierge is glaring at him, he slips, a small child sticks its tongue out at him, etc. In the end, it's the same thing to say that each sign is doubly articulated, i.e. that a sign always refers to another sign, indefinitely, and that the supposedly infinite ensemble of signs itself refers to a greater signifier. Such is the *paranoid* regime of the sign, but one could just as well call it despotic or imperial.

And then there is a completely different regime. This time, a sign, or a small group, a little bundle of signs, begins to flow, to follow a certain line. We no longer have a vast circular formation in perpetual extension, but rather a linear network. Instead of signs that defer themselves to one another, there is a sign that defers to a subject: the delirium comes about in a localized fashion, it is more a delirium of action than of idea, one line must be maneuvered to the end before another line can be initiated (quibbling delirium, what the Germans called "quarrelsome delirium"). It is in this way that a psychiatrist like Clérambault distinguished between two large groups of delirium: paranoid and passional.[4]

It could be that one of the major reasons for the crisis in psychiatry had been this meshing between completely different signs in this regime. The man of paranoid delirium, one can always lock him up, he presents all the signs of madness, but otherwise he is not mad at all, his reasoning is impeccable. The man of passional desire shows no signs of madness, except on certain points that are difficult to discern, and nonetheless he is mad, his madness manifests itself in a rash acting out (for example, the assassin). Here again, Foucault has defined profoundly both the difference and the complimentarity of the two cases. I mention them in order to give an idea of the plurality of semiotics, that is to say, of the clusters whose signs have neither the same regime nor the same function.

3. It matters little whether a regime of signs receives a clinical or historical name. Not that it's the same thing, but regimes of signs cross over very different "stratifications." Just now, I was talking in clinical terms about the paranoid regime and the passional regime. Now let's talk about social formations. I wouldn't say that emperors are paranoiacs, nor the reverse. But in the great imperial formations, whether archaic or even ancient, there is the great signifier, the signifier of the despot; and beneath it the infinite network of signs that refer themselves to one another. But you also need all sorts of categories of specialized people whose job it is to circulate these signs, to say what they mean, to interpret them, to thereby freeze the signifier: priests, bureaucrats, messengers, etc. It is the coupling of meaning and interpretation. And then there is still something else: there still must be subjects who receive the message, who listen to the interpretation and obey, carrying out the tedious assignments—as Kafka says in "The Great Wall of China," or "The Emperor's Message."[5] And each time, one could say that having reached its limit, the signified generates more meaning, allowing the circle to grow.

Any social formation always appears to work well. There is no reason for it not to work well, for it not to function. Nonetheless, there is always one side through which it escapes, undoes itself. One never knows if the messenger will arrive. And the closer one gets to the periphery of the system, the more subjects find themselves caught in a kind of temptation: whether to submit oneself to signifiers, to obey the orders of the bureaucrat and follow the interpretation of the high priest—or rather to be carried off elsewhere, the beyond, on a crazy vector, a tangent of deterritorialization—to follow a line of escape, to set off as a nomad, to emit what Guattari just called a-signifying particles. Take a belated example like that of the Roman Empire: the Germans are quite taken by the two-fold temptation to penetrate and integrate themselves into the empire—but at the same time pressured by the Huns to form a nomadic line of escape, a war machine of a new variety, marginal and non-assimilable.

Let's take an entirely different regime of signs, namely capitalism. Capitalism, too, appears to function very well, there is no reason for it not to. Furthermore, it belongs to what we just referred to as passional delirium. Contrary to what happens in paranoid imperialist formations, bundles of signs, both large and small, set off along lines on which all sorts of things appear: the movement of money-capital; the erection of subjects as agents of capital and of work; unequal distribution of goods and means of payment to these agents. One tells the subject that the more he obeys, the more he commands, since he obeys only himself. Perpetually one falls back from the commanding subject onto the obeying subject in the name of the law of capital. And without a doubt this sign system is very different from the imperialist system: its advantage is that it fills in the gaps, while carrying the peripheral subject toward the center and freezing nomadism in its tracks. For example, in the history of philosophy, we are all too familiar with the famous revolution that moved discourse from the imperial stage, where the sign perpetually referred to the sign, on to the stage of subjectivity as a properly passional delirium that always threw subject back onto subject. And yet even there, the better it works, the more it leaks on all sides. Money-capital's lines of subjectivization never cease emitting junctions, oblique lines, transversals, marginal subjectivities, lines of deterritorialization that threaten their planes. An internal nomadism, a new type of deterritorialized flow, a-signifying particles that come to compromise any given detail, and the whole configuration. The Watergate affair, global inflation.

2

Schizophrenia and Society

The Two Poles of Schizophrenia

Organ-Machines

This theme, i.e. the machine, does not mean that the schizophrenic lives like a machine in a global way. He or she lives traversed by machines. The schizophrenic lives in machines, alongside machines, or the machines are in him, in her. The schizophrenic's organs are not provisional machines but function only as machine parts, random components connected up with other external components (a tree, a star, a light-bulb, a motor). Once the organs have been connected to a power source, once they have been plugged into flows, the organs then comprise larger, complex machines. It has nothing to do with the idea of mechanism. *This* machinery is totally disparate. The schizophrenic reveals the unconscious for what it truly is: a factory. This is the picture Bruno Bettelheim gives us of little Joey, the machine-child who lives, eats, defecates, breathes and sleeps only when he is plugged into motors, carburetors, steering wheels, lamps, and electric circuits, whether they are real, contrived or imaginary: "He had to establish these imaginary electric connections before being able to eat, because it was the current that made his digestive tract work. This ritual was performed with such dexterity, that we had to check more than once to verify there were no wires or outlets."[1] A journey or just a walk in the park forms a circuit for the schizophrenic, who ceaselessly flows, fleeing along machinic lines. Even the schizophrenic's utterances seem not to be the combinations of signs, but the product of machine assemblages. *Connect-I-Cut!* cries little Joey. Here is how Louis Wolfson explains the language machine which he invented: a finger in one ear, a head-phone in the other, a foreign book in one hand, growling in his throat, etc. He invented it to flee his mother tongue, to put it to flight, to make it flow and spring a leak, to be able to translate each sentence into a mixture of sounds and words resembling him, but which were at the same time borrowed from foreign languages.

The peculiar character of schizophrenic machines derives from their putting elements in play that are totally disparate and foreign to one another. Schizophrenic machines are aggregates. And yet they work. But their function is to put something or someone to flight, to make a flow, to spring a leak. We cannot even say that the schizophrenic machine is comprised of the parts and elements of various pre-existing machines. Essentially, the schizophrenic is a functional machine making use of left-over elements that no longer function in any context, and that will enter into relation with each other *precisely by having no relation*—as if the concrete distinction, the disparity of the different parts became a reason in itself to group them together and put them to work, according to what chemists call a non-localizable relation. Psychoanalyst Serge Leclaire says the ultimate elements of the unconscious have not been reached as long as pure singularities have not been observed; they are fused or stuck together "precisely by an absence of connection," they are disparate and irreducible elements connected only by a non-localizable relation, such as "the very force of desire."[2] This suggests the need to rethink the fundamental assumptions of psychoanalysis regarding the association of ideas, including both relations and structures. The schizophrenic unconscious is an unconscious of left-over elements that comprise a machine simply by being irreducible and truly distinct. For instance, the sequences of Beckett's characters: pebble-pocket-mouth; a shoe-a pipe stem-a small indeterminate pouch-a bicycle bell lid-a half crutch. An infernal machine preparing for action. As in a W.C. Fields film, the hero prepares a dish whose recipe is an exercise program: a short-circuit between two machines, establishing a non-localizable relation of elements that will animate an explosive machine, a generalized flow, a properly schizophrenic non-sense.

The Organless Body

In the necessary description of schizophrenia, there is another theme besides the organ-machine, with its flows, vibrations, and breakdowns. There is the theme of the organless body, a body deprived of organs: eyes shut, nostrils plugged, anus blocked, stomach rotten, throat ripped out, "no mouth, no tongue, no teeth, no throat, no esophagus, no stomach, no intestines, no anus."[3] A body swollen like a giant molecule or an undifferentiated egg. This catatonic stupor has often been described. The machines grind to a halt, and the schizophrenic is frozen in rigid poses that can last for days or years. And what characterizes catatonic states and outbreaks of delirium is not simply their periodic alternation. Rather, at every moment, a struggle seems to be taking place between two poles: 1) the exacerbated workings of the machines, and 2) the catatonic stasis of the organless body. All the phases of this struggle are translated in the type of anxiety which is specific to the schizophrenic. There is always some stimulus or impulse stealing into the heart of the catatonic stupor; and vice versa, stupor and rigid stasis are forever creeping over the swarming machines, as though the organless body were perpetually shutting down machinic connections, and organ-machines were ceaselessly erupting on the organless body.

The organs themselves, however, are not the real enemy of the organless body. Organism is the enemy, in other words, any organization which imposes on the organs a regime of totalization, collaboration, synergy, integration, inhibition and disjunction. Only in this sense are the organs indeed the enemy of the organless body, which exerts a repulsive action on them and treats them like instruments of persecution. On the other hand, the organless body attracts the organs, appropriates them for itself, and makes them function in a regime other than the one imposed by the organism, in such a way that each organ is the whole body—all the more so, given that the organ functions for itself and includes the functions of all the others. The organs are thus "miraculously" born on the organless body, obeying a machinic regime that should not be confused either with organic mechanism or with the organization of the organism. For example, the mouth-anus-lung of the anorexic. Or certain drug-induced schizoid states, as William Burroughs describes them in relation to the organless body: "The human organism, what a scandal, it's so inefficient. Rather than a mouth and an anus, both constantly in danger of infection, why don't we have a single orifice for nourishment and defecation? We could plug our mouth and nose, fill in the stomach, and pierce an air-hole directly into the lungs—which should have been done from the beginning."[4] Artaud himself describes the ferocious struggle of the organless body against the organism, and against God, master of organisms and organization. President Schreber describes the alternating attraction and repulsion that ensues according to whether the organless body repudiates the organization of the organs or, on the contrary, appropriates the organs in a non-organic regime.

An Intensive Relation

One can say that the two poles of schizophrenia (the catatonic state of the organless body, and the non-organic functioning of the organ-machines) are never isolated from one another. Together they produce forms where sometimes repulsion has the upper hand (the paranoid form), and sometimes attraction (the miraculous or fantastic form of schizophrenia). If we think of the organless body as a solid egg, it follows that, *beneath* the organization that it will assume, that will develop, the egg does not present itself as an undifferentiated milieu: it is traversed by axes and gradients, by poles and potentials, by thresholds and zones destined later to produce one or another organic part. For the time being, however, the egg's organization is intensive. It's as if a flow of variable intensity permeated the egg. It is in this sense that the organless body ignores and repudiates the organism, in other words, the organization of *extended* organs, and instead forms a matrix of intensity that appropriates the *intensive* organs. It seems that the various proportions of attraction and repulsion on the body without schizophrenic organs produces various intensive states through which the schizophrenic passes. The schizophrenic journey can be stationary; but even in motion, it happens on the organless body—it is an intensive journey. The organless body is at zero-degrees intensity, but is enveloped by the production of intensive quantities. From zero, these intensities are effectively produced as that which will fill up space to this or that degree. Thus the organ-machines are like the direct powers of the organless body. The organless body is the pure intensive matter, or the stationary motor, whose organ-machines will constitute the working parts and the appropriate powers. And this is confirmed by schizophrenic delirium: beneath the sensory hallucinations, beneath even the delirium of thought, there is something more profound, a feeling of intensity, i.e. a becoming or a passage. A gradient is crossed, a threshold traversed, forward or backward. A migration is under way: *I feel* that I am becoming a woman, *I feel* that I am becoming god, that I am becoming clairvoyant, that I am becoming pure matter... Schizophrenic delirium can be grasped only at the level of this 'I feel' which every moment records the intensive relationship between the organless body and the machine-organs.

This is why pharmacology in the most general sense promises to be so extremely important for practical and theoretical research on schizophrenia. The study of the metabolism of schizophrenics opens up a vast field of research in which molecular biology has a crucial role to play. A chemistry at once intensive and experiential seems able to go beyond the traditional organic/psychic duality, at least in two directions: 1) the experimental schizoid states induced through mescaline, bulbocapnine, LSD, etc.; 2) the therapeutic initiative to calm the anxiety of schizophrenics, while dismantling their catatonic shell in order to jump-start the schizophrenic machines and get them running again (the use of "major tranquilizers" or even LSD).

Schizophrenia as a Process

Psychoanalysis and the 'Schizogenetic' Family

The problem is twofold: at once the indeterminate extension of schizophrenia, and the nature of the symptoms that constitute schizophrenia as a whole. The very nature of the symptoms makes them difficult to systematize, to combine in a coherent and readily localizable entity. They come apart at the seams. Schizophrenia is a syndrome in disarray at every point, ceaselessly retreating from itself. Emil Kraepelin formulated his concept of dementia praecox using two main poles: 1) hebephrenia as a post-pubescent psychosis exhibiting phenomena of disaggregation, and 2) catatonia as a form of stupor with problems in muscular activity. In 1911, Eugene Bleuler coined the term *schizophrenia*, which stresses a fragmentation or functional dislocation of associations. The primary disturbance is the absence of any relation among them. But these fragmented associations are also the flip-side of a dissociation of the person, a schism with reality, a certain priority or autonomy granted to an inner life that is rigid and closed-in on itself (the "autism" which Bleuler increasingly stresses: "I would almost say that the original disturbance applies primarily to the life of the instincts.") It appears that psychiatry, in its present state, has had little success in its efforts to determine a comprehensive unity for schizophrenia in terms of causes or symptoms, having sought it instead in the disturbed personality as a whole, which each symptom expresses in its own way. More promising are the efforts of Eugene Minkowski and especially Ludvig Binswanger, who have sought this unity in the psychotic forms of "being-in-the-world," its spatialization and temporalization ("leaps," "eddies," "shrinkage," "stagnation"). Nor should we neglect to mention Gisela Pankow, who locates it in the image of the body, using a practical method of spatial and temporal restructuring to exorcise the schizophrenic phenomena of dissociation and render them accessible to psychoanalysis ("to repair the zones of destruction in the image of the body and gain access to the familial structure").[5]

However, the real difficulty is to give an account of schizophrenia as something with positive traits, and as such, not to reduce it to the lacunal or destructive traits it engenders in a person. These negative traits include the deficits and dissociations which schizophrenia causes to appear in a hypothetical structure. It cannot be said that psychoanalysis offers us a way out of this essentially negative perspective because psychoanalysis has an ambiguous relationship to schizophrenia. On the one hand, psychoanalysis realizes that its clinical material derives from psychosis (this is the case for Freud in Zurich, and it is also the case for Melanie Klein and Jacques Lacan: paranoia attracts psychoanalysis more than schizophrenia). On the other hand, because the method of psychoanalysis has been tailored to the phenomena of neurosis, it has experienced serious difficulty in discovering a satisfactory gateway to psychosis (if only because of the dislocation of associations). Freud proposed a simple distinction between neurosis and psychosis: in neurosis, the reality principle is safeguarded in exchange for a repression of the "complex," whereas in psychosis, the complex shows up in consciousness in exchange for a destruction of reality caused by the libido turning away from the external world. Lacan's research posits a distinction between neurotic repression, involving the "signified," and psychotic foreclosure, which operates in the symbolic order at the very level of the "signifier," a kind of hole in the structure, an empty place, which causes whatever is foreclosed in the symbolic to reappear as hallucination in the real. The schizophrenic now appears as someone who cannot *recognize* or *place* his or her own desire. The negative perspective is reinforced to the extent that psychoanalysis asks: What is missing from the schizophrenic that would allow the psychoanalytic mechanism to "take hold" of him or her?

Could it be that whatever the schizophrenic lacks is something in Oedipus? Could it be a disfigurement, from the earliest age, of the maternal role in combination with an annihilation of the father, both of which would explain the existence of a lacuna in the Oedipal structure? Following Lacan, Maud Mannoni points to "an initial foreclosure of the signifier of the father," such that "the Oedipal characters are in place but, in the play of permutations that results, there is something like an empty place. This place remains enigmatic and is open to the anxiety which desire elicits."[6] However, it is not at all certain that a structure which is undeniably familial is a good unit of measure for schizophrenia, even if the structure is extended over three generations by including the grandparents. The effort to study "schizogenetic" families, or schizogenetic mechanisms in the family, is a common trait shared by traditional psychiatry, psychology, psychoanalysis, and even anti-psychiatry. What is so disappointing in these efforts is that the commonly cited mechanisms (for example, Gregory Bateson's double bind or the simultaneous emission of two orders of messages, the one contradicting the other: "Do this, but don't do it...") are in fact a banal part of the daily existence of every family, giving us no insight into the schizophrenic's mode of production. Even if we raise the familial coordinates to a properly symbolic power by making the father a metaphor, or by making the name-of-the-father a signifier coextensive with language, we still do not escape a narrowly familial discourse, in which the schizophrenic is negatively defined by the hypothetical foreclosure of the signifier.

Breaking Through to "More Reality"

It is strange how schizophrenics keep being brought back to problems that are not their own, as is abundantly clear: father, mother, law, signifier, etc. The schizophrenic is elsewhere, and there is no reason to conclude that the schizophrenic lacks something that does not concern him or her. Beckett and Artaud have said all there is to say about it. We must get used to the idea that certain artists or writers have had greater insight into schizophrenia than psychiatrists or psychoanalysts. We make the same mistake when we define schizophrenia in negative terms or in terms of a lack (dissociation, loss of reality, autism, foreclosure) and when we model schizophrenia on a familial structure in which this lack can be located. In fact, the phenomenon of delirium does not reproduce, even in an imaginary way, a family story organized around a lack. On the contrary, delirium is an overflowing of history; it is universal history set adrift. Races, civilizations, cultures, continents, kingdoms, powers, wars, classes, and revolutions are all mixed together. To be delirious in this sense requires no advanced learning. In delirium you always find a Black, a Jew, a Chinese, a Great Mongol, an Aryan. Delirium is composed of politics and economics. And there is no reason to believe that what delirium expresses is merely its manifest content. What delirium expresses is the way in which desire invests a whole social field that is historical, and the way in which unconscious desire embraces its irreducible objects. Even when delirium traffics in familial themes, the holes, cuts, and flows that traverse the family and constitute it as schizogenetic are extra-familial in nature, causing the whole social field in its unconscious determinations to be brought in. As Marcel Jaeger has put it so well: "Despite what the gurus of psychiatry think, the things that mental patients say do not merely express the opacity of their individual psychic disorders. The discourse of madness, in all its articulations, joins up with another discourse, the discourse of history—political, social, and religious—which speaks in each of them."[7] Delirium is not constructed around the name-of-the-father, but on the names of history: proper names. It's as if the zones, the thresholds or the gradients of intensity which the schizophrenic traverses on the organless body (I feel that I am becoming...) are designated by the proper names of races, continents, classes, persons. Not that the schizophrenic identifies with persons. Rather, the schizophrenic identifies domains and zones located on the organless body by these proper names.

Hence schizophrenia needs to be described in positive terms. "Dissociation," "autism," and "loss of reality" are convenient terms for those who wish to silence schizophrenics. "Dissociation" is a poor word to designate the state of those elements which make up these special, schizophrenic machines which can be positively determined—in this respect, we quickly recognized the machinic role played by the absence of connection. "Autism" is also a rather poor word to designate the organless body and all that flows over it; this has nothing to do with an inner life cut off from reality. And "loss of reality"—how can we say this about someone who lives in an almost unbearable proximity with the real ("this emotion, which communicates to the mind the shattering sound of matter," writes Artaud in *The Nerve Meter*)? Rather than conceptualizing schizophrenia in terms of the havoc which it wreaks in a person, or in terms of the holes and lacunae which it reveals in a structure, we must grasp schizophrenia as a *process*. When Kraepelin was trying to forge his concept of dementia praecox, he did not define it by its causes or symptoms, but as a process, i.e. an evolution and a terminal state. Unfortunately, this terminal state was conceived as a total and definitive disaggregation, which justified locking up the patient for the rest of his or her natural life. Today Karl Jaspers and Ronald D. Laing understand this rich notion of process in a totally different way: a rupture, an eruption, a break-through which smashes the continuity of a personality and takes it on a kind of trip through "more reality," at once intense and terrifying, following lines of flight that engulf nature and history, organism and spirit. This is how the schizophrenic organ-machines, the organless body, and the flows of intensity on the body interact, bringing about a connection of machines and a setting adrift of history.

Now we see the difference between paranoia and schizophrenia (even those forms of schizophrenia labeled paranoid): the "I-will-not-leave-you-alone" of the paranoid, and the "leave-me-alone" of the schizophrenic; the paranoid combination of signs, and the machinic assemblages of schizophrenia; the massive wholes of paranoia, and the tiny multiplicities of schizophrenia; paranoia's vast territories of reactive integration, and schizophrenia's active lines of flight. If schizophrenia seems like the sickness of today's society, we should not look to generalizations about our way of life, but to very precise mechanisms of a social, political, and economic nature. Our societies no longer function on the basis of codes and territories. Quite the opposite. They function on the basis of a widespread decoding and deterritorialization. Unlike the paranoid whose delirium consists of restoring codes and reinventing territories, the schizophrenic never ceases to go one more step in a movement of self-decoding and self-deterritorialization (this is the schizophrenic break-through, the voyage or trip, the process). The schizophrenic is like the limit of our society, but an abhorred limit, always suppressed, always cast out. Laing grasped the real problem of schizophrenia: What can we do so the break-through does not become a break-down? How can we prevent the organless body from shutting down in a catatonic stupor? How can the acute state of delirium overcome its attendant anxiety, and yet not give way to a chronic state of exhaustion which, as we too often see in the hospital, ends in a state of total break-down? In this respect, the conditions that prevail in the hospital, as well as those that prevail in the family, are less than satisfactory. It would seem that hospitalization, and familialization, too often produce the major symptoms of autism and the loss of reality. How can the power of a lived chemistry be combined with a schizological analysis in such a way that the schizophrenic process does not turn into its opposite, i.e. the production of a schizophrenic ready to be locked-up? And in what type of group, what kind of collectivity?

3

Proust Round Table

Roland Barthes: Since I am to speak first, I will only point out that, for me, any colloquium on Proust has something paradoxical about it: Proust can only be the subject of an infinite colloquium—infinite because more than any other author, he is the one about whom there is an infinite amount to say. He is not an eternal author but, I think, a perpetual one, the way a calendar can be perpetual. And I do not believe this comes from the richness of Proust, which may be an overly qualitative notion, but rather from a certain destructuration of his discourse. It is not only *digressed* discourse, as we have said, but it is discourse perforated and deconstructed. It is like a galaxy open to infinite exploration because the particles move about and change places. This means that Proust is one of the very few authors I reread. I read his work like an illusory landscape lit by a succession of lights governed by a sort of variable rheostat that makes the décor pass gradually, and tirelessly, through different volumes, different levels of perception, and different levels of comprehension. The material is inexhaustible, not because it is always new, which does not mean much, but because it is always displaced when it returns. In this sense, the work is a true "mobile," and may in fact be the incarnation of Mallarmé's long-sought Book. In my opinion, *In Search of Lost Time* (and all the other texts that accompany it) can only elicit ideas of research and not research itself. Therefore, Proust's text is excellent material for critical desire. It is a true object of desire for criticism, since everything is spent in the fantasy of research, in the idea of searching for something in Proust, thereby making the idea of an end for that research seem illusory. Proust is unique to the extent that all he leaves us to do is *rewrite him*, which is the exact contrary of exhausting him.

Gilles Deleuze: For my part, I would simply like to pose a problem in Proust that has occurred to me relatively recently. I have the impression that there is in this book a very important, very troubling presence of madness. This does not mean that Proust was mad, of course, but that in the *Search* itself there is a very vivid, very widespread presence of madness. Starting with two key characters. The presence of madness, as always in Proust, is very skillfully distributed. It is obvious from the start that Charlus is mad. As soon as you meet Charlus, you say: "Hey, he's mad." And the narrator tells us it is so. For Albertine, the reverse happens; it takes place at the end. It is not an immediate conviction; it is a doubt, a possibility. Maybe she was mad, maybe she had always been mad. This is what Andrée suggests at the end. So who is mad? Charlus, certainly. Albertine, maybe. But isn't there someone even more deranged? Someone hidden everywhere and who controls the certainty that Charlus is mad and the possibility Albertine might be too? Isn't there a ringleader? Everyone knows who this ringleader is: the narrator. How is the narrator mad? He is a very bizarre narrator. Totally bizarre. How is he presented? He has no organs, he can't see, he does not understand anything, he does not observe anything, he knows nothing; when something is shown to him, he looks but does not see it; when someone makes him feel something, they say: but look how beautiful this is, he looks and then when someone says: here, take a look—something echoes in his head, he thinks of something else, something that interests him, something that is not on the level of perception, not on the level of intellection. He has no organs, no sensations, no perceptions: he has nothing. He is like a naked body, a vast undifferentiated body. Someone who doesn't see, feel or understand anything. What sort of activity could he have? I think that someone who is in that state can only respond to signs, to signals. In other words, the narrator is a spider. A spider is good for nothing. It doesn't understand anything; you can put a fly in front of it and it won't budge. But as soon as the slightest edge of its web starts vibrating, it moves its heavy body. It has no perceptions, no sensations. It responds to signals, nothing else. Just like the narrator. He also spins a web—his work—and responds to its vibrations while spinning it. A spider-madness, narrator-madness that understands nothing, doesn't want to understand anything, isn't interested in anything except the little sign back in the background. Both the certain madness of Charlus and the possible madness of Albertine emanate from him. He projects his opaque, blind presence throughout the four corners of the web that he is constantly making, undoing, redoing. It is an even greater metamorphosis than in Kafka, since the narrator has already undergone a transformation before the story begins.

What do you see when you don't see anything? What is striking for me in the *Search* is that it is always the same thing, but also extraordinarily diverse. If we tried to transcribe the narrator's vision the way biologists transcribe the vision of a fly, it would be a nebula with little bright points here and there. For example: the Charlus nebula. What does the narrator see, this narrator who is not Proust, of course? He sees two eyes, two blinking, asymmetrical eyes and he vaguely hears a voice. Two singularities in the round-bellied nebula known as Charlus. In the case of Albertine, it is not an individual nebula, but a collective one—a distinction that is of no importance at all. It is the nebula of "young girls" with singularities, one of which is Albertine. It always happens the same way in Proust. The first, global vision is a kind of cloud with small points. There is a second moment that is no more reassuring. Depending on the singularities contained by the nebula, a kind of series is formed: for example Charlus's speeches, three long speeches built according to the same type, and whose rhythms are so similar that in each of the three cases, Charlus begins with an operation that would be called denial today: "No, you do not interest me," he tells the narrator. The second moment is opposition: there is so much difference between you and me that it cannot be overcome, and you are less than nothing compared to me. The third moment is madness: Charlus's speech, which until then is completely controlled, starts to go off-track. A surprising phenomenon that takes place in each of the three speeches. In the same way, you would have to show how there is an Albertine series and in fact multiple Albertine series that emerge from the nebula of young girls. These series are marked by eruptions of sadomasochism; they are abominable series, punctuated by profanation and sequestration; they are vast, cruel series born of myopic vision. And it does not stop there. There is a moment when, at the end of these series and like an ultimate third phase, everything dissolves, everything scatters, everything bursts apart—and ends—in a cluster of small boxes. There is no more Albertine. There are a hundred little Albertine boxes, spread out, no longer able to communicate with each other, aligned in a very curious dimension that is a transversal dimension. And I think it is there, in this final moment, that the theme of madness truly appears. It appears with a kind of vegetal innocence, in a plant-like compartmentalization. The most typical text in this regard, the one that best displays the triple organization of the vision of the spider-narrator is his first kiss with Albertine. One can easily distinguish the three essential moments (although you could find many others). First, the nebula of the face with a bright, moving dot. Then the narrator comes closer: "In the short path from my lips to her cheek, I saw ten Albertines." Lastly, the great final moment comes when his mouth reaches the cheek and he is nothing more than a blind body grappling with Albertine's breaking up, her dispersion: "[...] suddenly, my eyes stopped seeing, then my nose, crushed, no longer perceived any odors, and without knowing for all that more about the taste of the desired rose, I learned, from these detestable signs, that I was finally kissing Albertine's cheek."

This is what interests me now in the *Search*: the presence, the immanence of madness in a work that is not a dress, not a cathedral, but a spider web woven before our eyes.

Gérard Genette: What I will say is inspired both by the work of this colloquium and by a retrospective glance on my own work on Proust, past and present. It seems to me that Proust's work, given its scope and complexity, and also given its evolving character, with the uninterrupted succession of diverse *states* of a single text, from *Pleasures and Days* to *Time Regained*, presents criticism with a difficulty that is also, in my eyes, an opportunity: to impose the passage from classical hermeneutics, which was paradigmatic (or metaphorical), to a new hermeneutics that would be syntagmatic, or metonymical, if you prefer. I mean that it is no longer sufficient, where Proust is concerned, to note the recurrence of motifs and to establish on the basis of these repetitions, once they have been collected and verified, certain thematic objects whose ideal network we could then establish using the method which Charles Mauron has made famous, and which is the basis of all thematic criticism. The effects of distance and proximity, of the *place* in the text, between the various elements of the content must also be taken into account.

Of course these elements of disposition have always attracted the attention of analysts of narrative or stylistic technique. Jean Rousset, for example, told us of the *sporadic* aspect of the presentation of character in the *Search* and Leo Bersani spoke of what he called the "centrifugal force" or "horizontal transcendence" of style in the *Search* that distinguishes it from the style of *Jean Santeuil.* But what is pertinent to formal analysis is equally pertinent, I believe, indeed paramount, to the thematic analysis and interpretation of Proust. Let me cite only two or three examples which I have dealt with elsewhere. It should not be overlooked that from the first pages of *Combray*, the themes of alcohol and sexuality appear together, which supports (at least) their later relations of metaphorical equivalency. Conversely, I find the effects of displacement or delay significant when applied to the love between Marcel and his mysterious little cousin. It takes place in *Combray* but is only mentioned retrospectively much later, when Aunt Léonie's sofa is sold to Rachel's bordello. Or again, a thematic object like the Roussainville keep: it appears (twice) in Combray as witness and confidant of the protagonist's solitary erotic exultation, and then returns in *Time Regained* with a new erotic signification that resonates with the first meaning and modifies it after the fact, when we learn that the keep was the scene of Gilberte's orgies with the children of the village. There is an effect of variation here, a difference in identity that is as important as identity itself. It is not enough for interpretation to superimpose the two occurrences; that which resists superimposition must also be interpreted—especially since we all know that the *Search* was more often than not created by the dispersion and dissociation of syncretic initial cells: it is an expanding universe where the elements that were close at the beginning are constantly moving apart. We know, for example, that Marcel and Swann, Charlus and Norpois were initially joined; we know that the so-called "Preface to *Against Saint-Beuve*" juxtaposed the experiences of the madeleine and the Guermantes cobblestone. In a draft published by Philippe Kolb, we see that the disillusioning revelation concerning the sources of the Vivonne was primitively acquired in childhood and that all of the thematic architecture of the *Search* relies on the prodigious distance between the feet of these arches, on the enormous wait for the final revelation.

All of this demands that we pay close attention to the chrono-topological disposition of thematic signifiers and therefore to the semiotic power of the *context.* Roland Barthes insisted several times on the anti-symbolic role of the context, which is always treated like an instrument to reduce meaning. It seems to me that the opposite practice could be imagined using observations of this type. The context, in other words, the *space of the text* and the *effects of place* it determines, also generate sense. I think it was Hugo who said: "In *concierge*, there is *cierge* [candle]." Just as subtly, I would say: in context there is text and one cannot eliminate the first without taking the second into account, which is problematic in literature. It would therefore be better to return context to its symbolic reach by turning to a hermeneutics, or semiotics, that is less founded on paradigmatic invariance than on syntagmatic and therefore textual variations. Consequently, as we have known at least since Saussure, it is not repetition but difference, modulation, alteration, what Doubrovsky called the *false note* yesterday—in a word, variation, even in its most elementary form. It would be pleasant to think that the role of the critic, like the musician, is to *interpret variations.*

Serge Doubrovsky: I think the three interventions we have just heard and that at first glance have nothing in common are caught in the same spider's web, precisely the one described by Deleuze. And wasn't that in fact typical of Proust, both this fragmentation, this total isolation and then, in the end, this communication, this reunion?

Roland Barthes: I would simply like to say to Genette that if, in analyzing variations, one seeks a theme, one is entirely within a hermeneutic, for then one is following a vertical climb to a central object. However, and here I think Genette is right, if one postulates a description or simply a writing of variation, a variation of variations, then it is no longer a hermeneutic, it is simply a semiology. At least that is how I would define the word "semiology" taking up an opposition Foucault posed between "hermeneutics" and "semiology."

Jean-Pierre Richard: I would like to add a few words to what Gérard Genette said earlier. I certainly agree with the conception he developed of the *theme* as the sum or series of its modulations. I also think it is a good idea to undertake a contextual thematics. But I would like to mark a slight difference in the definition which has been provided or suggested. It seems to me, for example, that the Roussainville keep, at least in Genette's analysis, cannot truly appear as a theme...

Gérard Genette: I called it a "thematic object."

Jean-Pierre Richard: … I would see it more as a *motif*, in other words, an object Proust very consciously uses repeatedly in the text to create certain effects, important effects, and I agree with Genette, that these are effects of delayed or displaced meaning.

But what I see as properly *thematic* in the Roussainville keep is something else: the possibility it offers us to open it, almost to break it apart, to perform in any case a mobilization and something like a disseminating liberation of its various constitutive traits (qualities or functions), to dissociate it, in fact to connect it with other objects that are present and active in the expanse of Proustian fiction. Among these definitive traits—I mean that define the object, but without *finishing* it of course, without closing it, rather opening it on all sides to its outside—among these specific traits, there would be *redness* (suggested by the signifier *Roussainville*): the redness that connects the keep to the libido of all the little redheaded girls. Or its *verticality* (that you earlier and correctly referred to as phallic) that connects the keep to all standing objects; and also, we could say, *inferiority*: since everything erotic that takes place in this keep always takes place in its underground floor. Thanks to this characteristic, the keep will undergo a subterranean modification with all of the other deep and clandestine places in the *Search*, especially with the crypt of the Combray church, the little anal pavilion of the Champs-Elysées that Doubrovsky talked about the other day, and the Paris subway during the war where Charlus takes his odd walks. The modulation of the theme can even appear very authentically Freudian here since along with the infantile and auto-erotic state of the underground (Roussainville), we have an anal underground in the Champs-Elysées, then a homosexual underground in the Paris subway. This is what I see as the modulation of a theme. What I see as thematic in an object is less its ability to be repeated, to be reproduced as a whole, identical or varied, in various places, close or far apart, in the text, than its ability to spontaneously divide, to be abstractly, categorically distributed towards all other objects of fiction in a way that establishes a network of implicit solidarity—or if you prefer, this metaphor is apparently an obsession with us this evening—an ability to weave them, in the anticipatory and memorial space of reading, into a kind of vast signifying spider web. Themes are then read as the main lines of this infinite redistribution: series, yes, but always broken series, continually reencountered or traversed.

And this notion of *traversing* leads me to want to question Gilles Deleuze who did so well to evoke, at the end of his book on Proust, the importance of *transversals* in Proust's work. Perhaps the Roussainville keep provides us with an excellent example: remember the young boy who leads a visit to the Combray crypt where the murdered little girl was found, as Doubrovsky mentioned yesterday. But he is also one of the actors in the erotic games played out in the keep in which Gilberte takes part. Here, confirmed by the relay of a key character, we have a clear connection between two modalities of the Proustian underground, two of our spatio-libidinal series. My question for Deleuze about this is how exactly he conceives of the meaning of this notion of *transversality* in Proust. Why is it privileged by him in relation to all of the other structuring relationships in Proustian space (e.g. focality, symmetry and laterality)? And how is it specifically connected to an experience of madness?

Gilles Deleuze: I think we can call a dimension transversal that is neither horizontal nor vertical, supposing of course that it is question of a plane. I am not asking whether a dimension of this sort appears in Proust's work. I am asking what it is used for. And if

Proust needs it, why he needs it. It seems to me that in the end he has no choice. There is one thing he likes a lot: the idea that things or people or groups do not communicate. Charlus is a box; the young girls are a box containing smaller boxes. And I do not think it is a metaphor, at least in the ordinary sense of the term. Closed boxes or non-communicating vessels: here we grasp, I believe, two of Proust's possessions in the sense that a man is said to have properties, possessions. Well, these properties, these possessions which Proust manipulates throughout the *Search*, it is through him, strangely, that they communicate. This communication does not occur within any dimension usually included in the dimensions of communicating things: it could be called an aberrant communication. A famous example of this type of communication: the bumblebee and the orchid. Everything is compartmentalized. And that does not mean Proust is mad, but that this is a mad vision, since mad vision is much more plant-based than animal-based. What makes human sexuality an affair of flowers for Proust is that each person is bisexual. Everyone is a hermaphrodite but incapable of self-fertilization because the two sexes are separated. The amorous or sexual series will therefore be a particularly rich one. In speaking of a man, there are the male and female parts of the man. And for this male part, two cases or rather four: it can enter into a relationship with the male part of a woman or the female part of a woman, but also with the female part of another man or the male part of another man. There is communication, but it is always between non-communicating vases. There are openings but they always take place between closed boxes. We know that the orchid presents the image of an insect drawn on its flower, with its antennae, and the insect comes to fertilize this image, thereby ensuring the fertilization of the female flower by the male flower: to indicate this type of crossing, of convergence between the evolution of the orchid and the evolution of the insect, a contemporary biologist[1] has spoken of an aparallel evolution, which is exactly what I mean by aberrant communication.

The train scene where the narrator runs from one window to the other, going from the right landscape to the left and vice versa provides another example of the same phenomenon. Nothing communicates: it is a kind of great exploded world. The unity is not in what is seen. The only possible unity has to be sought in the narrator, in his spider behavior weaving his web from one window to the other. I think all the critics have said the same thing: the *Search*, as a work, is entirely made in this dimension, haunted by the narrator alone. The other characters, all of the other characters, are only boxes, mediocre or splendid boxes.

Serge Doubrovsky: Could I ask you this question then: what is *Time Regained* in this perspective?

Gilles Deleuze: *Time Regained* is not the moment when the narrator understands, nor the moment when he knows (I am using the wrong words but it's for the sake of time); it is the moment when he knows what he has been doing from the beginning. He didn't know. It is the moment he knows he is a spider, the moment he knows that madness has been present from the beginning, the moment he knows that his work is a web and at that moment he is fully affirmed. *Time Regained* is the transversal dimension par excellence. In this kind of explosion, of triumph at the end, one could say that this spider has understood everything. It has understood it was making a web, and that it was prodigious feat to understand it.

Serge Doubrovsky: What do you make of the major psychological laws that the narrator brings in throughout the story and scatters throughout the text? Do you see them as symptoms of his madness or analyses of human behavior?

Gilles Deleuze: Neither. I think they are very localized. As Genette said, there are very important problems of topology. Psychological laws are always laws of series. And series, in Proust's work, are never the last word. There is always something deeper than these series organized according to a vertical axis or with increasing depth. The series of planes that we see crossed by Albertine's face leads to something else, something much more important which is the last word. The same applies to the series marked by the laws of lies and the laws of jealousy. That is why as soon as Proust manipulates the laws, a dimension of humor intervenes that I see as essential and that raises a problem of interpretation, a real problem. Interpreting a text, I think, always comes back to evaluating its humor. A great author is someone who laughs a lot. In one of his first appearances, Charlus says something to the narrator like: "You don't care about your grandma, do you, you little devil." You might think Charlus is making a vulgar joke. But perhaps Charlus is in reality making a prediction, precisely that the narrator's love for his grandmother, or for his mother, the whole series is not at all the last word, since the last word is: you don't care, etc. And this is why I think that all the methods that have been invoked so far find themselves faced with this need to take into account not only a rhetoric, but a humoristics.

Question from the audience: Mr. Barthes, you suggested a relationship between the *Search* and Mallarmé's Book. Could you be more explicit concerning this relationship, or is it only an idea?

Roland Barthes: It is a projected connection; a metaphor, if you will. Mallarmé's Book is a space for permutation between a text that is read and the spectators who change places at each moment. I would simply suggest that Proust's book, the space of reading of this Proustian book, throughout the story, might be this Mallarmean Book, this book that only exists in a kind of non-hysterical, purely permutative theatricality founded on permutations of places. That is all I wanted to say.

Serge Doubrovsky: I would like to take advantage of this brief pause to respond to Genette. I will be in complete agreement with what he said before. All of the scenes of the *Search* are relived, but each time there is a qualitative difference that comes from the evolution of the book, of the text as such. And that is why, in order to avoid any misunderstanding, I did not present my own commentary as the final stage of my research but as an effort to establish the landmarks that will then allow the establishment of a network of differences. As for what Deleuze said earlier, I would not have used the same words. But the more I read Proust, the more I am sure, not that he was mad but—forgive the expression—a little "loony." To remain at this level, there are sentences that appear perfectly logical, but when you look closer, they do not hold up to scrutiny. If I used the language of psychoanalysis yesterday to describe this type of phenomenon, it was because psychoanalysis is the ideal language of the madman, it is madness codified. I therefore used a handy system, though maybe only to reassure myself.

Jean Ricardou: The various statements being exchanged here can be more or less easily connected. For example, what I would like to formulate combines best with what Gérard Genette discussed. I will therefore ask Genette if he considers this separation or dispersion that currently inspires his critical desire as specific to Proust. As for me, I have the impression that his phenomenon (I would willingly call it the "Osiriac arrangement") is characteristic of every text. I am thinking in particular of a contemporary of Proust (but who is unfortunately much less mentioned): Roussel. He operates in perhaps a similar way, in the sense that some of his texts, like the *New Impressions of Africa*, are composed of a legible proliferation of parentheses inside parentheses separating the themes, dispersing them more and more. It is apparent in the composition of other texts by Roussel. Moreover, what worries me a little is that the phenomenon of dispersion could lead one to believe, perhaps, that there is first of all a presence of unity and that this unity is then dispersed. In other words, the Osiriac arrangement presupposes, before its dislocation, the presence of an original body, the body of Osiris. For me, it seems necessary to correct this arrangement with another notion: the notion of the "impossible puzzle." In it, there is a group of pieces separated from one another by the act of constantly putting them between new parentheses. At the same time, however, if you attempt to recompose a supposedly broken unity from the dispersed pieces, you would realize, through the impossible puzzle effect, that the pieces do not fit well together, do not have a compatible geometry. What interests me, in the end, is to aggravate the case of unity: not only (as you show) space and dispersion, but also impossible reunification. There is no original unity.

Gérard Genette: The relationship between Proust and Roussel is obviously too difficult to be dealt with quickly. There is, however, one element large enough for us to mention. As far as I know, Roussel had a certain way of mastering his arrangement and the characteristic of the Proustian arrangement is that its author never quite mastered it. One could say he did not master it because he died too soon but naturally that is a joke. Even if he were still alive, I am sure he still would not have mastered it because it is infinite. The other question is: Is this phenomenon specific to Proust's work or a general phenomenon? I think this is a false problem in fact because, for me in any case, I can sense a phenomenon characteristic of Proust, and starting from this phenomenon, I am tempted to reread all other texts in this light. But from another point of view, one could say that these phenomena of distance, separation, etc. are the very definition of any text.

Roland Barthes: I see we are still turning around this form of theme and variation. In music, there is the academic and canonical form of the theme and variation, for example Brahms' variations on a theme by Haydn. The theme is given first and then ten, twelve or fifteen variations follow. But we must not forget that in the history of music, there is a great work that pretends to use the "theme and variations" structure but it fact undoes it: Beethoven's variations on a waltz by Diabelli, at least as they are admirably explained and described by Stockhausen in Boucourechliev's little book on Beethoven. You can see that we are dealing with thirty-three variations without a theme. And there is a theme that is given at the beginning, which is a very silly theme, but one that is given precisely, to some extent, for the sake of derision. I would say that Beethoven's variations here function a little like Proust's work. The theme is diffracted entirely in the variations and there is no longer a varied treatment of a theme. This means that in a way the metaphor (for every idea of variation is paradigmatic) is destroyed. Or, in any case, the origin of the metaphor is destroyed. It is a metaphor, but without an origin. I think that is what should be said.

Another question from the audience: I would like to ask a question that will be a little like a pebble in the pond. In other words, I expect diverse responses that will give me a better idea of what you are all searching for in Proust. This is my question: Does the narrator have a method?

Gilles Deleuze: I think the narrator has a method; he does not know it at the beginning, he learns it by following different rhythms, on very different occasions, and this method, literally, is the spider strategy.

Serge Doubrovsky: The narrator's method? Well, there are several. The narrator is both someone who claims to live and someone who writes. This raises all kinds of problems. And it leads me back to the origins of metaphor: the original relationship, the relationship with the mother, with the body, with this "I" that is an other and that one eternally seeks to reconstitute—but can one really do so?—using various methods of writing.

Gérard Genette: When referring to the narrator of the *Search*, you have to state whether you are using the term in the strict sense or in the larger sense, which is ambiguous. Do you mean the one who is telling the story, or the protagonist? Concerning the protagonist's method, I can only repeat what Deleuze has written: he learns a method of deciphering, etc. That is the protagonist's method, and you could say it develops little by little. As for the method of the narrator as such, it is obviously outside the scope of the question asked.

Same interlocutor: If you say that the protagonist's method, in other words, the narrator in the broadest sense, develops little by little, then aren't you in disagreement with Gilles Deleuze? Because, if I understand you correctly, Mr. Deleuze, your idea is that this method is only discovered at the end. There would have been a kind of instinctive approach, an approach that is only understood, reviewed and analyzed in *Time Regained.*

Gérard Genette: I just said how I agreed with Deleuze.

Gilles Deleuze: Yes, I do not see where you see an opposition in what we have said.

Same interlocutor: I see an opposition between the idea of a method that is developed little by little and the idea that it is only revealed at the end.

Gilles Deleuze: I'm sorry, but I see them as the same thing. To say a method is locally constituted is to highlight that there is first, here and there, a fragment of content that is taken into a fragment of method. For the narrator to say at the end: "Ah, that's it!" does not mean that suddenly everything is reunited. The bits and pieces remain bits and pieces; the boxes are still boxes. But he grasps at the end that it is precisely these pieces that, with no reference to a superior unity, constitute the work as such. I therefore see no opposition between this local constitution of fragments of method and the final revelation.

Same interlocutor: I would like to return to a word you used in your first communication. You said at one point: But what does the narrator do? He doesn't see anything, he doesn't understand anything. And you added: He doesn't want to understand anything.

Gilles Deleuze: It does not interest him. That is what I should have said.

Same interlocutor: Well, I wonder if the will not to understand is not part of the method. The idea of rejection: I reject things because they do not interest me. By instinct, I know that it does not interest me. Consequently, there *is* a method from the beginning, which would be to rely on a certain instinct. What is discovered at the end is that this method was the right one.

Gilles Deleuze: It is not that this method was the right one, but that this method functioned well. But it is not universal. You thus cannot say: it was the right method. You should say: it was the only method capable of functioning in such a way that this work was produced.

Same interlocutor: But doesn't the ambiguity come from the fact that, precisely, if the narrator has a method in the beginning, it is a method that does not postulate the goal towards which it is reaching? No goal is set; it only becomes apparent at the end.

Gilles Deleuze: But nothing is set. The method isn't either. Not only is the goal of the method not set, but the method itself is not set.

Same interlocutor: It may be, if not set, then at least evoked.

Gilles Deleuze: Is it evoked? I will take a simple example: the madeleine. It gives rise to an effort from the narrator that is explicitly presented as a methodical effort. That is truly a scrap of method in practice. We learn, hundreds of pages later, that what was found at that moment was radically insufficient and that something else needs to be found, more searching is necessary. Thus, I do not at all believe—and it seems to me that you are now contradicting yourself—that the method is set first. It is not set; it functions here and there, with mistakes that are an integral part of the work and even when it has worked, it has to be taken up again in another mode. And that continues until the end, where a... a kind... how should I put it?... a kind of revelation intervenes. At the end, the narrator offers a glimpse of his method: to be open to what constrains him, to be open to what hurts him. That is a method. We can in any case call it that.

Another question from the audience: Gilles Deleuze, I would like to return to your spider image, which is very striking, to ask you a question: What do you do then with the notion of belief, which is so prevalent in Proust? You said that the spider did not see anything; and Proust often says that such or such spectacle is bathed in a belief, in other words in a certain impression prior to the spectacle itself, for example the hawthorns, the impression felt on the morning at mass.

Gilles Deleuze: Once again, there is no opposition. What is opposed, if you will, is the world of perception or intellection, on the one hand, and the world of signals on the other. Each time there is belief, it means a signal has been received and that there is a reaction to this signal. In this sense, the spider believes, but it only believes in the vibrations of its web. The signal is what makes the web vibrate. Until the fly is in the web, the spider absolutely does not believe in the existence of a fly. It does not believe it. It does not believe in flies. However, it believes in any movement of the web, no matter how small, and it believes in it as in a fly. Even if it is something else.

Same interlocutor: In other words, an object only exists if it is caught in the web...

Gilles Deleuze: ... if it emits a signal that moves the web, that moves it in the state that it is in at that moment. Because it is a web that is made, that is built, just like with spiders, and it does not wait until it is done for there to be prey, in other words things that make the web move.

Same interlocutor: But he is the one who secretes this prey, because he makes it become prey.

Gilles Deleuze: No. He secretes the web. There is an outside object, but it does not intervene as an object, it intervenes as an emitter of signals.

Same interlocutor: Caught in the web he is in the process of secreting.

Gilles Deleuze: That's right.

Same interlocutor: And it only exists at that moment.

Gilles Deleuze: That's right.

Another question from the audience: I would like to ask a question to Mr. Deleuze and Mr. Doubrovsky. Mr. Deleuze, you used the word madness several times. Could you define your use of this word? Also, Mr. Doubrovsky, you stated that the narrator is not mad but "loony." That requires an explanation.

Gilles Deleuze: I started with the use Proust himself made of the word "madness." There is an excellent page in *The Prisoner* on this theme: what worries people is not crime, not misdeeds, it is something worse, it is madness. And these words, as if by chance, describe Charlus and the mother of a family who discovered, or sensed—she also happens to be very stupid—that Charlus was mad, and that when he stroked the cheek of her boys and pulled their ears, there was something more than homosexuality, something incredible that was on the order of madness. And Proust tells us that this is worrisome.

As for determining what madness is and what it consists of, I believe that one could speak of schizophrenia. This universe of closed boxes that I tried to describe, with its aberrant communications, is a fundamentally schizoid universe.

Serge Doubrovsky: If I used the word "loony," it is because I believe it is not exactly a question of madness. I do not think the narrator is completely mad, even though we could add to the texts cited by Deleuze the passage where Vinteuil is said to have died a madman. The narrator struggles with madness; otherwise, you can be sure, he would not have written his book. I wanted to introduce, through the use of a slang term, some of the humor Deleuze had requested.

I will not repeat what I said yesterday about neurosis. What strikes me, staying at the level of writing alone, is that the same stories, the same characters, the same situations reappear constantly with a slight variation each time. This phenomenon, which Genette referred to earlier, was very well analyzed by Leo Bersani in his book on Proust. Things are repeated obsessively, the coincidences are too great. Everything happens as if the story were becoming more and more fantastical. We no longer have any sort of narrative realism, but a delirium that presents itself as narration. This should be shown through a series of examples. Limiting ourselves to the main Proustian maxims alone, which could have been gathered into a collection, the effect, when read one after the other, is quite extraordinary: the narrator deploys his treasures of ingeniousness to justify behavior that is fundamentally aberrant.

Another question from the audience: Roland Barthes, I would like to ask a question that I will have some difficulty formulating since it calls on a text I have had some difficulty understanding: the preface to your *Sade, Fourier, Loyola.* There you speak of the "pleasure of the text" in terms that evoke Proust rather clearly. You also speak of a kind of critical activity considered as subversion or redirection, which is not without resemblance to the interpretation of variations of which Genette spoke. This seems rather ambiguous to the extent that the interpretation of variations is not far from a certain form of pastiche that threatens to lead to the worst critical indulgence.

Roland Barthes: I do not see the ambiguity of the pastiche.

Same interlocutor: I would like to talk about the interpretation of variations, which you seem to ascribe to as a critical activity, and that I would relate to the pleasure of the text you describe. I would like to know how that is situated.

Roland Barthes: The pleasure of the text has no direct relationship with the object of this colloquium, although Proust is a great source of pleasure for me personally. I even spoke earlier of critical desire. The pleasure of the text is a sort of claim I made, but it must now be taken to a more theoretical level. I will simply say, in a word, that it may now be time, given the evolution of textual theory, to question the economy or economies of pleasure in the text. How does a text please? What is the pleasure limit (*plus-à-jouir*) of a text, where is it situated, is it the same for everyone? Certainly not. Where then does that lead us methodologically? We could for example start with the observation that for millennia, there was an undisputed pleasure in narration, anecdotes, stories, tales. If we now produce texts that are no longer narrative, what substitutive economy controls pleasure? There has to be a displacement of pleasure, a displacement of the pleasure limit (*plus-à-jouir*), and that is when we should seek a kind of extension of the theory of text. I ask the question, and I have nothing further to offer at the moment. It is something one could consider working on collectively, in a research seminar, for example.

As for the second question concerning the interpretation of variations, I would say that a critic is not at all like a pianist who simply interprets, executes the variations that are written. In reality, the critic at least temporarily reaches a destructuration of the Proustian text; he or she reacts against the rhetorical structuring (the "outline") that has until now been prevalent in Proust studies. At that point, the critic is not at all like a traditional pianist performing variations that are indeed in the text, but he or she becomes more like the operator of a part as in post-serial music. It is the same difference there would be between the interpreter of a romantic concerto and the musician, the operator in a formation (the word orchestra is no longer used) capable of playing completely contemporary music, according to a written canvas that has nothing to do with old-fashioned notation. At that moment, the Proustian text becomes, little by little, through the sort of Heracliteanism that critics are caught up in, a type of sheet music full of holes with which one will be able to operate variations instead of performing them. This would lead us back to the problem that was raised in a much more concrete, and in a sense, much more serious debate that took place this afternoon, by those of us who referred to the problems of the Proustian text, in the material sense of the word "text." Perhaps at that point we would need these Proustian papers, not only for the literality of the sentences they would provide us but for the type, I would say, of graphic configuration, of graphic explosion they represent. That is in a way how I see a certain future, not of Proustian criticism (its future is of no interest: criticism will always remain an institution, one can always move outside or beyond it), but of reading and therefore of pleasure.

Jean-Pierre Richard: Following Roland Barthes' remarks, I would like to say that for me there seems to exist a rather fundamental agreement or at least a convergence between everyone around this table: everyone has described Proust's writing practices for us from the perspective of dispersal, fragmentation, and discontinuity. It seems obvious to me, however, in reading Proust's text, that there is a Proustian ideology of the work that goes against all of these descriptions, a very explicit, insistent, even heavy-handed ideology, which on the contrary values echoes, lines of resemblance, reminders, repercussions, the division into *ways*, the symmetries, the points of view, the "stars," and which ends in the well-known passages of *Time Regained* with the appearance of a character who ties together all of the threads that until then were separate. It therefore seems that there is a disparity between the explicit Proustian ideology of the text and the descriptions you have made of it. I therefore ask you simply this: If this disparity exists, what place do you give this Proustian ideology in the practice of the text? How do you explain this contradiction between what he says and the way he says it?

Roland Barthes: Personally, I see the ideology you describe. It comes out more at the end...

Jean-Pierre Richard: Not all along?

Roland Barthes: ... more like a Proustian *imaginary*, in the Lacanian sense; this imaginary is *in* the text, it takes its place there as in a box but, I would add, a Japanese box in which there is only another box, and so on. And in that way, the text's misunderstanding of itself ends up being figured in the text itself. That is how I would see this theory of writing rather than this ideology, which is in the Proustian text.

Jean-Pierre Richard: This theory also, however, structures the text. It sometimes resembles a practice. Deleuze quoted earlier, for example, and quite appropriately, the example of the madeleine, saying that the main character only understood its meaning much later. But during the first experience, Proust already says: I had to postpone until much later my understanding of the meaning of what happened to me that day. There is thus indeed a theoretical presupposition and certainty of what is the value of the experience to be interpreted later. It seems difficult to say here that it is only at the end, by an after-the-fact effect, that the web is woven or undone.

Jean Ricardou: I do not completely agree with the idea of a Proustian ideology of the work. I would say: the ideology of Proust's work. This ideology, which is internal for the most part, has two functions, depending on whether it conforms or not with the text's functioning. In the first case, one of the effects of this self-representation I already mentioned in my presentation and I won't insist. But this is not to say—to add some nuance to my previous remarks—that any ideology within the text necessarily agrees with the text's functioning. They may very well be opposed. With this reverse self-representation, the relationship between fiction and narration would no longer be similitude, as in strict self-representation, but opposition. Not a metaphor, but an antithesis. In this case, it could be a strategy of deception. The ideology of the work would draw all the more attention to unification, to gathering together because the best way to grasp dispersion is the desire for gathering together. It could also be the indication of a dual operation. In my presentation, I put the accent on the analogical comparison, but it is only possible through separation and distinction. Deleuze and Genette have both insisted on this complimentary operation. Using this insistence, one might find a contradictory ideology in the *Search*. This time, it is not the other becoming the same (Swann's way joining Guermantes' way) but the same becoming other: deaths, separations, exclusions, transformations (everything tending to become its opposite). There would thus be self-representation of the contradictory functioning of the text through a conflict of ideologies of the text.

Gérard Genette: A word on what Jean-Pierre Richard was just saying. I believe that in Proust, as in many other writers, theory lags behind practice. To put it simply, one could say he is a writer of the

20th century with an aesthetic and literary ideology of the 19th century. But we are and we must be 20th century critics, and we have to read him as such, not as he read himself. Moreover, his literary theory is nevertheless more subtle than the grand finale and closing synthesis of *Time Regained.* In his theory of reading and in reading his own book, when he states for example that his readers will have to be readers of themselves, there is something that in part subverts the idea of a final closure of the work, and therefore the (classical-romantic) idea of the *work* itself. Then there is a third element. Proust's text is no longer what it was, say, in 1939 when only the *Search* was known along with two or three works considered minor. In my opinion, the major event in Proust criticism over the last few years is not that we can write or have written about Proust, but that he has, I dare say, continued to write himself. It is the discovery of the mass of pre-texts and para-texts that have opened the *Search* more than it was before when it was read in isolation. I mean that not only does it open from the end, as we have always known, in the sense that its circularity prevents it from ending by stopping, but that it is also open at the beginning, in the sense that not only does it not end, but in a sense it never begins, because Proust was always already working on this work. And in a way, he is still working on it. We do not yet have all of Proust's text. Everything we are saying now will in part be invalid when we have the whole text. Luckily, for him and for us, we will never have the whole text.

Another question from the audience: I find that among the things that have been said, there were two rather disturbing things. One from Deleuze and the other from Doubrovsky. They each spoke of madness. It is one thing to say with Deleuze that the theme of madness is present throughout Proust's work. It is another thing to point a finger and say, "Look, Charlus is mad. Albertine is mad." One might as well say that anyone is mad: Sade, Lautréamont or Maldoror. Why is Charlus mad?

Gilles Deleuze: Listen, I am not the one who says it; Proust does. Proust says it from the start: Charlus is mad. Proust makes Andrée write: Maybe Albertine was mad. It is in the text. As for the question of whether Proust was mad or not, you will admit that I did not ask that question. I am like you; it does not interest me. I simply asked whether madness was present in this work and what was the function of this presence.

Same interlocutor: OK. But then Doubrovsky continues by saying that madness, which this time is the writer's madness, appears in the novel when the coincidences start to pile up towards the end. Is this compatible with a non-psychological view of Proust's work? Isn't what happens then just an acceleration in the recurrence of themes? Are these coincidences, or what you call coincidences, proof of madness?

Serge Doubrovsky: Personally, I think the narrator has a strategy—and I mean the writer writing the book—which consists of attributing homosexuality to others, attributing madness to Charlus or Albertine. He reserves "nervosism" for himself, and it is easy to recognize all the aspects of a psychosomatic illness in it.

What I mean is that the entire work seems to be a kind of game through which a writer is trying to build a universe, to tell a story we can read, that has been read as a story. Jean-Pierre Richard was right to highlight the presence of a structuring ideology in the work. Proust, man of the 19th century. But the more we read the *Search*, the more we realize we are in a mental universe, a psychical one, if you prefer, or better yet an unconscious one—I don't know—but a textual universe in any case. This plays off two completely opposed views: a story is being told, but as it is being told, it is being destroyed.

Same interlocutor: Do you mean that as soon as a story is no longer "realist," it becomes madness?

Serge Doubrovsky: I think that a certain feeling of the derealization of the text leads one to ask questions about madness. But, again, I do not like this word. I would simply add that the loss of the reality principle seems to me to be one of the major discoveries of modern writing.

Another question from the audience: I would like to ask two questions: one to Barthes and the other to Deleuze.

When you, Roland Barthes, say that an economy must be reintroduced into the theory of the text as it has been practiced until now, you choose pleasure as the anchor of this new dimension. But whose pleasure? You say: the reader's pleasure, the critic's pleasure. But is it possible to take pleasure in someone like Proust who writes beyond the pleasure principle? And, more generally speaking, isn't it finally time to locate the economic investments on the side of the writer instead of the reader, something no critic has succeeded in doing?

Roland Barthes: Perhaps in looking around the theme of pleasure, I am posing the question in a somewhat naïve, alienated way at first. Maybe one day it will lead me to the affirmation you suggest. You asked a question but in fact you gave a response that I might only find months from now; in other words, that this notion of the pleasure of the text might not hold. But I would like, at least once, to take this notion from the start, simply and naïvely, even if the path I must take will destroy me, dissipate me as a subject of pleasure and dissipate the pleasure in me. Maybe there will no longer be any pleasure; maybe there will only be desire, the pleasure of fantasy.

Same interlocutor: Yes, of course, it is called fantasy, but there is something else: a kind of pleasure caught in a dead desire. And that may precisely be what defines the critic's viewpoint.

Roland Barthes: You show no qualms about making my pleasure in Proust seem guilty, in any case. I would not have had it for long, I think.

Same interlocutor: Now for my question to Deleuze. You said that Proust opened himself to violence towards himself. But what does violence to Proust, what does he discover, in the end, that does violence to him?

Gilles Deleuze: Proust always defines the world of violence as part of the world of signals and signs. Every signal, no matter what it is, does violence.

Same interlocutor: But isn't there another possible reading of Proust? I am thinking of a text by Blanchot where he talks of inscriptions instead of signs. A spider spins its web without method or aim. Granted. But there are nonetheless a certain number of texts that are inscribed somewhere. I am thinking of the famous sentence that says that the two sexes will each die separately. Here there is something that does not refer solely to the world of signs, but to a much more secret and much less reassuring series, a series that would connect, among other things, with sexuality.

Gilles Deleuze: Maybe the world of signs is a reassuring world for you. It was not for Proust. And I do not see the need to distinguish between that world and the world of sexuality when, for Proust, sexuality is entirely caught up in the world of signs.

Same interlocutor: Yes, but at a first level. It is also inscribed somewhere else.

Gilles Deleuze: But what type of inscription are we talking about? The sentence you mentioned on the two sexes is a prediction. It is the language of prophets, not the "logos." Prophets emit signs or signals. And moreover, they need a sign to guarantee their word. There is no rhetoric, no logic here. The world of signals is not a reassuring one at all, nor is it asexual. On the contrary, it is the world of the hermaphrodite, of a hermaphrodite that does not communicate with itself: it is the world of violence.

4

On the Vincennes Department of Psychoanalysis

The recent happenings in the Department of Psychoanalysis at the University of Vincennes are very simple in appearance: a certain number of lecturers have been excluded in the name of pedagogical and administrative reorganization. In an article for *Le Monde*, however, Roger-Pol Droit asks if such reorganization is not a Vichy-style purge. The procedures for dismissal, the selection of instructors, the treatment of dissenters, the immediate nomination of replacements would also suggest—all things being equal—a Stalinist operation. Stalinism is not exclusive to Communist parties; it has also infected leftist groups and spread into psychoanalytic associations. The fact that the excluded instructors themselves or their allies have not shown great resistance would tend to confirm this hypothesis. They did not actively participate in their own indictment, but it seems possible a second wave of purges would lead to that sort of progress.

The question is not one of doctrine but concerns the organization of power. Those in charge of the Department of Psychoanalysis who organized these expulsions have declared in their official statements that they were acting on the instructions of Dr. Lacan. He is the inspiration behind the new statutes. It is to him that applicants will eventually have to submit their candidacies.

And he is the one calling for a *return to order* in the name of a mysterious matheme of psychoanalysis. It is the first time a private individual of any stature has granted himself the right to intervene in a university in a sovereign manner in order to carry out, or have carried out, a reorganization involving dismissals and nominations of teaching personnel. Even if the Department of Psychoanalysis were to consent, it would not change a thing in this affair, nor would it alter the threat which such a move conceals. The Freudian School of Paris is not only a group with a leader; it is a very centralized association with a clientele, in all meanings of the word. It is hard to imagine that a university department would submit to an organization of this type.

The knowledge to which psychoanalysis lays claim is inseparable from a kind of terrorism, an intellectual and emotional terrorism made to break down a resistance which psychoanalysis deems unhealthy. It is already troublesome when this operation occurs among psychoanalysts, or between psychoanalysts and patients, for a goal they call therapy. But it is a much greater cause for concern when the same operation aims to break resistance of another nature altogether in a segment of the teaching profession that itself claims to have no intention to "treat" or to "train" psychoanalysts. This is nothing less than blackmail of the unconscious of the opposition by using the prestige and the presence of Dr. Lacan to impose decisions without any possible discussion (it is "take it or leave it," and if you leave it "the disappearance of the department would be necessary from the point of view of analytical theory as well as from the point of view of the university...," *a disappearance decided by whom? For whom?*) All terrorism involves some kind of washing: in this case, unconscious-washing is no less authoritarian and frightening than brainwashing.

5

Author's Note for the Italian Edition of *Logic of Sense*

It is difficult for an author to reflect on a book written several years ago. One is tempted to act clever, or to feign indifference, or even worse, to become the commentator of oneself. Not that the book has necessarily been surpassed; but even if it remains relevent, it is an "adjacent" relevance. What is needed is a benevolent reader who will give back to the book its relevance and its continuity. *Logic of Sense* is a book I still like because for me it continues to represent a turning point: it was the first time I sought, however tentatively, a form that was not in keeping with traditional philosophy. And it is a cheerful book in many passages despite the fact that I wrote it during a period of illness. There is nothing I would change.

It would be better for me to ask myself why I needed Lewis Carroll so much, and his three great books: *Alice's Adventures in Wonderland*, *Through the Looking Glass* and *Sylvie and Bruno*. The fact is that Carroll has a gift for renewing himself according to spatial dimensions, topological axes. He is an explorer, an experimenter. In *Alice's Adventures in Wonderland* things happen in profundity and in height: the subterranean spaces, the lairs, the tunnels, the explosions, the falls, the monsters, the food; even those things which come from above or lurk above, like the Cheshire cat.

In *Through the Looking Glass* there is instead a surprising conquest of surfaces (no doubt prepared by the role of the magic cards at the end of *Alice's Adventures*): one no longer sinks, one slides; it is the flat surface of the mirror or of the game of chess; even the monsters become lateral. For the first time literature thus declares itself an art of surfaces, a measurement of planes. *Sylvie and Bruno* is something entirely different (perhaps prefigured by Humpty Dumpty in *Through the Looking Glass*): two surfaces coexist, with two adjoining stories—and one might say that these two surfaces roll up in such a way that the reader passes from one story to the other, while they disappear on one side, only to reappear on the other, as if the chess game had become spherical. Eisenstein speaks in these terms of Japanese scroll paintings, in which he saw the first approximation of film editing: "The ribbon of the scroll is 'swung around' into a rectangle! *But it is not swung around itself,* as ribbon into scroll; but *on its surface* (on the flatness of the picture) *the visual representation is swung around.*"[1]

In *Logic of Sense* I am trying to explain how thought organizes itself according to similar axes and directions: for example, height and Platonism which will shape the traditional image of philosophy; the Pre-Socratics and depth (the return to the Pre-Socratic as return to the subterranean spaces, to the prehistoric caves); the Stoics and their new art of surfaces ... Are there other directions for the future? We all move forward or backward; we are hesitant in the middle of all these directions; we construct our topology, celestial map, underground den, measurements of surface planes, and other things as well. While moving in these different directions, one does not speak in the same way, just as the subject matter which one encounters is not the same. In fact, the process is a matter of language and style.

For my part, when I was no longer content with the history of philosophy, my book *Difference and Repetition* still aspired nonetheless toward a sort of classical height and even toward an archaic depth. The theory of intensity which I was drafting was marked by depth, false or true; intensity was presented as stemming from the depths (and this does not mean that I have any less affection for certain other pages of this book, in particular those concerning weariness and contemplation). In *Logic of Sense*, the novelty for me lay in the act of learning something about surfaces. The concepts remained the same: "multiplicities," "singularities," "intensities," "events," "infinities," "problems," "paradoxes" and "propositions"—but reorganized according to this dimension. The concepts changed then, and so did the method, a type of serial method, pertaining to surfaces; and the language changed, a language which I would have wanted to be ever more *intensive* and one which would move along a path of very small spurts.

What is it that was just not right in *Logic of Sense*? Apparently it still reflects a naïve and guilty sense of self-satisfaction with respect to psychoanalysis. My only excuse for such self-satisfaction would be this: I was then trying, very timidly, to render psychoanalysis *inoffensive*, presenting it as a surface art, one which deals with Events as surface entities (Oedipus was not a bad person, he had good intentions ...).

In any case, the psychoanalytic concepts remain intact and respected, Melanie Klein and Freud. So then, what about now? Fortunately I am nearly incapable of speaking for myself, because what has happened to me since *Logic of Sense* now depends on my having met Félix Guattari, on my work with him, on what we do together. I believe Félix and I sought out new directions simply because we felt like doing so. *Anti-Oedipus* no longer has height or depth, nor surface. In this book everything happens, is done, the intensities, the events, upon a sort of spherical body or scroll painting: The Organless *Body*. Together we would like to be the Humpty Dumpty of philosophy, or its Laurel and Hardy. A philosophy-cinema. I believe also that this change of method brings with it a change of subject matter, or, vice versa, that a certain kind of politics takes the place of psychoanalysis. Such a method would also be a form of politics (a micropolitics) and of analysis (a schizoanalysis) and would propose the study of multiplicities upon the different types of organless bodies. A *rhizome*, instead of series, says Guattari. *Anti-Oedipus* is a good beginning, provided we can break away from it. Some readers might say: "This note is idiotic, and immodest." I would only answer: "You do not know how truly modest and even humble it is. The secret is to become invisible and to make a rhizome without putting down roots."

6

The Future of Linguistics

1. Henri Gobard distinguishes four types of language: *vernacular*, a mother tongue, of rural origin, territorial in nature; *vehicular*, a language of exchange, commerce, and circulation, quintessentially urban; *referential*, a national and cultural language, effecting a recovery or reconstruction of the past; *mythical*, a language that points to a spiritual, religious, or magical homeland. Some of these languages may simply be patois, dialect, or even jargon. It doesn't matter, because Gobard does not conduct his research as a comparative linguist would. He acts more like a polemicist or a kind of strategist, one who is already implicated in a situation. He puts himself in a real situation where languages are in actual conflict. He does not examine structures of language, but rather functions. And these functions compete with one another through different languages, in the same language, or in the derivatives or residues of language. It goes without saying that history and particular milieus force the map of the four languages to undergo modifications. It goes without saying that the map undergoes a modification at a particular moment and within the same milieu, according to the scale or the point of view that has been adopted. Several languages can simultaneously compete for the same function, in the same place, etc.

2. Gobard readily acknowledges all he owes to those researchers who have focused on the phenomenon of bilingualism. But then why does he favor 4 over 2 (and 4 is in no way exhaustive)? Because dualism, or the binary, runs the risk of trapping us in the simple opposition between a low and a high language, between a major and a minor language, between a language of power and a language of the people. Gobard's four factors are not meant to reinforce the above oppositions, but they do propose a complex *genesis* of them. How does a language come to power, whether on a national or a global scale? By what means is linguistic power warded off? This raises the question of the imperialism of English, or rather that of the American language today. It may be the greatest vehicular language in terms of financial and economic circuits, but that alone is not enough. It has to take on referential, mythical, and vernacular functions as well. The American Western can play the same role for a Frenchman today as "our Gallic ancestors" do for an immigrant of African descent. American pop-music, or the American influence in advertising, has a mythical role to play. American slang can take on a vernacular function. It is not about conquerors imposing their language on the conquered (though this is often the case). The mechanisms of power are more subtle and diffuse than that, operating through reversible, versatile functions which are themselves the objects of active political struggles, and even micro-struggles.

3. A few practical exercises for "tetra-glossian" analysis. Consider the impact African-Americans have had on American English: the way they penetrate English with and through other dialects and languages, the way they shape within English new vernacular languages for their own use, and the way they recreate the mythical and the referential (cf. the beautiful book by J.L. Dillard, *Black English*).[1] Take a very

different case, one made famous by Kafka: the way Czech Jews, at the end of the Austrian Empire, feared Yiddish as a vernacular language, but having forgotten Czech, the other vernacular of the rural area from which they came, they found themselves caught using a desiccated German as their vehicular language, cut off from the Czech people, all the while dreaming of Hebrew as a mythical language in the early days of Zionism. Or how about France today, or any other country, where immigrants or their children have lost their mother tongue and find their relationship to the imposed vehicular language both difficult and political? What about the possibility of a resurgence of regional languages: not just the resurgence of various patois, but the possibility of new mythical and new referential functions? And what about the ambiguity of these movements, which already have a long history, displaying both fascistic and revolutionary tendencies? Gobard develops an example of a micro-struggle, or micro-politics, at some length in pages of great gusto: the nature and the function of the teaching of English in France (the different kinds of professors, the attempt to make English uni-lingual, "optional French," and Gobard's counter-proposals intended to prevent English, as the recognized vehicular language of the world, from crystallizing the other functions, which on the contrary must act on English through "the right to an accent," through particular references, and through polyvocal desires). When Gobard relates the internal struggles of the faculty at Vincennes, it is theatre worthy of Ionesco.

4. Gobard's distinction of four languages or four functions of language might very well recall the classical distinctions which linguists make when they show that a message implies a sender and a receiver (conative and emotive function), an exchange of information (vehicular function), a verbalizable context (referential function), a

selection of the best elements and combinations (poetic function), and a code which sender and receiver must agree on (metalinguistic function). Gobard sees the language of the child in the light of a joyful tetra-genesis, where an emotive vernacular function ("mama"), a vehicular informational function ("baba"), a poetic referential function ("goo-goo gaga"), and a mythical inventive function (childhood codes, magical languages, "eenie-meenie-minie-moe") can be distinguished. However, what distinguishes Gobard's categories from those used by other linguists (sociolinguists in particular), is precisely that other linguists presuppose the existence of a system of language, and even if they claim not to, these other linguists still remain committed to universals like subject, object, message and code, competence, etc., which refer to a genre of languages and, above all, to a form of power in these languages (there is a specifically linguistic capitalism). Gobard's originality, on the other hand, consists in his examining collective or social assemblages, which when they combine with movements of the "earth," form heterogeneous types of power. Not in the usual sense that a language has a territory or territories, but in the sense that the functions of language are inseparable from movements of deterritorialization and reterritorialization. These material and spiritual movements constitute a new geolinguistics. In a word, Gobard sees collective assemblages of utterance rather than subjects, coefficients of deterritorialization rather than codes. (To take the previous examples: the way vehicular English deterritorializes African Americans, who in turn reterritorialize themselves on Black English; the way Jews who broke away from rural Czech, tried to reterritorialize themselves on a German possessing every sort of linguistic, cultural, and poetic artifice (cf. the Prague school of literature); and by extension, Hebrew as a magical, mythical, or spiritual reterritorialization).

5. There are signs today that some linguists (e.g. Ducrot) are beginning to doubt both the informational character of language in general, and the assimilation of a particular language to a code. They are choosing instead to subordinate the problems of semantics and syntax to a genuine pragmatics or politics which draws out the assemblages of power at work in a particular language, as well as the linguistic possibilities of struggle against these powers. And they are challenging the idea of the structural homogeneity of a particular language and the idea of universals of language (including "competence"). Gobard's analysis breaks new ground in all these directions, while he invents an original sense of humor and fits of anger. Languages are gibberish, Joycean quirks; they are not anchored to structures. It is only functions and movements that manage to create a bit of polemical order in them. Gobard is right, because as soon as you have something to say, you are like a foreigner in your native language. Up to now, linguists have known too many languages. This has allowed them to compare languages, but also to turn knowledge into nothing more than pure research. Gobard knows many languages, too: he is an extremely creative English professor who knows he is French and wants to be Sicilian. Like so many other great doctor-patients of language, Gobard has another question in mind: How to stammer? Not to stammer words, in speech, or in a particular language, but how to stammer language in general? (Our greatest poet in French is Gherasim Luca—of course, he is from Romania. Luca knows how to stammer not just words, but language itself; he invented it). Gobard has a new way of evaluating the relations of language and the Earth. Still holding back in Gobard are a Court de Gébelin, a Fabre d'Olivet, a Brisset, and a Wolfson: What future awaits linguistics?

7

Alain Roger's *Le Misogyne*

"I am dirty, I am vulgar, I am poor, a beggar, if you know what I mean. Yes, although a student at the Ecole Normale, I used to ride the subway in the evening like a beggar, I would ring the doorbell like a beggar, get drunk like a beggar, screw like a beggar, *more pauperum*, yes, there is no need to translate..." Is this the narrator Alain speaking of himself? Is it the author Alain Roger speaking of his novel? There are four poor women who are murdered, and these acts are all either preceded or accompanied by four disgusting rapes. Even the motivation is poor: the misogynist kills women simply because he hates them. But he carries a woman inside him—the infamous bisexual—and it is under the spell of a young woman who is also bisexual, his inverted double, that he commits murder, a murder which is the reenactment of a primordial scene, an original androgyny ("I wanted to know, to know how I had been conceived. That's what my body wanted, to see it, to see the original monstrous act. I was crazy with disgust, I used to imagine it was my mother...").

This forced, deliberate poverty, this familiar psychoanalytic variation, are the necessary preconditions for the emergence of something brilliant. The reader has an early sign. The novel seems written in alexandrines. It is done discretely. They linger just below the surface of the text, or they suddenly erupt in the text ("It was the month of

June, and I was twenty-one," "I felt the pleasures of a woman in my thighs..."). Is this meant to reinforce the archaism of the novel and the conformity of its theme, a kind of psychoanalysis in verse? Is it a touch of humor, the omnipresent power of laughter? Or is it something else? It is almost as if the virtual alexandrines awaken us to a new element. There is something rich and sumptuous about this novel.

In a previous novel, *Jerusalem Jerusalem*,[1] a young woman with an antiquated name, Cecilia, after a poor life, a poor relationship, and finally a poor suicide, becomes a cult figure, the object of a group-sanctification: recitations, confessions, prayers, evangelism, etc. These pages are extraordinary. It seems that a constant theme of Roger's work is the birth of religion in what is most everyday and banal. *Le Misogyne* is cut from the same cloth as *Jerusalem Jerusalem*: an *election* can be applied to anything, such as a people, but also to an individual, such as a person or an antiquated first name that designates an event. For there to be an election, a sanctification, all you need is a flash of intensity, even if imperceptible or unconscious, in what is most everyday; a proper name functioning as a proper name, that is, as a marker of this intensity; and a hostile mechanism, like an enemy, threatening *to crush* these intensities, to reduce them to what is most poor in the everyday.

In Roger's work, language as a whole seems to function in this way, like a proper name: old-fashioned, humble, with the power to flash, and which at the same time is threatened by the mechanism of everyday words turned against it; this threat must be constantly destroyed to rediscover the brilliance of the Name. This style, particular to Alain Roger, captivates by its beauty and perfection. Take one example from *Le Misogyne*, the paranoid text about the cat-man: 1) the group of *Cats* (proper name) constitutes the chosen people; 2) the car is the enemy mechanism which crushes the *Cats*; 3) for every crushed *Cat*, a procedure leading to the incineration of a car is initiated.

This "procedure" (it is not at all a trick, it is more writing as process) can work in the opposite direction, in the direction of profanation and vulgarization. For example, at the end of *Le Misogyne*, another young woman with an antiquated name, this time Solange, also kills herself. The narrator goes in search of another Solange, a woman having the same first name, whom he will present with verbal snippets from the "true" Solange for the purpose of free association. And this time, unlike in *Jerusalem Jerusalem*, the words which the true Solange could make flash with intensity now fall back into the platitudes and the poverty of the other Solange's everyday words. The proper name-language is profaned as a common noun-utterance. This is the death of style, just as there are suicides, cat killings, etc. But this reversal is not what is most important; it matters only as the inverse or the shadow of the one movement that does matter: sanctification, sacralization, an immanent atheist election.

The name of this movement or process is well known: it is called an *epiphany*. At the beginning of *Le Misogyne*, we see a rather successful epiphany, in the Joycean sense, when the narrator, who has committed his first crime by proxy, goes to see his friend Paul in the hospital, who is recovering from an automobile accident in which he killed his wife: "Then, like a spring, Paul shot up out of bed. It made me jump. His smile lost amid the bandages—it was unreal. It was like the solitary walnut tree, so far away." A flash of intensity. But how can we speak of Alain Roger's originality, if he is content with reproducing almost exactly the same procedure-process that Joyce invented? Nor is there any lack of precursors or co-inventors among other famous authors, such as Proust.

What strikes me as original is the way Roger gives an epiphany radically new dimensions. Up until now, the epiphany had merely oscillated between two poles: 1) passion, or the sudden revelation of objective contemplation; and 2) action, or the crafted form of subjective experimentation. In any event, an epiphany would happen to a character, or the character would make it come about. The character itself is not the epiphany, at least not principally. But when a person becomes an epiphany, at that moment he or she ceases to be a person. A person undergoes this change not to become a transcendent entity, a god or goddess, but to become an Event, a multiplicity of events each folded in the other, an event of the order of love. This extension of the epiphany, its coincidence with a whole character, and consequently the depersonalization of the character that results, the person-event becoming a non-personal event—this is where the power of Alain Roger's novel can be felt most viscerally. But I am not claiming to offer an analysis, merely an impression, an indication of a disturbance. In this sense, the novel is a book of love.

The young woman, Solange, is the epiphany-character. The narrator Alain is a professor, a school teacher, and Solange is a student in his class. Alain wants to kill women, but he doesn't dare, and begins by having one killed by his friend Paul. Solange makes a strange pact, a contract with the professor, to which she subjects the whole class, "the polypary," the collective. A series of ugly, poor, vulgar scenes ensues. Soon she will inspire the other crimes, participate in them afterwards, even anticipate them, until she finally commits the last one. More ugly and poor scenes. She will not sleep with Alain because he loves her and she loves him *too much* ("She said: 'My saying that I love you hardly does it justice. I love you not like a child, or a brother, or a spouse, but all three at the same time, and I especially love the woman buried deep within you, whose presence I recognize in all your gestures and your crimes'"). Thus, Alain has a woman inside him, whom he wants to kill; Solange has a boy in her, whom she wants Alain to kill. Each is bisexual. Alain is a misogynist, and Solange a tomboy. They are each in search of the primordial act, the union of father and mother, the father whom Solange hates, and the mother who causes Alain such suffering.

The story can always be told along those lines. That is its sordid side, its poverty, its vulgarity, which the narrator exploits as the system of common words, even if psychoanalysis, structuralism, as well as modern subjectivity and significance, explicitly partake of the same common words (the same goes for *Jerusalem Jerusalem*). However, you have only to repeat the proper name—Solange Solange, or Cecilia Cecilia—for something unexpected to emerge: the intensities contained in the name, a whole other story, a whole other version of the story.

A little known author, whom Roger does not seem to be familiar with—the encounter is all the more beautiful for being fictional—has created several of his works a strange epiphany of the young woman. His name is Trost, and he describes a modern, or future, young woman as "freely mechanical," or machinic.[1] She is not defined as virgin, or as bisexual, but as having a supple machine-body with multiple degrees of freedom: a state that is freely mechanical, autonomous and in motion, deformable and transformable. Trost was hoping and praying. Or he thought he saw the arrival of this "Chance-Woman," this "girl-woman, a retort that is ready-made and found in the exterior world, a true and simple product of extreme modern complexity which she reflects like a brilliant erotic machine."

Trost believed that the young girl-woman in her visible and sensible reality encompassed an abstract line that was like the blueprint of a human group to come, a group about to be discovered, a revolutionary group whose militants would know how to fight the enemy within: i.e. the phallus of the difference of the sexes, or what amounts to the same thing, a bisexuality that is divided, distributed, and set in opposition, one side against the other. Not that the young woman figures or prefigures this group. She was non-figurative, encountered in "the non-figurative aspect of our desire." She was "the totally profane intensity of desire," dressed in a profane skirt or pants. As pure desire, she was opposed to all that is biographical or related to memory in desire: no past, no recognition, no reawakened memory. Her mystery was not the mystery of a lost origin or object, but the mystery of a function in operation.

Unconscious and desiring, she is opposed in her very strangeness to the unconscious of psychoanalysis, to the whole personological, familial, self-centered mechanism "that makes us desire the objects of our loss, the pleasures of the nuclear family, guiding us toward neurosis, and keeping us attached to reminiscence." Child-like and forgetful, she is opposed to the memories of childhood, thanks to the blocks of childhood that traverse her in intensity and set her astride several age groups. Incestuous, essentially incestuous, she is all the more opposed to biological and regressive Oedipal incest. Self-destructive, she is as much opposed to the death-drive as she is to narcissism, because self-destruction in her case is still life, a line of flight, a trip. In short, she was the young woman-machine of *n*-sexes: Miss Arkadin, Ulrike von Kleist...

This is what happens in the other version of Roger's novel, which coexists with the first. Solange Solange designates this flash of a young woman, one who contains "every sex," the "pre-pubescent adult," the "tomboy," "one who embodies every embrace, from the most innocent to the most incestuous," and every sexuality, including the non-human and the vegetable. This has nothing to do with the difference of the sexes, and even less with bisexuality, wherein each sex also possesses the other. Rather, the epiphany, the election, is the eruption of an intense multiplicity which finds itself reduced, crushed by the distribution of the sexes and one's assignment as either one or the other. It all begins with the young woman: "I remember when I was younger, I possessed every sex, mine, yours, and many more. But by the time I was thirteen, it was already over. I fought puberty, but it was no use. They all disappeared. I became so heavy…" The young woman is above all caught in a struggle with a mechanism that is not merely biological pubescence, but a whole social mechanism destined to reduce her to the demands of marriage and reproduction.

Boys do not lag far behind. The girls serve as an example and a model for the boys. The first victim draws in the second, like a trapped animal serving as bait. The boys are forced to go through the girls to undergo an inverse and symmetrical reduction. Consequently, if we take this line of argument to its limit, there is only one sex, the female sex, but there is only one sexuality, male sexuality, which takes women as its object. So-called female sexuality has always been the means of male chauvinism. Thus the difference is not at all between the two sexes, but between the state of *n*-sexes on the one hand and, on the other, its reduction to one or the other of two sexes. The Solange with the power to flash is opposed to all the other false Solanges who have accepted, even wished for this heavy reduction (cf. the end of *Le Misogyne*)—just as the epiphany of the young woman is opposed to the banality of both man and woman—just as the freely machinic function is opposed to the reductive mechanism—just as the intense proper name that embraces a multiplicity is opposed to the system of common words that assign duality…

Read the novel for yourself: it is indeed the vulgar story of a misogynist who kills women because he has a woman inside him, but it is also the epiphany of a murderous young woman who kills, and eventually kills herself—but hers is a whole other story. Solange must be imagined as living and eternal, as born anew from herself, without the need for suicide. She must be imagined as Lightness in the flesh. This novel and Roger's previous novel, intimately connected, are links in a chain of life and renewal.

8

Four Propositions on Psychoanalysis

I would like simply to present four propositions on psychoanalysis.

This is the first: *psychoanalysis stifles the production of desire*. Psychoanalysis is inseparable from a political danger, unique to it, which has nothing to do with the dangers of the old psychiatric hospital. The old psychiatric hospital locks you away in an eclosed space that has coordinates on a grid. Psychoanalysis, however, works invisibly in the open air. The psychoanalyst today shares a similar position with the merchant in feudal society as Marx understood it: psychoanalysts work in the open pores of society, not only in private practice, but in schools and institutions and every sector of society. This way of working has created the unique situation we find outselves in today with respect to the psychoanalytic enterprise. The fact is that psychoanalysis is always talking about the unconscious; but in a certain way, this serves only to reduce the unconscious, to destroy it, to ward it off. The unconscious is thought of as a counter-consciousness, a negative of consciousness, like a parasite. It is the enemy. "Wo es war, soll ich werden." Give this phrase your best translation—*where it was, there I as a subject must be*—it changes nothing! It doesn't change the "soll," this strange "duty in the moral sense." What psychoanalysis calls production or formation of the unconscious is nothing more than failure, idiotic conflict, lame compromise, or obscene word-play. Any success at all is labeled sublimation, desexualization, or thought—but certainly not desire, that enemy lodged at the heart of the unconscious. You always have too many desires, you are a polymorphic pervert. What you must be taught is Lack, Culture, and Law, in other words, the reduction and the abolition of desire.

This has nothing to do with theory. It has to do with the infamous practical art of psychoanalysis, the art of interpretation: interpret, initiate regression, regress. Perhaps the most grotesque pages in all of Freud are those he wrote on fellatio: how in this instance a penis (*pénis*) stands for a cow udder (*pis de vache*), and a cow udder for the maternal breast. In other words, fellatio means you can't find a cow udder to pull, or that you want your mommy, or she has no more milk. This is merely a way of showing that fellatio is not a "true desire" but means something else, that it is hiding something, some other desire. The grid which psychoanalysis has at its disposal is perfect for this: the true contents of desire are supposedly partial infantile impulses, and Oedipus is the genuine expression of desire (it structures "the whole"). As soon as desire *assembles* something, in relation to an Outside, to a Becoming, they undo this assemblage, they break it up, showing how the assemblage refers on the one hand to a partial infantile mechanism and, on the other, to a global Oedipal structure. Fellatio is no different in this respect: an oral impulse to suckle the breast + a structural Oedipal accident. It is the same for homosexuality, bestiality, masochism, voyeurism, even masturbation: Are you not ashamed to act like a child? Are you not ashamed to do this to Oedipus? Before psychoanalysis, they used to refer to fellatio as a dirty old man's obsession; now they refer to it as a perverse infantile activity. It amounts to the same thing. They are always trying to separate true desires from false desires. They are always trying to break up the machinic assemblages of desire.

But what we are saying is this: you do not have the unconscious, you never had it. It is not some "it was" where an "I" must show up instead. Freud's formulation should be reversed. You *must* produce the unconscious. Produce it, or be happy with your symptoms, your ego, and your psychoanalyst. Each of us works and creates with the shred of placenta which we smuggled out of the womb and which we carry with us as a milieu of experimentation—but we do not experiment by obeying the egg, the progenitors, the interpretations and regressions which still bind us to it. Try to produce some unconscious, it is not so easy. It doesn't happen just anywhere, it doesn't happen with a slip of the tongue, a witty remark, not even with a dream. The unconscious is a substance which must be created, placed, made to flow; it is a social and political space which must be won. A revolution produces the unconscious in an awesome display, and revolution is one of the few ways to do so. The unconscious has nothing to do with Freudian slips, in speech or in action. It is not a subject that produces little off-shoots in consciousness. It is an object of production; it must be produced (unless there is some obstacle). To put it another way, there is no subject of desire, and no object either. The objectivity of desire itself is only its flows. There is never enough desire. Desire is the system of a-signifying signs out of which unconscious flows are produced in a social-historical field. Every unfolding of desire, in whatever place it may occur, such as a family or a school in the neighborhood, tests the established order and sends shock waves through the social field as a whole. Desire is revolutionary because it is always seeking more connections. Psychoanalysis unhooks and reduces every connection and assemblage. That is its job. It hates desire, and it hates politics. Producing the unconscious = the expression of desires = the formation of utterances = the substance or material of intensities.

The second proposition thus concerns the way in which psychoanalysis impedes the formation of utterances. How are utterances formed? In producing the unconscious, the machinic assemblage of desire and the collective assemblage of utterance are one and the same. In their content, assemblages are populated by becomings and intensities, by intensive circulations, by multiplicities of every kind (packs, masses, species, races, populations). And in their expression, assemblages use 1) indefinites, but which are not indeterminate (*some* stomachs, *an* eye, *a* child, etc.), 2) infinitives, which are not infinite or undifferentiated but are processes (to walk, to fuck, to shit, to kill, to love...), 3) proper names, which are not persons (they can be groups, animals, entities, singularities, whatever is written in capital letters). *Un Hans Devenir-Cheval* (A HANS HORSE-BECOMING).[1] The sign (utterance) everywhere connotes multiplicities (desire), or it guides flows. The collective machinic assemblage is as much the material production of desires as it is the expressive cause of utterances. Whatever has desire as its content is expressed as an IT, the "it" of the event, the indefinite of the infinitive proper name. The "it" constitutes the semiotic articulation of chains of expression whose intensive contents are among the least formalized. In this sense, Guattari shows that *it* does not represent a subject, but *diagrams* an assemblage; it does not overcode utterances, but keeps them from falling under the tyranny of semiotic constellations known as significant.

However, it is not difficult to impede the formation of utterances, nor the production of desire. Just split the IT in two: on the one hand, an *expressing subject*, which overcodes and transcends all utterances and which allows, on the other hand, a *subject of utterance* to re-emerge in the form of a personal pronoun, any personal pronoun, in all their permutations. The flows of desire are now dominated by an imperialist signifying system; they are reduced to a world of mental representations where the intensities lose their steam and the connections are broken. A fictitious expressing subject, an absolute I, has been made the cause of utterances whose relative subject can be any one of the personal pronouns (I, you, he, etc.) that are usually assigned according to the hierarchy and stratification of the dominant reality. Far from maintaining a relationship with the proper name, personal pronouns effect its nullification in a function of capitalist exchange. Do you know what must be done to keep someone from speaking in his or her name? Have them say "I". The more the cause of expression is attributed to a subject, whose utterances are then referred to other subjects which depend on it as the originator, the more the assemblage of desire is broken, the more the conditions required for the formation of utterances tend to dissolve—the more the expressing subject can be foisted on the subjects of utterance, which have become docile and sad. We are not saying that this procedure is peculiar to psychoanalysis. In fact, it fundamentally belongs to the "democratic" State apparatus (the identity of legislator and subject). Theoretically it is woven in with the long history of the Cogito. But "therapeutically," psychoanalysis has figured out how to make it work to its own advantage. We are referring not to the "topic" under discussion, but to the procedure by means of which the patient is first treated as an expressing subject with respect to the psychoanalyst and psychoanalytic interpretation (you, Patient, are the true *psychoanalysand*), but then is treated as a subject of utterance in his or her own desires and activities, which are to be interpreted in such a way, and until such time as, the expressing subject can be foisted on a subject of utterance which has given up on everything, i.e. whatever the patient had wanted to say, or had desired. One of the many places where this sort of thing can be seen is the Medical Pedagogic Institute (MPI). Here the child is split up: on the one hand, the child in all its concrete activities is a subject of utterance; on the other hand, the child in psychotherapy is elevated to the symbolic level of an expressing subject only to be reduced more effectively to the ready-made, standard utterances which are expected of a child, and which are imposed on the child. There you have your glorious castration, which merely cuts off the "it," prolonging this interruption with the famous cleavage of the subject.

When we have ourselves psychoanalyzed, we believe we are speaking, and we willingly pay for this belief. In fact, we haven't the slightest chance of speaking. *All of psychoanalysis is designed to keep people from speaking and to take away the conditions of true expression.* This is what we wanted to make clear in the text that follows this one: in each case you have an example of how children are kept from speaking, and how they have no way to escape. This was the case with the Wolf-Man, but it is also the case with Little Hans and the child patients of Melanie Klein, who is perhaps worse than Freud. How a patient can be kept from producing utterances is most striking when children are involved. This is how psychoanalysis does it: it begins with ready-made collective utterances, Oedipal in nature, and it claims to discover the cause of these utterances in a personal subject of utterance which owes everything to psychoanalysis. You are trapped from the start. We should try to do the opposite, and this is the task of schizo-analysis: begin with someone's personal utterances and discover their genuine production, which is never a subject but always machinic assemblages of desire, collective assemblages of utterance that traverse the subject and circulate within it. If they are blocked in one location, they are tunneling in another. They always take the form of multiplicities, packs, mobs, masses of elements of very different orders, haunting the subject and populating it (this has nothing to do with a technological or sociological hypothesis). There is no expressing subject. There are only utterance-producing assemblages. You know, when Guattari and I attempted a critique of Oedipus, we were forced to say so many stupid things in response to stupid objections like: "Now hold on, Oedipus is not mommy-daddy, it's the symbolic," or "It's the signifier, it's the mark of our finitude, this lack in being which we call life...." Well, beside the fact that these formulations are even worse, what psychoanalysts say theoretically is not the point. We see clearly enough what they do in practice, and the ignoble use they make of Oedipus—there is no other use. The partisans of the signifier are especially egregious offenders in this respect: you can't say "Mouth of the Rhône" (*Bouches du Rhône*) without them firing back "mouth of the mother" (*bouche de la mère*), or "hippy group" (*groupe hippy*) without being corrected: "big weenie" (*gros pipi*). Whether structural or not, personology replaces every assemblage of desire. The distance that separates the desire or the sexuality of a child from Oedipus is in no danger of being discovered—just look at Little Hans. Psychoanalysis is the murder of souls. You can be analyzed for ten years, a hundred years: the longer it continues, the less there will be any opportunity to speak. That's the whole point.

My time is almost up, let me pick up the pace. The third proposition should develop how psychoanalysis goes about crushing utterances, destroying desire—the precise effect which it aims to produce. It has a two-fold machine at its disposal. On the one hand, there is an *interpretation machine*, whose purpose is to translate whatever the patient says into another language: whatever the patient says is already supposed to mean something else. In this kind of paranoid regime, every sign refers to another sign in an unlimited network of signs, perpetually expanding its scope in a spiral sweep: the sign which has been deemed a signifier refers to a signified, which itself spits back signifiers (the hysteric is meant to ensure this feed-back or echo which perpetuates psychoanalytic discourse *ad infinitum*). On the other hand, there is also a *machine of subjectivation*, and this represents a whole other regime of signs. In this case, the signifier is no longer grasped in relation to some signified, but in relation to a subject. The point of significance has become the point of subjectivation: the psychoanalyst himself. And from that point, rather than a sweeping spiral of signs referring to each other, you have a sign or a block of signs that shuttles along its own linear path, thus constituting an expressing subject, then a subject of utterance on which the first can be flattened—and here obsession neurosis is meant to serve as the process by which the subject of utterance always gives back expressing subjects.

Nor do these two machines or regimes exist side by side, properly speaking. We are familiar with regimes of interpretation, those despotic systems whose complimentary roles are played by the paranoid emperor and by the great interpreter. And we know regimes of subjectivation animate capitalism as a whole, both at the level of the economy and the level of politics. But the originality of psychoanalysis resides in the clever penetration of these two systems, or as it has been so aptly put: "the subjectivation of the id" and "the autonomy of an irreducibly subjective experience." These two machines, the one *in* the other, are what block every possibility of real experimentation, just as they impede the production of desire and the formation of utterances. Interpretation and subjectivation: these two diseases of the modern world were not invented by psychoanalysis, but psychoanalysis did find techniques of maintenance and propagation that are perfectly suited to such diseases. The whole code of psychoanalysis, partial drives, Oedipus, castration, etc., have no other purpose.

The fourth and last proposition—as quickly as possible: What about the power which psychoanalysis wields? As Robert Castel persuasively argues in his recent book,[2] psychoanalysis involves power relationships. To say that the source of power in psychoanalysis is transference, as so many psychoanalysts do, well, it's a joke. It's like saying that the source of power in banking is money (given the relation between transference and money, the two imply one another). Psychoanalysis is based on the liberal-bourgeois form of the contract; even the *silence* of the psychoanalyst represents the maximum of interpretation as prescribed by the contract. This silence is the culmination of the contract. However, within this external contract between psychoanalyst and patient, there is another contract of a very different kind silently at work: this other contract *converts* the libidinal flows of the patient, changing them into dreams, fantasies, words, etc. A libidinal flow that is changeable and indivisible is converted into an exchangeable and divisible flow, and the intersection of these two flows is where the power of the psychoanalyst resides. And like all power, the whole point is to render powerless the production of desire and the formation of utterances, in other words, to neutralize the libido.

I would like to conclude with one last remark: let me explain why Guattari and I are not the least interested in undertaking a theoretical enterprise from a Marxist-Freudian perspective. There are two reasons. First, such a theoretical enterprise begins with a return to origins, that is, a return to sacred texts: the sacred texts of Freud and the sacred texts of Marx. We think the point of departure should be totally different. It's not about reexamining sacred texts which have been more or less interpreted; it's about taking a good look at the actual situation as it now stands: the situation of the bureaucratic apparatus in the Communist Party, the situation of the bureaucratic apparatus of psychoanalysis, and the attempt to undermine these apparatuses. Both Marxism and psychoanalysis speak in the name of a certain kind of *memory*, though in very different ways, but this difference hardly matters. And it is in the name of a necessary *development* that their modes of expression function, again in very different ways, though it matters even less. We, on the other hand, believe that it is high time to speak in the name of a positive force of forgetting, in the name of what for each of us is his or her underdevelopment, what David Cooper so aptly calls the private third-world of each and every one of us,[3] and which is the same thing as experimentation. The second reason to distinguish our theoretical enterprise from typical Marxist-Freudian approaches is that they are attempting to reconcile two economies: the political and the libidinal. Even Reich maintains this duality and this combination. Our view, on the other hand, presupposes only one economy, and thus the problem of a genuine anti-psychiatric analysis is to show how unconscious desire sexually invests the forms of this economy as a whole.

9

The Interpretation of Utterances

What the psychoanalysis of children, more than any other type of psychoanalysis, makes obvious is the way *utterances* are crushed and stifled. It is impossible to produce an utterance without having it reduced to a prefabricated and predetermined grid of interpretation. The child cannot escape it: he or she is "beaten" in advance. Psychoanalysis is a formidable enterprise for preventing any production of utterances or real desires. We will take the example of three children, since that is where the problem is most apparent: Freud's well-known Little Hans; Melanie Klein's Richard; and Agnes, who is an example of the current sectorization. It goes from bad to worse.

What was said by the child has been put in the left-hand column. In the right-hand column, we have placed what the psychoanalyst or psychotherapist *hears* or retains or translates or manufactures. The reader can judge the extent of the difference between them. Under the guise of meaning and interpretation, this difference indicates maximum repression and betrayal.

The comparative work on these three children's cases was done as a group [Gilles Deleuze, Félix Guattari, Claire Parnet, André Scala] in the hope that similar groups will form, calling into question the letter of psychoanalysis.

LITTLE HANS, 5 YEARS OLD—FREUD

A–Hans' first movement is not complicated: he wants to go downstairs to meet his girlfriend Mariedl and sleep with her. A movement of deterritorialization through which the boy-machine endeavors to enter into a new assemblage (*for Hans*, his parents already formed a machinic assemblage with him, but one that was not supposed to be exclusive: "I will go back upstairs tomorrow morning to have breakfast and go to the bathroom.") His parents react poorly: "Goodbye, then...." Hans leaves. "Of course they bring him back." His first attempt at deterritorialization in the building thus fails. Hans understands that the little girls in his building are not "proper": he deciphers the local political economy and locates a more suitable partner in the restaurant, an "urbane lady." A second attempt at deterritorialization by conquering and crossing the

Freud cannot believe Hans desires a little girl. This desire *must* hide something else. Freud does not understand anything about assemblages or the movements of deterritorialization that accompany them. He only knows one thing: the family-territory, the logical family person. Anything else must be *representative* of the family. Desire for Mariedl must be an avatar of a supposedly primary desire for the mother. The desire for Mariedl has to be a desire for Mariedl to be part of the family. "Beneath this wish—I want Mariedl to sleep with me—*another wish certainly exists*: I want Mariedl to be part of our family"!!

street. But once again, there are problems.... His parents decide on a compromise: Hans will come to their bed from time to time. No one has ever been better reterritorialized to mother's bed. That is what an artificial Oedipus is. Forced into it, Hans expects at least as much from it as he did from the building-assemblage with little Mariedl, or the street-assemblage with the other young girl: "Why don't you put your finger there, Mom?"—"Because it's filthy!"—"What does filthy mean? Why?" Hans is cornered at every turn, surrounded. In a single movement, he is forced to take his mother as an object of desire and forbidden from doing so. He is inoculated with the Oedipus virus.

B–Hans never showed any fear that someone would cut off his penis. He responds to the threat of castration with august indifference. He never spoke of an organ, only about a functioning and a collective agent of functioning:

Psychoanalysis returns to theological modes of thought. Sometimes the belief is in only one sex, the male, the penis-organ (Freud). But this idea is accompanied by an *analogical method* in the ordinary sense: the clitoris would be the analog of the penis, a lousy little *the pee-maker*. Children have no interest in organs and organic functions, the things of sex. They are interested in machinic operations, in the states of the things of desire. Obviously, girls have a pee-maker and moms do too, since they pee: the materials are still the same, but simply have varying positions and connections. The sameness of the materials is the unity of the plane of consistency or composition. It is the *univocity* of being and desire. The variations in position and connection, the multiplicities are machinic assemblages that create the plane with varying degrees of power or perfection. There are not two sexes, there are *n* sexes; there are as many sexes as there are assemblages. And since each of us enters into several assemblages, each of us has *n* sexes. When children discover that they are reduced to one sex, male or female, they discover their powerlessness: they lose the machinic sense and are left only with the signification of a tool.

penis that will never grow. Sometimes they believe that there are two sexes, restoring a specific, vaginocentric feminine sexuality (Melanie Klein). This time the method changes, an analogical method in the scientific or *homological* sense is used, founded on the phallus-signifier and not on the penis-organ.[1] The structuralist profession of faith as expressed by Lévi-Strauss is given privileged application here, surpassing imaginary analogies for structural and symbolic homologies.

But in any case, nothing has changed: it matters very little whether one recognizes 1 or 2 sexes, even if the two sexes are situated inside each of us (bisexuality; the desire for a vagina in men that would be the equivalent of penis envy in women).[2] It makes no difference whether we think in terms of ordinary analogies (organs and organic functions) or scientific homology (signifiers and structural functions). These differences are all theoretical and only exist in the psychoanalyst's mind. In any case, they bind desire and castration together, whether the latter is interpreted as imaginary or symbolic

And then a child really does fall into depression. They have been damaged; their countless sexes have been stolen! We have tried to show how this ordeal *first* occurs in young girls. They are the first ones reduced to *one* sex; the little boys come next. It is not a question of castration, which would be the boy's fear of losing the penis he has, or the girl's distress about no longer or not yet having the penis she does not have. The problem is altogether different: the theft of the sexes that the child-machine had. (Thus Hans' fantasy of the plumber that is so misunderstood by his father and Freud. It is a deterioration fantasy, a nightmare of being damaged, of being reduced to one sex).

(the only question is which of the two methods administers this troublesome bond the best). In any case, they reduce sexuality, i.e. desire as libido, to the difference between the sexes: a fatal error whether this difference is interpreted organically or structurally, in relation to the penis-organ or in relation to the phallus-signifier.

That is not how the child thinks and lives:

1) Not an analogy of organs or homology of structures but a *univocity of material* with variable connections and positions (assemblages). Not organic function or structural function but machinic functioning. Univocity is the only atheist thought, the thought of the child;

2) Univocity is also the thought of the multiple *n* assemblages into which the material enters, *n* sexes; locomotive, horse and sun are no less sexes than boy and girl; the question-machine of sexuality always overflows the problem of the difference between the two sexes; *reducing everything to the difference between the* sexes is the best way to misunderstand sexuality;

3) When the child sees itself reduced to one of the two sexes, masculine *or* feminine, it has already lost everything; man or woman already designates beings from whom *n* sexes have been stolen; there is not a relationship of each of the sexes to castration, but first a relationship to the omnisexual, the multisexed (*n*) with this theft;

4) There is a dissymmetry between girls and boys, but it consists in the following: girls are the first ones from whom *they* steal the *n* sexes, from whom they steal the machine-body to turn it into a tool-body. The feminine revolutionary movements are radically mistaken when they demand rights for a specifically feminine sexuality (Lacanized Women's Liberation Movement!). What they should demand of all the sexes, no more feminine than masculine, of which the girl is first deprived, is that they end up a girl.

Freud continually misunderstands infantile sexuality. He interprets, and therefore misunderstands. He clearly sees that the child is completely indifferent to the difference between the sexes; but he interprets it as if the child were reacting to castration anxiety by maintaining its belief in the existence of a small penis on the girl. This is not true: the child has no castration anxiety before being reduced to a single sex. The child lives as having *n* sexes that correspond to all the possible arrangements into which the materials common to girls and boys enter but also those common to animals, things... Freud clearly sees that there is a girl-boy dissymmetry; but he interprets it as a variation of Oedipus-girl and Oedipus-boy and as the difference between girl-castration and boy-castration. This is not true either: there is no relation to Oedipus or the familial theme, except with the transformation of the body from machine to tool. There is no relation to castration tied to the sex one has, except with the theft of all the sexes one had. Freud binds sexuality to the family, to castration, to sexual difference: three major mistakes, three superstitions worse than in the Middle Ages, a theological mode of thought.[3] You could not even say that Freud interprets poorly; while interpreting he is at no risk of hearing what the child says. There is a lot of cynicism in Freud's declaration: "We use the indications the patient gives us in order to present his or her unconscious complex *to his or her consciousness in our own words* thanks to our *art of interpretation*."

C–Thus Hans failed in his deepest desire: attempts for machinic assemblages through deterritorialization (exploration of the street, each time in connection with a young girl). He is reterritorialized by his family. He is ready, however, to take even his family as a machinic assemblage or functioning. But the father, mother and "the Professor" are there in varying degrees to remind him that the family is not what he thinks it is, not an assemblage or a functioning. They are agents of desire, as well as people or representatives of the law: not machinic functioning but structural functions, the Father-function and Mother-function. Suddenly Hans is afraid to go out into the street. And he is afraid to go because a horse might bite him. How could it be any different since

Here, the father and the professor do not pull their punches. No scruples. Once again the horse must represent something else. And this something else is limited: first it is the mother, then the father, and then the phallus. (Not to worry, no matter what animal is under consideration, the Freudians' response will always be the same: horse or giraffe, rooster or elephant, it's always papa). Freud states it plainly: the horse by itself is of no importance; it is purely incidental....[4] A child seeing a horse fall under the whip and struggling back up with clattering hooves and sparks has no affective importance! Instead of seeing intensive affects and a machinic assemblage in the horse's determinations, such that the horse in the road distinguishes itself from any other animal and even other types of horses, Freud sings his refrain: look here, what the horse has near its eyes are papa's spectacles; what it has around its the street was blocked, forbidden to him from the point of view of his deepest desire? And the horse is not at all a horse as an imaginable tangible form (by analogy) or as a conceivable intelligible structure (homology). A horse is an element, a specific material in a street-horse-omnibus-load assemblage. A horse, as we have seen, is defined by a list of affects depending on the assemblage into which it enters. These affects represent nothing other than themselves: being blinded, having a bit, being proud, having a big pee-maker, large haunches for making dung, biting, pulling over-sized loads, being whipped, falling, making a hullabaloo with its legs... The true problem through which the horse is "affective" and not representative is: How do affects circulate in the horse? How do they pass and transform from one into the other? *The horse's becoming and the becoming-horse of little Hans*, one into the other. Hans' problem is determining the dynamic

mouth is papa's mustache![5] It is astonishing. What is a child to do against so much bad faith? Instead of seeing in the horse's determinations a *circulation* of intensities in a machinic arrangement, Freud proceeds through static analogies of representations, identifying the analogs: it is no longer the horse making perfect droppings with its massive rear (degree of power), but the horse itself *is* a dropping, and the door through which it comes out is a rear end! Instead of having the pee-maker and biting in a kind of intensive relationship in the horse, suddenly the *pee-maker* bites! Here, Hans gives a start, a way of saying that his father really has not understood a thing: "But a pee-maker does not bite." (Children are reasonable; they know that pee-makers do not bite, no more than pinky fingers speak). The father's shameful response: "Perhaps it does nonetheless ..." Who is sick? Little Hans? Or his father and the "professor" together? Ravaged by *interpretosis* and meaning. Nasty. Pity the children.

What does Freud want with his sly and determined resolve? (He himself relationship between all of these affects. For example, to be able to "bite," is it necessary to go through "falling," which then transforms into "making a hullabaloo with its feet?"[6] What is *possible* for a horse? Far from being an Oedipal fantasy, it is an anti-Oedipal program; becoming a horse to escape the stranglehold they want to impose on him. All human paths were closed for Hans. Only a becoming-animal, a becoming-human, will allow him to conquer the street. But psychoanalysis is there to close this final outlet.

boasts of not telling the father everything in order to reach his goals more easily and manipulate the interpretations). What he wants is to:

1) Break all of the little boy's machinic assemblages in order to reduce them to the family that will then be considered something other than an assemblage and imposed on the child as a representative of logic;

2) Prevent all of the child's movements of deterritorialization, which are, however, the essence of libido and sexuality; closing all exits, passages and becomings, including the becoming-animal, the becoming-inhuman; reterritorializing him in his parent's bed.[7]

3) Worry him, make him feel guilty, depress him, immobilize him, freeze him, fill him with sad affects... through interpretation. All Freud knows is anthropomorphism and territoriality, yet libido is always going somewhere else. Freud does not understand animals, their becoming or the becoming-animal. He does not understand the wolves of the Wolf-Man any more than the rats of the Rat-Man or Little Hans' horse.

D—How could Hans not be afraid at the same time (and for completely different reasons than those invented by Freud)? Becoming animal, entering into an assemblage like this is something serious. Even more important, desire directly confronts its own repression here. In the horse assemblage, the power to be affected is filled by affects of domestication, loss of power and sudden brutality no less than power and pride, active force. The road is not at all desire-anxiety-fear. But desire first meets fear, which only later becomes anxiety under the familial or psychoanalytic operation. Take for example biting: is it the act of a vicious animal in triumph, or the reaction of a beaten animal? Does little Hans bite or is he bitten? Will becoming-animal grant Hans the secret of the street as a line of flight, or will it give him the real reason for the blockage and obstruction ensured preventively by the

How does Freud go about achieving his goal? He breaks Hans' machinic assemblage into three parts: the horse will in turn and with increasing depth be mother, father and then phallus. Or more precisely:

1) Anxiety is first linked to the street and the mother ("he misses his mother in the street!");

2) The anxiety changes, settles, deepens into a fear of being bitten by a horse, a horse-phobia connected to the father ("the horse *had* to be his father");

3) The horse is a big, biting peemaker. Hans' ultimate assemblage, his last attempt at deterritorialization as becoming-animal is broken to be retranslated into family territoriality, familial triangulation. Why is it so important from this point of view for the mother to move toward the father and the father to move toward the phallus? Because the mother cannot possess autonomous power, which would allow territorial dispersion to subsist. We have seen that even if the mother dominates, the power of the family is phallocentric. It is therefore necessary for the father to get his power from the crucial phallus in order for triangulation

family? Becoming-animal as a superior deterritorialization pushes desire to its limit: desire coming to desire its own repression—a theme absolutely different from the Freudian theme, where desire would repress itself.

to occur as a structural or structuring operation. Castrated desire can only be socialized and sublimated on this condition. It is essential for Freud to assert that desire represses itself. In order to do so, it is necessary to show that *desire cannot bear "intensities."*[8] Freud still has the hysterical model in mind, where intensities are weak, as 19th century psychiatry had noted. The intensities therefore have to be broken to prevent them from circulating freely and really changing. They must be immobilized, each in a kind of significant or symbolic redundancy (desire for the mother, desire against the father, masturbatory satisfaction). An artificial system has to be constituted where they spin in circles. He has to show that desire is not repressed but represses itself by taking as its object something that is Loss, Castration and Lack in its essence (the phallus in relation to the mother, to the father, to itself). The psychoanalytic operation is then done: Freud can cynically claim to wait patiently and let Hans speak. Hans never had the slightest chance to speak, to pass on a single one of his "utterances." The reactions of the child in this kind of analysis are fascinating: the moments of irony when he senses that the adults are going too far.[9] And on the contrary, the total absence of humor, the extreme tedium of the analysis, the monomaniacal interpretation, the self-satisfaction of the parents and the Professor. But no one can live on irony: Little Hans has less and less, or he hides it more, he agrees with everything, he recognizes everything, resigns himself, yes, yes, I wanted to be the mama, I want to be the papa, I want a big pee-maker like papa's... just so they leave him alone, so that he can finally forget, forget everything, including those annoying hours of psychoanalysis.

RICHARD, 10 YEARS OLD—MELANIE KLEIN

This book by Melanie Klein is the shame of psychoanalysis.[10] You might think that Klein's themes—partial objects, paranoid and depressive positions—would allow psychoanalysis to avoid, even just a little, the Oedipal and familial quagmire. In fact, it only gets worse. The combatants: a young English Jew with a sense of humor is pitted against an old Austrian woman, whose resentment breaks the boy. The battle takes place over the course of 93 sessions. Richard's sense of humor protects him at first. He smiles politely at Mme. Klein's interpretations (p. 26); he remarks that it is "difficult to have so many kinds of parents in one's head" (p. 30); he asks to have a look at Mme. Klein's lovely watch to see if the session will soon be over (p. 31); he seems worried about his cold (p. 35); he says that "when he had told everything to Mme. Klein, he expected to hear the very same interpretations she had just given him" (p. 166). However, the imperturbable and humorless Mme. Klein continues her work, pounding away: *he is afraid* of my interpretations.... This is the leitmotif of her book: "*Mme. K interpreted*, Mme. K interpreted, Mme. k interpreted." Richard will be defeated, saying: Thank you, Madame. The goals of Mme. K are several: 1) to translate Richard's affects immediately into fantasies; 2) to move him, after a time, from the paranoid-schizoid position to the depressive position, from the machinic position (functioning) to the position of the little tool ("repaired"); 3) in terms of finality, to prevent him from forming utterances, thus breaking up any collective assemblage which would generate utterances in a child.

This is war! Richard reads three newspapers a day and listens to the radio. He learns the meanings of the words "ally," "enemy," "tyrant," "liar," "traitor," "neutral." And he learns them politically, that is, in terms of the proper names of contemporary History (Churchill, Hitler, Ribbentrop, Darlan), in terms of countries, territories, and the polycentrism of the Socius (map, borders, thresholds, the crossing of thresholds), in terms of war machines (bombs, planes, ships, etc.). He constructs several types of machinic assemblages: first, assemblages of countries on the full body of the Earth; second, assemblages of ships on the full body of the sea; third, assemblages of every means of transport (plane, bus, train, truck, parachute) on the full body of the World. And these assemblages are indeed libidinal:

not because, as Mme. K believes, they represent the eternal family, but because they are affects, becomings, passages, crossings; they are fields of territorialization and lines of deterritorialization. Richard's map, "viewed from the back," looks bizarre, confused, all mixed up, deterritorialized. Richard draws each type of assemblage in relation to the other types: the "giant star fish," or the full body of the Earth, is the "empire" with different colored countries, where the colors are affects. If the countries are assigned to family members, it is not because, as Mme. K believes, "the empire represents the family" (p. 105), but because the family itself is nothing other than an assemblage that is opened and deterritorialized along the Socius's lines of attack and flight. What happens in the family depends on what happens in the empire. It is true that Richard has an erection, but his penis gets hard or soft *politically*. This eros is political. Far from reducing the

Socius to the family, this political eros opens up the names of the family on top of the names of geography and history and redistributes them along the lines of a political polycentrism. The countries are affects. They are the equivalent of Richard's animal-becoming (this is why he assigns so many of them to himself). Richard's libido bathes the earth. He masturbates to Countries. This is Sex-Pol in action.

Thus, for Mme. K, the empire is the family. Mme. K does not hesitate. Unlike Freud, she is no hypocrite, she does not feign hesitation. From the start, she says: let's see, Hitler is whoever hurts mama, he is the bad father, the bad penis. The map "viewed from the back" is "the parents joined in the midst of sexual relations." "Mme. K interpreted: the English port where Prince Eugen was entering, represented his mother's genital organs." The colors are family members, etc., etc., for more than 400 pages! Richard is suffocated, the reader nauseated. Richard will be broken, crushed under enormous pressure, trapped *artfully* in the office of Mme. K: this is worse than being trapped in school, in the family, or in the media. No one has better demonstrated that a child has no right to participate in politics: it is understood that war is nothing to a child, to the libido of a child. All that counts for him are his "destructive impulses." The facts cannot be denied: Klein's conceptions of positions and partial objects do not loosen the Freudian stranglehold; on the contrary, they reinforce the familialism, Oedipalism, and phallocentrism proper to psychoanalysis. Mme. K has discovered a more direct way to convert affects into fantasies and to interrupt the child to keep him from producing utterances. The reasons are simple:

1) The theory of positions is intended to lead the child from its paranoid-schizoid position to a depressive position, where the family can again assume its unifying role, structurally and personologically integrating every other assemblage;

2) Mme. K borrows her bi-polar concepts from the school: *good and bad*, and every possible variation on this dualism. Her office is as much a family

room as a class room. Mme. K moralizes. Herein lies Melanie's originality: she cannot use the couch as the equivalent of the family bed to psychoanalyze children; she needs the equivalent of the school. This is the cost of psychoanalysis, only then is it possible (Anna, Freud's daughter, never understood).[11] Thus Mme. K reinterprets the family in terms of the school; she impregnates the family with the school. But she also furnishes the family with artful forces that enable it to ward off and recycle every libidinal investment originating from the Socius;

3) The conception of fragmented partial objects, you might think, would be one way to acknowledge multiplicities, segmentations, assemblages, and social polycentrism. In fact, it is quite the opposite. As Mme. K understands it, objects appear partial when they are abstracted from the machinic assemblages in which they participate, are dispersed, and distributed, when they are torn from the multiplicities to which they belong only to be reduced to and flattened on the "ideal" of an organic totality, a signifying structure, a subjective or personological integrity, none of

which, admits Mme. K, is yet present, but which will show up later as the "position," the age of the patient, and the cure progress (reduction to strata...).[12] "At the end of the analysis, despite the painful feelings he experienced, the child had not despaired, since he considered the cure essential to his well-being." Good Lord, at what price!

AGNES, 9 YEARS OLD, SECTORIZATION—J. HOCHMANN[13]

Sectorization has several focal points: the hospital, the emergency room, the free clinic, special education programs, house calls. Its model is not the family or the school, but the socius; hence it is polycentric. This does not preclude its forcing the child back on the family, understood as the unit of care. Because of her epilepsy, Agnes is taken out of public school, placed in a special education program, then sent to a free clinic, until finally a team of psychotherapists come to her home. They begin by translating everything into the language of organicism: everything is forced onto the stratum of organicism, everything is reduced to "a struggle over an organ." They speak in terms of organ and func-

Agnes' fit coincides with her period. She expresses her fit "machinically": a machinic defection, a loss of well-being, a diminished functioning, the failure or alteration of material (not the lack of an organ). This is what she says to the psychotherapist: "please fix me up, my belly-button hurts" (p. 888). "They took everything from me, they robbed me, they broke my machine" (p. 903). She rejects a tool-body, an organic body, and demands that her machine-body be given back. She manipulates the psychotherapist "like a marionette" (p. 901). Agnes, like a marionette out of Kleist, only without strings, now watches strings emerging from her in every direction: she rejects her breasts, her vagina, her eyes for seeing, her hands for touching. It's not about the difference between the sexes. It's about machinic differences, states of potential and perfection, the differences between "functioning" and "no longer functioning" (this is what is sexual: apples make babies, cars make love, her sister makes a baby for her). Were it indeed about the difference between the sexes, she

tion, rather than functioning. And yet the psychotherapists are forced to admit that the organ in question is rather bizarre and uncertain. In fact, it is a changeable material, whose variations correspond to different positions and connections: "It is hard to localize, to identify; sometimes it's a bone, an engine, a piece of excrement; sometimes it's a baby, a hand, papa's heart, or mommy's jewels..." (p. 905). However, this does not stop them from asserting that the problem most certainly has to do with the difference between the sexes, castration, and the lost object (p. 891, p. 905).

would not call on her sister for help in these words: *Michelle, my sister, before puberty*, that is, before being ruined, damaged, stolen (p. 892).

Agnes lives the family as a machinic assemblage (a group of connections and multiple intersections) which then serves as the foundation or point of departure for other assemblages: thus Agnes could deterritorialize herself on these other assemblages that in turn would modify the assemblage of the family—hence Agnes' wish "to return to the public school where her brother and sister used to be." The elements and material at Agnes' disposal are distributed in the family assemblage in such a way as to experience every possible coupling, position, and connection. It is the presence of the indefinite article that tracks these variations as well as the circulation of affects throughout the assemblage: *a* belly, *a* mouth, *an* engine, *a* thingamabob, *a* baby (p. 890, p. 908).

The family itself will be translated into organic terms: fusion, symbiosis, dependence (and not connection). Agnes will be thrown back on the Oedipal family, both as destination and point of departure. Rather than make the family play the role of an assemblage, they make Agnes' assemblages play familial roles: "We wanted to offer the child a substitute mother, through which she could then establish a relation to the symbolic, since in our view (at least this is our hypothesis) it is this relation to the symbolic that was missing and which she was desperately trying to reconstruct through the negation of personal identity" (p.894). Thus Agnes is forced not only onto the stratum of organicism, but onto the strata of familial significance and subjective personal identity. However, because she rejects subjective identity and familial significance, as well as organicism, Agnes' elements and materials will all be interpreted in terms of negation and partial objects, at least in as much as they have been abstracted from the combinations into which Agnes was trying to insert them (p. 900). What gets overlooked is the fact that Agnes' protests do not originate in negations such as partiality, castration, or fragmented Oedipus. They have a perfectly positive source: the machine-body that was stolen from her, the functioning states of which she has been deprived.

"Agnes had become violent. She exploded like a bomb at the slightest frustration." How could it be otherwise? At every turn she is told: it is not you speaking, it's the others in you; but don't be afraid, you are Agnes; we understand the desires of a young girl like you, and we are here to explain them to you. How could Agnes not scream: "I am not Agnes!" She has wasted her breath talking, producing utterances, which the psychotherapist does not hear. Agnes takes her revenge by manipulating her "like a marionette." When Agnes says of the psychotherapist, "she says whatever I do, she knows whatever I think," we should not take it as a compliment regarding the psychotherapist's clear sightedness. Agnes is accusing her of acting like a cop, of gross distortion (unless the psychotherapist knew everything, how else could she so distort it?). Agnes is trapped on every side—family, school, socius. The essential factor in this generalized entrapment is psychotherapy, which has taken upon itself to realign the various focal points of power. Agnes used to have *n* sexes; they have given her one, and they have violently forced her back on the difference between the sexes. Agnes used to have *n* mothers, that is, materials capable of transformation; they have left her with one. Agnes used to have *n* parcels of territory; they occupy every last inch. "Her monotonous complaint" has nothing to do with "Oedipus torn between contradictory demands" (p. 908). She is screaming: Thief! Thief!

10

The Rise of the Social

The question here has nothing to do with the adjective that used to qualify the group of phenomena encountered in sociology: THE social refers to a *particular sector* in which very diverse problems are categorized as needed, special cases, specific institutions, a category of qualified personnel ("social" assistants, "social" workers). We speak of social plagues, like alcoholism and drugs; social programs, from repopulation to birth control; social adjustment or maladjustment (of the pre-delinquent, emotionally disturbed or handicapped, including different types of advancement). Jacques Donzelot's book has great force because he proposes an account of the origins of this recently formed, increasingly important, and strange sector, the social: a new landscape is taking shape. Since the contours of this domain are vague, we must first recognize it from the way it took shape in the 18th-19th centuries, the way it carved out its own originality in relation to older sectors even if it meant reacting to them and distributing them in a new way. Among the most striking pages by Donzelot, there are those that describe the case of the "children's tribunal": the *social*, par excellence. At first glance, it might only seem a miniature jurisdiction. But like an engraving under a magnifying glass, Donzelot discovers another organization of space, other finalities, other characters, even disguised or assimilated in a judicial apparatus: notables as assessors, educators as witnesses, an entire group of tutors and technicians that closely follow the broken or "liberalized" family.

The social sector does not merge with the judicial sector even if it does propose new offshoots for it. Donzelot shows how the social does not merge with the economic sector either, precisely because it invents an entire social economy and creates a new basis for the distinction between rich and poor. Nor does it merge with the public or the private sector, since it induces a new, hybrid figure of public and private and produces its own distribution, an original intertwining of state interventions and retractions, charges and discharges. The question is not at all whether there is indeed a mystification of the social, or which ideology it expresses. Donzelot asks how the social formed in reaction to the other sectors, leading to new relationships between the public and private sectors; the judicial, the administrative and the customary sectors; wealth and poverty; city and country; medicine, school and family, etc. The social thus manages to intersect and rework the previous or independent distinctions, providing the forces present with a new field. It is then with all the more force that Donzelot can leave the reader to draw conclusions about the social's pitfalls and machinations.

Since the social is a hybrid domain, especially in the relationship between public and private, Donzelot's method consists of drawing out *pure, short lineages*, either successive or simultaneous, that each act to form a contour or a side, a character of the new domain. The social will be found at the intersection of all these short lines. We must still distinguish the milieu on which these lines act by investing it and changing it: the family. Not that the family is incapable of being a motor for evolution, but it is necessarily so only by combining with other vectors, just as the other vectors enter into relationships of coupling or crossing to act on the family. Donzelot's book is therefore not at all about the crisis of the family: the crisis is only a negative effect of the rise of these the little lines; or rather, *the rise of the social and the crisis of the family are the dual political effect of the same elementary causes.* Hence the title "*The Policing of Families,*" which above all explains this correlation and escapes the dual danger of an overly global sociological analysis and an overly hasty moral analysis.

We must then show how, at each intersection of these causes, assemblages or arrangements form that function in one way or another, sliding into the spaces between larger or older mechanisms that in turn receive the effects of mutation. This is where Donzelot's method almost becomes a method of engraving, sketching the mounting of a new scene in a given framework (like the scene of the children's court in the judicial framework; or, again among the most beautiful pages by Donzelot, the "philanthropic visit" that slides into the framework of "charitable" institutions). Finally, we must determine the consequences of the lines of mutation and of the new functions on the field of forces, alliances, hostilities, resistances and above all the collective becomings that change the value of a term or the meaning of an utterance. In short, Donzelot's method is genealogical, functional, and strategic. Another way of expressing his debt to Foucault and Castel. But the way Donzelot establishes these lineages, the way he draws an entire strategic map of the "social" gives his book its profound originality.

Donzelot proves at the very beginning of his book that a lineage or a small line of mutation of the family can begin with a detour, a turn. Everything begins with a *bass* line: a line of critique or attack on nurses and domesticity. And already at this level, there is an intersection, since the critique does not take place in the same way for the rich and the poor. For the poor, he denounces the unsound political economy that leads them to abandon their own children, leave the countryside and place a heavy burden on the state. For the rich, he denounces an unsound economy or private hygiene that pushes them to confide the education of children confined in small rooms to domestics. There is therefore already a sort of hybridization of public and private that comes into play with the rich-poor distinction and also the city-country distinction, to trace the first line.

But a second line immediately appears. Not only does the family tend to detach itself from its domestic framework, but conjugal values tend to be distinguished from more properly familial values and take on a certain autonomy. Of course alliances remain regulated by family hierarchies. But it is less to preserve the order of families than as a preparation for conjugal life in order to give this order a new code. Preparation for marriage as an end rather than the preservation of the family by means of marriage. Concern for descendants rather than pride in ascendance. Everything happens as if women and children, caught in the failure of the old familial code, sought out the elements of a new, properly "social" coding in conjugality. The theme of the big sister-little mother is born. The social focuses on conjugality, its apprenticeship, its exercise and its duties, more than on the family, its inherentness and its rights. But here again, this mutation resonates differently for the rich and the poor: the conjugal duties of a poor woman confine her to her husband and children (preventing her husband from going to the cabaret, etc.) while those of a rich woman give her wide-ranging functions of control and a "missionary" role in the domain of charitable actions.

A third line extends to where the conjugal family tends to disengage itself partially from the paternal or marital authority of the head of the household. Divorce, the development of abortion for married women, and the possibility of paternal destitution are the most remarkable points on this line. But at a deeper level, subjectivity and objectivity are compromised: the subjectivity that the family finds in its responsible "head," capable of governing it and the objectivity the family draws from a network of dependency and complementarities that made it governable. On the one hand, new subjective drives must be found. This is where Donzelot shows the role of the *call to save*, which becomes the centerpiece of the new aid arrangement (here lie the differences between past charity and new philanthropy, where aid must be seen as an investment). On the other hand, the network of old dependencies is replaced with direct interventions where the *industrial system* itself comes to remedy the flaws for which the family is made responsible (thus the legislation on child labor where the system is supposed to defend children against their own families—the second aspect of philanthropy). In the first case, the state tends to free itself of overly burdensome responsibilities by using the call to save and private investment. In the second case, however, the state is led to intervene directly, making the industrial sphere a "moral civilization." As a result, the family can become both the object of neo-liberal praise as a place for saving and the object of social and even socialist critique as an agent of exploitation (protecting women and children). It is simultaneously an opportunity for the neo-liberal state to unload and the target or the burden of the interventionist state. Not an ideological argument, but two poles of a strategy on the same line. The hybridization of the public and private sectors takes on a positive value to form the social.

And then there is a fourth line bringing about a new alliance between the medical field and the state. Under the action of very diverse factors (the development of obligatory schooling, the soldier's regimen, a disengagement from conjugal values that puts the accent on descendents, population control, etc.), "hygiene" becomes public at the same time that psychiatry comes out of the private sector. There is still hybridization to the extent that medicine maintains a private neo-liberal character (*contract*) while the interventionist state necessarily intervenes through public and statutory actions (*tutelage*).[1] But the proportions of these elements vary. Oppositions and tension continue to exist (for example, between judicial power and psychiatric "competency"). Moreover, the wedding of medicine and the state takes on a different aspect, not only according to the common policies in vigor (eugenics, Malthusianism, planning, etc.) but depending on the nature of the state that is supposed to carry out these policies. Donzelot has written some excellent pages on the exploits of Paul Robin and anarchist groups who represented a certain "leftist" current at the time, with actions in factories, strike support, neo-Malthusian propaganda and where anarchism supported the notion of a strong state. As in the previous cases, the points of authoritarianism, the points of reform, and the points of resistance and revolution confront each other on the same line over the new stakes of "the social," where medicine and the state combine to become hygienists in several ways, even contradictory ones that reinvest or remodel the family. We learn many troubling things by reading Donzelot on schools of parenting, on the start of family planning; it is surprising that the political divisions were not necessarily the ones we thought. To serve a more general problem: the political analysis of statements—how a statement refers to a policy and can radically change its meaning from one policy to another.

There is another line: the line of psychoanalysis. Donzelot gives it a great deal of importance based on an original hypothesis. There is some concern today to establish a true history of psychoanalysis that breaks with the intimist anecdotes about Freud, his disciples and his dissidents or with ideological questions in order to define organizational problems more clearly. The history of psychoanalysis in general has until now carried the mark of intimism, even at the level of the formation of psychoanalytic associations, because we have remained trapped in a ready-made schema: psychoanalysis was created in private (contractual) relationships, formed private offices and only recently left them to reach into a public sector (IMP,[2] dispensaries, sectorization, and teaching). Donzelot, on the contrary, thinks that psychoanalysis established itself very quickly in a hybrid public and private environment and that this was one of the fundamental reasons for its success. Psychoanalysis came to France late. But it took hold precisely in semi-public sectors like family planning in relation to problems such as "How can unwanted children be avoided?" We should try to confirm this hypothesis by looking at other countries. In any case, it allows a break with the perfunctory dualism "Freud, neo-liberal—Reich, Marxist dissident" in order to carve out a political and social field of psychoanalysis where ruptures and confrontations occur.

In Donzelot's hypothesis, where does psychoanalysis get the power to invest a mixed sector—"the" social—and immediately trace a new line? Psychoanalysts are not social workers like those the other lines produced. Several things distinguish them from social workers: they do not come to your home, they do not verify what you say, and they do not impose any restrictions. But we have to return to the previous situation: there was still much tension between the judicial and psychiatric orders (deficiency of the psychiatric grid, an overly broad notion of degeneracy, etc.) and much opposition between the requirements of the state and psychiatric criteria.[3] In short, the rules of equivalency and translation between the two systems were lacking. Everything then occurred as if psychoanalysis registered this lack of equivalency and proposed as a substitute a new system of *flotation* by creating the theoretical and practical concepts necessary for this new state of things. Just as for the economy, a currency is called a floating currency when its value is no longer determined by a fixed measure but in relation to the prices of a variable, hybrid market. This obviously does not exclude any new regulatory mechanisms (like the "snake" that indicates the maximum and minimum of currency flotation). This is the significance of Donzelot's comparison between Freud and Keynes: it is much more than a metaphor. In particular, the special role of money in psychoanalysis no longer needs to be interpreted under old free market standards or with inept symbolic forms. It becomes a veritable psychoanalytic "snake." But *how did psychoanalysis ensure this very special flotation, when psychiatry was unable to do so?* According to Donzelot, its primary role was to float public norms and private principles, expert appraisals and confessions, tests and memories through the play of displacement, condensation and symbolization connected to the parental images and psychic authorities used by psychoanalysis. Everything takes place as if Public-Private, State-Family, and Law-Medicine relationships had long been under a fixed system—the law—that set relationships and equivalencies, with even a wide margin of flexibility and variety. But "the" social emerges with the floating regime where norms replace the law and regulatory and corrective mechanisms replace the fixed standard.[4] Freud and Keynes. No matter how much psychoanalysis speaks of Law, it belongs to another regime. But it does not have the final word in the social: while the social is formed by this system of regulated floatation, psychoanalysis is only one mechanism among others, and not the most powerful. But it has permeated all of the other mechanisms, even when it disappears or combines with them.

From the "bass" line to the floating line, with all of the other lines in-between (conjugal, philanthropic, hygienic, industrial), Donzelot has drawn the map of the social from its emergence to its expansion. He shows us the birth of the Modern Hybrid: how desires and powers, the new demands for control but also the new abilities for resistance and liberation are organized and confront each other on these lines. "Having a room to oneself" is a desire, but also a control. Conversely, a regulatory mechanism is haunted by what overflows it and makes it burst from the inside. The fact that Donzelot lets his readers draw their own provisional conclusions is not a sign of indifference, but the direction of his upcoming work in the field he has charted.

11

Desire and Pleasure

[A] One of the major theses of *Discipline and Punish*[1] has to do with power arrangements. This thesis seemed essential to me in three respects: 1) In and of itself and in relationship to the radical Left, it is a profound political innovation of the conception of power, as opposed to any theory of the State.

2) With regard to Michel, this thesis allowed him to get beyond the duality of discursive and non-discursive formations, still present in *The Archaeology of Knowledge*,[2] and explain how these two types of formations were distributed or articulated segment by segment (without reducing one to the other, or equating the two..., etc.). It was not a matter of erasing the distinction, but of finding a reason for the relationships between them.

3) With a specific consequence: power arrangements rely neither on repression nor on ideology. Breaking away from these kinds of alternatives, more or less accepted by everyone, *D and P* formed a concept of normalization, and of disciplines.

[B] This thesis about power arrangements, I believed, was moving in two directions that were not at all contradictory, and yet distinct. In any case, these arrangements could not be reduced to a State apparatus. In one direction, they made up a diffused, heterogeneous multiplicity or micro-arrangements. In another direction, they referred to a diagram, a sort of abstract machine, immanent to the whole social field (for example, panoptism, defined by the general function of seeing without being seen and applicable to any multiplicity).It was as if these directions of a micro-analysis were equally important, since the second one showed that Michel was not satisfied with "dissemination" alone.

[C] *The Will to Knowledge*[3] takes a new step with regard to *D and P*. The point of view remains the same: neither repression nor ideology. However, to say it quickly, power arrangements are no longer content to be normalizers, they tend to be constituents (of sexuality). They are no longer content to form bodies of knowledge, they constitute truth (the truth of power). They no longer refer to categories which, in spite of everything, are negative ones (madness, delinquency as the object of imprisonment), but instead refer to a so-called positive category (sexuality). This last point is confirmed by an interview in the *Quinzaine littéraire*.[4] In this respect, I really believe that there is a new advance made in the analysis in *WK*. The danger is: does Michel return to something analogous to a constituting subject, and why does he feel the need to revive truth, even if he makes it into a new concept? These are not my own questions, but I think that these two false issues will be raised as long as Michel does not provide some additional explanation.

[D] A first question for me was the nature of the micro-analysis Michel first established in *D and P*. The difference between micro and macro was obviously not one of size, where micro-arrangements would be concerned with small groups (the family has no less a capacity for extension than any other formation). It was also not a question of an extrinsic dualism, since there are micro-arrangements immanent to the State apparatus and segments of the State apparatus also penetrate micro-arrangements—a complete immanence of the two dimensions. Is the difference then one of scale? A page in the *WK* explicitly refutes this interpretation. However, this page seems to link the macro to a strategic model and the micro to a tactical model. This bothers me because it seems to me that Michel's micro-arrangements have a wholly strategic dimension (especially if one takes into account this diagram from which they cannot be separated). Another direction would be one of the relations of power, as determining the micro (see especially the interview in the *Quinzaine*). But Michel, I believe, has not yet developed this point: his original conception of relations of power must be as new a concept as all the rest.

In any case, there is heterogeneity, a difference in the nature between micro and macro, which in no way excludes the immanence of the two. So, my question would be the following: Does this difference in nature allow us to keep talking about power arrangements? The notion of the State is not applicable at the level of a micro-analysis since, as Michel says, the issue is not to miniaturize the State. But is the notion of power any more applicable? Is it not also a miniaturization of a global concept?

I am getting to the first way in which I differ from Michel at the present time. If I talk about assemblages of desire with Félix Guattari, it is because I am not sure that micro-arrangements can be described in terms of power. For me, an assemblage of desire indicates that desire is never a natural or spontaneous determination. For example, feudalism is an assemblage that inaugurates new relationships with animals (the horse), with land, with deterritorialization (the knight riding away, the Crusades), with women (courtly love and chivalry)... etc. These are totally crazy assemblages but they can always be pinpointed historically. I would say for myself that desire circulates in this heterogeneous assemblage, in this kind of symbiosis: desire is one with a determined assemblage, a co-function. Of course, an assemblage of desire will include power arrangements (for example, feudal powers), but these must be located among the different components of the assemblage. Along one axis, we can distinguish states of being and enunciation in assemblages of desire (this would concur with Michel's distinction of two types of formations or multiplicities). Along another axis, we would distinguish territorialities or re-territorializations, and movements of de territorialization that lead into an assemblage (for example, all the movements of deterritorialization leading up to the Church, chivalry, peasants). Power arrangements would surface wherever re-territorializations, even abstract ones, take place. Power arrangements would therefore be a component of assemblages and yet these assemblages would also include points of deterritorialization. In short, power arrangements would not assemble or constitute anything, but rather assemblages of desire would disseminate power formations according to one of their dimensions. This is what allows me to answer a question that is necessary for me, but not for Michel: How can power be desired? The first difference is that, for me, power is an affection of desire (granted that desire is never a natural reality). All this is quite approximate. I have not spoken about the more complicated relationships between the two movements of deterritorialization and re-territorialization. However, it is in this sense that desire comes first and seems to me to be the element of a micro-analysis.

[E] I couldn't agree with Michel more about an aspect I consider fundamental: neither ideology nor repression. For example, statements, or rather utterances, have nothing to do with ideology. Assemblages of desire have nothing to do with repression. Yet, obviously, I do not have Michel's confidence concerning power arrangements; I become lost in the vagueness of the ambiguous status they have for me. In *D and P*, Michel says that they normalize and discipline. I would say that they encode and reterritorialize (I suppose that here too, there is more to it than just a difference in terminology). However, given that I emphasize the primacy of desire over power, or the secondary character that power arrangements have for me, their operations continue to have a repressive effect since they stamp out, not desire as a natural given, but the tips of assemblages of desire. Let's take one of the most beautiful theses of *WK*: the sexuality arrangement reduces sexuality to sex (to the sexual difference, etc. and psychoanalysis is a key player in this reduction). I see a repressive effect here, precisely at the border between micro and macro. Sexuality, as an historically variable assemblage of desire which can be determined, with its points of deterritorialization, fluxes and combinations, is going to be reduced to a molar agency, sex, and even if the means by which this reduction occurs are not repressive, the (non-ideological) effect itself is repressive inasmuch as the assemblages are broken apart, not only in their potentialities but in their micro-reality. So they can only keep on existing as fantasies, which changes and twists them completely out of shape, or they become shameful things… etc. A small problem that concerns me a great deal: Why are some troubled people, more than others, more vulnerable to, and perhaps dependent on, shame? (For example, people who have enuresis or anorexia are not easily affected by shame). I therefore need a certain concept of repression, not in the sense that repression would crack down on spontaneity but inasmuch as collective assemblages would have many dimension, and power arrangements would be only one of these dimensions.

[F] Another fundamental point: I think that the thesis neither repression—nor ideology has a correlate, and may in fact depend upon this correlate. A social field is not defined by its contradictions. The notion of contradiction is a global, inadequate notion and already implies a strong complicity of contradictories in power arrangements (for example, two classes, the bourgeoisie and the proletariat). Indeed it seems to me that another of Michel's great innovations in the theory of power is that a society does not contradict itself, or hardly does so. Yet his answer is: it strategizes itself, it makes up strategies. And I find that very beautiful. I see the immense difference (between strategy and contradiction) and should re-read Clausewitz on the subject. Yet I don't feel comfortable with this idea.

I would say that for me, a society, a social field does not contradict itself, but first and foremost, it leaks out on all sides. The first thing it does is escape in all directions. These lines of flight are what come first (even if first is not chronological). Far from being outside the social field or coming from it, flight lines constitute its rhizome or cartography. Flight lines are almost the same thing as movements of deterritorialization. They do not imply any return to nature. They are shooting points of deterritorialization in assemblages of desire. What comes first in feudalism are these flight lines it supposes; likewise for the 10th-12th centuries; likewise for the formation of capitalism. Flight lines are not necessarily revolutionary, on the contrary, but they are what power arrangements are going to seal off and tie up. Around the 11th century, all kinds of lines of deterritorialization were cropping up: the last invasions, groups looting and sacking, the deterritorialization of the Church, peasant migrations, the transformation of chivalry, the transformation of towns and cities which were progressively abandoning territorial models, the transformation of money that was injected into new circuits, the change in the status of women with the themes of courtly love that deterritorialized, even chivalrous love, etc. Strategy is secondary to flight lines, their conjugations, their orientations, their convergences and divergences. Here again, I find the primacy of desire, since desire is precisely within these flight lines, the conjugation and dissociation of fluxes. It is indistinguishable from them. So, it seems to me that Michel encounters a problem that does not have the same status for me at all. For if power arrangements were in some way constituents, only resistance phenomena could possibly counter them and the question involves the status of these phenomena. In fact, they too would be neither ideological nor repressive. Hence the importance of two pages in *WK* where Michel says: Do not make me say that these phenomena are imaginary… But what status is he going to give them? Here, there are many directions: 1) the one in *WK* where phenomena of resistance would be like a reverse image of arrangements, where they would have the same characteristics, diffusion, heterogeneity… etc., where they would be vis-à-vis; but this direction seems to lead as much to a dead-end as to a way out of one; 2) the direction indicated in the interview in *Politique Hebdo*:[5] if power arrangements are constituents of truth, if there is a truth in power, there must be a kind of power of truth as a counter-strategy against powers. Hence the problem of the intellectual for Michel and his way of reintroducing the category of truth, since, in renewing it completely by making it dependent on power, he finds ammunition which can be turned against power? But I don't see how. We will have to wait for

Michel to give his new conception of truth, on the micro analytical level; 3) the third direction, which would be that of pleasures, the body and its pleasures. Once again, I am in a state of waiting. How do pleasures animate counter-powers, and how does he conceive of this notion of pleasure?

I think that there are three notions which Michel uses in a completely new way, yet has not completely developed: power relationships, truths, and pleasures.

Some issues I have are not raised by Michel because he has already resolved them through his own research. Conversely, to encourage myself, I tell myself that there are other problems he has, out of his theses and feelings, that I do not share. Flight lines, movements of deterritorialization with collective, historical determinations have no equivalent in Michel's work. I myself don't wonder about the status resistance phenomena may have, since flight lines are the first determinations, since desire assembles the social field, power arrangements are both products of these assemblages and that which stamps them out or seal them up. I share Michel's horror regarding those who claim to be on the fringe of society: I am less and less able to tolerate romanticizing madness, delinquency, perversion or drugs. But flight lines, that is, assemblages of desire, are not, in my view, created by marginal characters. Rather, these are objective lines that cut across a society, where marginal figures are located here and there, making a loop, a swirl, a re-coding. I therefore have no need to posit the status of resistance phenomena if the first given of a society is that everything escapes from it and everything is deterritorialized. Hence the status of the intellectual and the political problem are not the same things theoretically for Michel and me. (I will attempt further on to explain how I see this difference between us).

[G] The last time we saw each other, Michel kindly and affectionately told me something like the following: I can't stand the word desire; even if you use it differently, I can't stop myself from thinking or experiencing the fact that desire = lack, or that desire is repressed. Michel added: So, what I call "pleasure" is maybe what you call "desire," but in any case, I need a word other than desire.

Obviously, once again, it is more than a matter of vocabulary. For one thing, I can barely stand the word pleasure. But why is that? For me, desire includes no lack; it is also not a natural given. Desire is wholly a part of a functioning heterogeneous assemblage. It is a process, as opposed to a structure or a genesis. It is an affect, as opposed to a feeling. It is a hecceity—the individual singularity of a day, a season, a life. As opposed to a subjectivity, it is an event, not a thing or a person. Above all, it implies the constitution of a field of immanence or a body-without-organs, which is only defined by zones of intensity, thresholds, degrees and fluxes. This body is as biological as it is collective and political. It is on this body that assemblages are made and come apart, and this body-without-organs is what bears the offshoots of deterritorialization of assemblages or flight lines. It varies (the body -without-organs of feudalism is not the same as that of capitalism). If I call it a body-without-organs, it is because it opposes all strata of organization, the organism's organization as well as power organizations. It is precisely the whole group of body organizations that will smash the plane or the field of immanence, and will impose upon desire another type of plane, each time stratifying the body-without-organs.

If what I'm saying is confusing, it is because there are many issues which crop up in my relationship with Michel: 1) I cannot give any positive value to pleasure because pleasure seems to interrupt the immanent process of desire. Pleasure seems to me to be on the side of strata and organization; and in the same breath desire is presented as inwardly submitting to the law and outwardly regulated by pleasures. In both cases, there is a negation of the field of immanence proper to desire. I tell myself that it is not a coincidence if Michel emphasizes Sade, and I, on the contrary, Masoch.[6] It would not be enough to say that I am a masochist and Michel is a sadist. It would be all right, but it is not true. What interests me about Masoch is not the pain, but the idea that pleasure interrupts the positivity of desire and the constitution of its field of immanence. (Likewise, or rather in a different way, in courtly love, there is the constitution of a plane of immanence or a body-without-organs where desire is lacking nothing and avoids pleasures which would intervene to interrupt its process). Pleasure seems to me to be the only means for persons or subjects to orient themselves in a process that exceeds them. It is a re-territorialization. From my point of view, this is precisely how desire is brought under the law of lacking and in line with the norm of pleasure.

2) On the other hand, Michel's idea that power arrangements have an immediate and direct relationship with the body is essential. I am more concerned with how they impose an organization on bodies. Thus, the body-without-organs is the place or agent of deterritorialization (and thereby the plane of immanence of desire). While all organizations, all the systems Michel calls bio-power, in effect reterritorialize the body.

3) Could I envision setting up equivalences of the following type: What for me is a body-without-organs/desire corresponds to what for Michel is the body/pleasure? Can the distinction body/flesh about which Michel spoke to me be placed in relationship

to the body-without-organs/organism? In a very important passage in *WK*, Michel writes about how life gives a possible status to forces of resistance. D.H. Lawrence wrote about this life which is not at all Nature, but rather the variable plane of the immanence of desire, through all the determined assemblages. Lawrence's conception of desire relates to positive flight lines. (A small detail: the way in which Michel uses Lawrence at the end of *WK* is contrary to how I use Lawrence).

[H] Has Michel made progress with the issue under consideration: how can one uphold the rights of a micro-analysis (diffusion, heterogeneity, fragmentary character) and still allow for some kind of principle of unification that will not turn out to be like the State or the Party, a totalization or a representation?

First, as for power itself: I return to the two directions in *D and P*, on the one hand, the diffused and fragmentary character of the micro-arrangements, but on the other hand, the diagram or abstract machine that covers the whole social field. It seems to me that there was still a problem in *D and P*: the relationship between there two directions of the micro-analysis will be, on one hand, the micro-disciplines, and on the other, the bio-political processes. That is what I meant in point C, in these notes. The point of view in *D and P* suggested that the diagram, which could not be reduced to the global authority of the State, was perhaps operating a micro-unification of small arrangements. Should one now understand that the bio-political processes have this function? I admit that I felt the diagram notion was a very rich one: Is Michel going to rediscover it on new ground?

However, as for lines of resistance, or what I call flight lines, how can one envision the relationships, conjugations, conjunctions and processes of unification? I would say that the collective field of immanence, where assemblages are made at a given point in time and where they trace their flight lines, also has a veritable diagram. It is then necessary to find the complex assemblage that is capable of implementing this diagram, by operating the conjunction of lines or points of deterritorialization. It is in this vein that I spoke of a war-machine, also power arrangements, but completely different from the State apparatus or military institutions. On one hand, we would have the State-power diagram—the State being a molar apparatus that promotes micro-elements of a diagram as an organizational plane—and on the other, the war-machine diagram of flight lines (the war-machine being an assemblage that produces micro-elements of the diagram as a plane of immanence). I can stop since two very different types of planes would be interacting here: a kind of transcendent plane of organization against the immanent plane of assemblages. We would fall back into the previously mentioned problems. And, from there on, I no longer know how to situate myself in terms of Michel's present research.

(Additional note: The two opposite states of the plane or the diagram interest me because of their historical confrontation in very diverse forms. In one case, we have a plane of organization and development, which is naturally hidden, but allows everything visible to be seen. In the other case, we have a plane of immanence where there are only degrees of speed and slowness, no development, and everything is seen and heard, etc. The first plane is not the same thing as the State but is linked to it. The second, on the contrary, is a war-machine, a dreamlike war-machine. On the level of nature, for example, Cuvier and also Goethe conceived of the first type of plane whereas Hölderlin in *Hyperion*, and Kleist, even more so, conceived of the second type.

Hence, there are two types of intellectuals. In music too, there are two conflicting conceptions of the sound plane. The power-knowledge link, as Michel analyzes it, might be explained as follows: powers imply a plane-diagram of the first type (for example, the Greek city and Euclidean geometry). Conversely, there are counter-powers, more or less related to war-machines and another type of plane, all kinds of minor knowledge (Archimedian geometry or the geometry of cathedrals against which the State eventually did battle) and a whole kind of knowledge proper to lines of resistance that does not have the same form as the other kind of knowledge).

12

The Rich Jew

A film by Daniel Schmidt, *Shadow of Angels*, which is playing at two local theaters (Mac-Mahon and Saint-André-des-Arts), has been accused of anti-Semitism. As usual, the attack comes from two quarters: long-established public agencies have called for cuts, if not the suppression of the film altogether, while anonymous groups threaten from the shadows, with menacing bomb scares. It has thus become extremely difficult to discuss the beauty, the novelty, or the importance of this film. To do so would be like saying: the film is so beautiful, we can overlook a little anti-Semitism… As a consequence of this systematic pressure, not only does the film seem likely to disappear in fact, it has already disappeared in spirit, carried away by an absolutely false problem.

Anti-Semitic films exist, certainly. And if some other group objects to this or that film, it is often for a precise reason that can be determined. In this case, however, a threshold has been crossed, due to the radical inanity of the accusation. One can hardly believe one's eyes and ears. It is true that the words "the rich Jew" are often used in the film to designate one of the characters. Nor is it insignificant that this character displays an "intentional" charm in the film. Schmidt used the following terms to explain an essential feature of his film: the faces are almost next to the actors, and what they say, almost next to the faces. Consequently, the rich Jew himself can say "the rich Jew." The actors draw on a store of stock-phrases and stock-faces, which govern a series of transformations. The words "the gnome, the dwarf" designate an unsettling giant whose gestures and function in the film are precisely those of a dwarf. The Nazi jargon and anti-Semitic declarations come from the anonymous character sprawled out and holding forth on a bed; or they show up in the mouth of the transvestite singer, who happens to be a former Nazi dignitary.

If we must examine the basis for this deranged accusation of anti-Semitism, let us examine who the characters are. There is the consumptive prostitute, daughter of the Nazi dignitary. And there is "the rich Jew," who made his fortune in real estate, and who speaks of his business in terms of eviction, demolition, and speculation. The tie that binds them is a feeling of intense fear, fear of what the world will become. The woman unconsciously draws on this fear, discovering a strength that upsets all who approach her, such that no matter how kind she is, no matter what she does, everyone comes away feeling scorned. What "the rich Jew," for his part, extracts from this fear is an indifference toward destiny, like a grace that flows through him, a distance that places him already in some other world. Hence the shadows of angels. Both of them display this power of transformation, because they have strength and grace (the transformation of the pimp is similar). The "rich Jew" owes his fortune to a system that is not presented as Jewish, but rather as dependent on the city, the municipal authorities, and the police. But he receives his grace from somewhere else.

The prostitute owes her condition to the collapse of Nazism, but she too receives her strength from somewhere else. The two of them are vulnerable, they are the only ones "alive" in this

Necropolis of a city. Only the Jew knows that he is not scorned by the woman, only the Jew is not threatened by her strength. Only the woman knows what the Jew is, and where his grace comes from. In the end, she asks him to kill her, because she is exhausted and no longer desires a strength which to her seems pointless. For his part, he goes to the police, entrusts himself to their protection in the name of business, but no longer wants his grace, which has become strangely awkward and uncertain. See the movie for yourself. Examine the images on the screen. What I have just described is the explicit content of the film.

Where is the anti-Semitism? Where can it be? You scratch your head, you search in vain. Is it the words "rich Jew"? Granted, these words are very important in the film. In good families once upon a time, you didn't say "Jew," you said "Israelite." But these families were precisely the anti-Semites. And how do you describe a Jew who is not an Israelite, not an Israeli, not even a Zionist? How do you describe Spinoza, the Jewish philosopher, banned from synagogue, the son of a rich businessman, and whose genius, strength, and charm were not unrelated to the fact that he was Jewish and described himself as a Jew? It's like trying to ban a word from the dictionary: the Anti-Semitic League has declared all those who use the word "Jew" to be anti-Semites (unless it is used in a ritual for the dead). Does the Anti-Semitic League refuse all public debate, and do they reserve the right to decide who or what is anti-Semitic without any explanation?

Schmidt has articulated his political intention, and it is plain throughout in the film, in the simplest and most obvious way. Old-style fascism, however real and powerful it may still be in many countries, is not the real problem facing us today. New fascisms are being born. The old-style fascism looks almost quaint, almost folkloric (e.g. the transvestite singer in the film) compared to the new fascism being prepared for us. The new fascism is not the politics and the economy of war. It is global agreement on security, on the maintenance of a "peace" just as terrifying as war. All our petty fears will be organized in concert, all our petty anxieties will be harnessed to make micro-fascists of us; we will be called upon to stifle every little thing, every suspicious face, every dissonant voice, in our streets, in our neighborhoods, in our local theaters. "I don't like films about fascism from the '30s. The new fascism is much more subtle, more disguised. Perhaps fascism, as in my film, is the driving force behind a society where social problems are solved, but where the question of anxiety is merely stifled."[1]

If Schmidt's film is banned or impeded in any way, it will not be a victory in the fight against anti-Semitism. But it will be a victory for the new fascism, and the first case where we can ask ourselves: even if it was merely a pretext, was there even the shadow of a pretext? A select few will recall the beauty of the film, its political importance, and how it was quashed.

13

On the New Philosophers (plus a More General Problem)

What do you think about "the New Philosophers"?

Gilles Deleuze: Not much. I can think of two reasons why their thought is empty. First, they work with big concepts, all puffed up like an abscess: THE law, Power, Master, THE world, THE revolution, Faith, etc. Then they create these monstrous packages, gross dualisms: THE law *and* THE rebel, Power *and* Angels. Second, the weaker the thought, the more important the thinker. *The expressing subject* takes itself all the more seriously in relation to empty propositions ("It is I who speak, and *I* am courageous and lucid..., *I* am a soldier of Christ..., *I* belong to the lost generation..., *We* were there in May '68..., *We* won't get fooled again..."). These two rhetorical procedures spoil the work. For a long time now, people in every discipline have been working to avoid these very pitfalls. We've been trying to create concepts with fine articulations, extremely differentiated concepts, to escape gross dualisms. And we've been trying to uncover *creative functions* which would no longer require an *author-function* for them to be active (in music, painting, audio-visual arts, film, and even philosophy). This wholesale return to the author, to an empty and vain subject, as well as to gross conceptual stereotypes, represents a troubling reactionary development. It is perfectly consistent with Haby's proposed reforms: a significant streamlining of the philosophical curriculum.

Are you saying this because Bernard-Henri Levy has violently attacked both you and Guattari in his book, Barbarism with a Human Face*?*[1]

Don't be ridiculous. Levy says there is a deep connection between *Anti-Oedipus* and "the defense of what is rotten in the manure of decadence" (his very words), a deep connection between *Anti-Oedipus* and drug addicts. At least he keeps the drug addicts laughing. But when he says that CERFI[2] is racist, he is pulling a fast one. I have wanted to discuss the New Philosophers for a while now, but I didn't know how. They must be saying to themselves: look how jealous he is of our success. They devote their time and energy to attacks, counter-attacks, and to counter-counter-attacks. I don't have time to respond more than once. This is it. What changed the situation for me is Aubral and Delcourt's book *Against the New Philosophy*.[3] They make a genuine attempt to analyze this new thought, and the result is truly comical. The book is a breath of fresh air. They were the first to say: "Enough!" They have even confronted the New Philosophers on the TV show "Apostrophes." So, in the words of the enemy, a little god told me to side with Aubral and Delcourt, to be brave, courageous, and pessimistic.

If their thought is so empty, how do you explain their success? Why do they receive encouragement and support from big names, Sollers for instance?

We have several different problems to address here. First, France has long been subjected to the fashion of literary "schools." A school is just awful: there is always a pope, manifestoes, declarations like "I am the avant-garde," excommunications, tribunals, political about-faces, etc. As a general rule, you would be right to think you've wasted your life, if your only claim was: "I belonged to this or that school." This explains why Stalinists are the only ones who spend their time giving the rest of us lessons in anti-Stalinism. In any event, however bad a school may be, we cannot say that these New Philosophers are a school. They do have a certain newness about them: rather than form a school, they have introduced France to literary or philosophical marketing. Marketing has its own particular logic: 1) You have to talk about the book, or get the book talked about, rather than let the book do the talking. Theoretically, you could have all the newspaper articles, interviews, conferences, and radio shows replace the book altogether, it needn't exist at all. The work which the New Philosophers do has less to do with their books than with the articles they can obtain, the newspapers and TV shows they can monopolize, an interview they can give, a book review they can do, or an appearance in *Playboy*. The effort they put into it, at this level anyway, and with this degree of organization, implies an activity exclusive of philosophy, or at least excluded from it. And 2), from a marketing perspective, the same book or product should have several versions, so as to appeal to everyone: a pious version, an atheist version, a Heideggerian version, a leftist, a centrist and a neo-fascist version, a Jacques Chirac version, a nuanced "unity of the Left" version, etc. Hence the importance of the distribution of roles according to one's inclinations. There is something of the diabolical Dr. Mabuse in Clavel, with an evangelical twist. His two assistants, Spori and Pesch, are Jambet and Lardreau (they want to rough up Nietzsche). Benoist is the racehorse, he is Nestor. Levy is sometimes the impresario, sometimes the script-girl, sometimes the happy talk show host, sometimes the DJ. Jean Cau thinks it's "totally awesome, dude." Fabre-Luce is Glucksmann's disciple. And Benda is being re-published, for his clerical virtues. What a goon squad.

Sollers had been the latest to found a school in the old style, papacy and all.[4] I suppose that once Sollers had understood a new enterprise was under way, he figured, why not strike up an alliance, he would be stupid not to. He is a late comer, but he got it right. There is something new here: marketing the philosophy book. It's a new idea. It had to occur to someone first. This reactionary development—reinstating an empty author-function, and brandishing empty concepts—does not preclude a profound modernism, a watered-down analysis of the landscape and the market place. A few philosophers may feel a certain curiosity and good-will toward this move, at least from the perspective of the naturalist or the entomologist. But my perspective is teratological: it's a horror show, and I'm fascinated in spite of myself.

If it really is a question of marketing, why did we have to wait for the New Philosophers, why is it only now that their thought has arrived?

For several reasons which are beyond the control of any one person. André Scala recently analyzed the reversal of the relationship between journalists and writers, between the press and books. Journalism, through radio and television, has increasingly realized its potential to create events (controlled leaks, Watergate, polls, etc.). And just as journalism needs to refer to external events less and less, since it already creates many of them, it also needs less and less to refer to external analysis, including polls of "intellectuals" or "writers." *Journalism has discovered an autonomous and sufficient thought within itself.* This is why, if we pursue this line of argument to its limit, a book is worth less than the newspaper article written about it or the interview which comes after it. Intellectuals and writers, even artists, are thus forced to become journalists if they want to conform to the norm. This is a new type of thought, the interview-thought, the conversation-thought, the sound bite-thought. We can imagine a book that would be about a newspaper article, and not the reverse. The power relations between journalists and intellectuals have totally changed. It all began with television, and the special editions that sought to tame willing intellectuals. The media no longer needs intellectuals. I'm not saying that this reversal, this domestication of the intellectual, is a disaster. That's how things go: precisely when writing and thought were beginning to abandon the author-function, when creations no longer required an author-function for them to be active, the author-function was co-opted by radio and television, and by journalism. Journalists have become the new authors, and those writers who wanted to become authors had to go through journalists, or become journalists themselves. A function that had been somewhat discredited has managed to recapture some modernity and find a new conformity by changing its place and its object. This is what made the enterprise of intellectual marketing possible. Are there other possible uses to be made of television, radio, and the press today? Of course, but the New Philosophers are not interested in them. We can talk more about that in a minute.

There is another reason why their thought is arriving now. We've been in election mode for some time now. Elections are not a particular locale, nor a particular day in the calendar. They are more like a grid that affects the way we understand and perceive things. Everything is mapped back on this grid and gets warped as a result. The particular conditions of the elections today have elevated the usual level of bullshit. The New Philosophers have inscribed themselves on this grid from the beginning. It hardly matters that some of them were immediately opposed to the union of the Left, whereas the others wanted to offer Mitterrand one more brain-trust. The two tendencies were identical in their opposition to the Left, but were especially united in a theme found early on in their books: the hatred of May '68. It was a competition to see who could piss on May '68 the most. And they have constructed their expressing subject in terms of this hatred: "We were there in '68 (they were?), and we can tell you it was stupid, there's no point doing it again." This is all they have to sell: the bitterness of '68. In this sense, then, they are a perfect fit for the present electoral grid, whatever their political orientations. Everything is filtered through this grid: Marxism, Maoism, Socialism, etc., and not because actual struggles have revealed new enemies, new problems, or new solutions. It is simply because THE revolution must be declared impossible—everywhere, and for all time. This explains why those concepts which were beginning to function in a very differentiated way (powers, resistances, desires, even "the plebe") are once again globalized, amassed in the insipid unity of Power, THE law, the State, etc. This also explains why the thinking subject has made a come-back: the only possibility of revolution, as far as the New Philosophers are concerned, is the pure act of the thinker who thinks revolution as impossible.

What I find really disgusting is that the New Philosophers are writing a martyrology: the Gulag and the victims of history. They live off corpses. They have discovered the witness-function, which perfectly compliments the author- and thinker-function (cf. the issue of *Playboy*: *we* are the witnesses...). But there never would have been any victims if the victims had thought or spoken like our New Philosophers. The victims had to live and think in a totally different way to provide the material that so moves the New Philosophers, who weep in their name, think in their name, and give us moral lessons in their name. Those who risk their life most often think in terms of life, not death, not bitterness, and not morbid vanity. Resistance fighters are usually in love with life. No one was ever put in prison for powerlessness and pessimism—on the contrary! From the perspective of the New Philosophers, the victims were duped, because they didn't yet grasp what the New Philosophers have grasped. If I belonged to an association, I would bring a complaint against the New Philosophers: they show just a little too much contempt for the inmates of the Gulag.

When you denounce marketing, are you defending the idea of the old-style book, or the old-style school?

Neither. I don't see the necessity of the alternative: either marketing, or the old-style. It's a false choice. The interesting things happening right now escape this false choice. Look how musicians are working, or those who work in the sciences, or how certain painters are trying to work, how geographers are organizing their research (cf. the journal *Hérodote*). What leaps out at you are the various encounters. It's not about conferences or debates. By working in a discipline, you encounter people working in a some other discipline, as if the solution always came from somewhere else. It's not about intellectual comparisons and analogies. These intersections are real; various lines of research intersect with one another. For example (and this example is important because the New Philosophers keep talking about the history of philosophy), André Robinet has renewed the history of philosophy today with computers; thus he necessarily encounters Xenakis. Just because mathematicians are able to develop or modify a problem of a very different nature does not mean that the problem has received a mathematical solution; it means that the problem contains a mathematical sequence that can be combined with other sequences. The way the New Philosophers deal with Science (always a capital 'S') is frightening. To encounter, through the work you do, the work that musicians, painters, or scholars are doing, is the only actual combination that does not lead to old-style schools or the new marketing. These *singular points* are what constitute the source of creation, creative functions independent of and detached from the author-function. And this is true not only for the intersection of different disciplines; every discipline, every section of every discipline, however small, is already comprised of such encounters. Philosophers must come from anywhere, not in the sense that philosophy would depend on the popular wisdom you can find pretty much everywhere, but in the sense that each encounter produces a new position of assemblages, even as it simultaneously defines a new use for these assemblages—like savage musicians, or pirate radios. And so, every time creative functions desert the author-function, you see the author-function take refuge in the new conformity of "promotion." This series of battles is more or less visible: film, radio, and television are the possibility of creative functions that have deposed the Author; but it is the conformist use of these media that provides cover for the reconstitution of the author-function. The big production companies recently began to promote a director's film; so Jean-Luc Godard now has the opportunity to put something creative on TV. But the powerful organization of television has its own author-functions with which to suppress creation. When literature, music, etc., conquer new territories of creation, the author-function is reconstituted in the press, and the press is sure to stifle its own creative functions, not to mention the creative functions of literature. We come back to the New Philosophers: where once a little breeze was blowing, they have closed the window. It's stifling, suffocating. This is the total negation of politics and experiment. To sum up, my problem with the New Philosophers is that the work they do is manure, and this work partakes of a new relationship between book and press that is fundamentally reactionary. They are new, yes, but conformist in the highest degree. But the New Philosophers themselves are not important. Even if they disappear tomorrow, their marketing enterprise will be repeated again and again. This marketing enterprise represents the submission of thought to the media. By the same token, thought offers the media a minimum intellectual guarantee and peace of mind to stifle any attempts at creation which would make the media themselves evolve. The lame debates we see on TV, and the stupid narcissistic director's films, lessen the chances of any real creation on television and elsewhere. Given the new power relations between journalists and intellectuals, and the situation of intellectuals regarding the media, I would like to propose a charter: refuse, make more demands, become producers, instead of authors who now display only the insolence of domestics or the brilliance of a hired clown. Beckett and Godard figured out how to create, and they each managed it in very different ways. There are so many possibilities in film, audio-visual arts, science, books, etc. But the New Philosophers incarnate the disease that is trying to stifle all that. There is nothing alive in their work, but they will have fulfilled their function if they can occupy center stage long enough to give whatever is creative the kiss of death.

14

Europe the Wrong Way

The German government has requested the extradition of Mr. Croissant, Esq. A French court of appeals will examine the matter on November 2. Why will this judgment be an event of immense importance?

The German government submitted a first case, then submitted several more. It faults Klaus Croissant for behaving like a lawyer, in other words for making known the state of the detention of the prisoners in Stuttgart: their hunger strikes, the threats of assassination weighing down on them, and the motives of their acts. The government also faults Klaus Croissant for maintaining a relationship with terrorists or presumed terrorists (the French lawyers of the FLN faced the same reproach). Can we surmise that the French government notified the German government of the absurdity of its first case and that, as a result, the German government hurriedly submitted other evidence using every possible scheme at its disposal?

And yet the decision of the court of appeals will be of great importance not only because the motives for extradition seem to be based on politics and even popular opinion. And not only because the extradition of Klaus Croissant under the current conditions would mean handing him over to a country whose legal system is in a state of exception and where he would risk rapid elimination in prison[1] (what would happen to Croissant if new terrorist acts occurred in Germany?).

That would be enough, but there is more. Recent events have given the German government a strong position in relation to the other European governments, and even to some African governments. It is in a position to call on these governments to align themselves with its very particular policy of repression or to let its police operate on their soil (cf. the requests for the Barcelona, Alger, Dakar airports, etc.). The German government lectures other governments, giving them lessons; strangely, only Italy has been spared for the moment, perhaps because of the Kappler affair.[2] The German press finds itself in a position to have its articles reproduced in French newspapers, which merely copy them without saying so: *France-Soir* as the edition for the provinces in the Springer group; d'Ormesson's proposal in *Le Figaro* concerning the need to strike back against each act of terrorism by killing the prisoners whose freedom is demanded. A conspiracy of silence has fallen on the two survivors of the Boeing and Stuttgart, whose declarations would be essential elements for any inquiry.

In short, West Germany is in a position to export its judicial, legal and "information" model and to become the qualified organizer of repression and poisoning in other countries. This context underscores the importance of the decision of the French court of appeals. If it gives the authorization to extradite Croissant, it would abandon its recent jurisprudence and at the same time encourage, for better or worse, the importation of the German governmental and judicial model.

In Germany, the government and the press have done their best to suggest that the Stuttgart prisoners killed themselves "in the same way" certain Nazi leaders did: out of devotion to a demonic choice, and out of the despair (these people not only lost, they had become social pariahs). The government and the press speak, foolishly, of a "Wagnerian drama." At the same time, the German government has metamorphosed into a Nuremburg tribunal. Even the leftist papers in France have followed suit, asking whether Baader is the son of Hitler or of Schleyer himself.[3] Are we looking for filiations? Then let us not forget that the questions of violence and terrorism, as a response to imperialist violence, have in various forms continued to preoccupy and divide revolutionary and workers' movements since the last century. The same questions are now being raised with respect to the people of the Third World, whom Baader and his group claim to represent, considering Germany to be an essential agent of their oppression. The Stuttgart prisoners were not fascist leaders or people pushing for fascism as a form of provocation. The German government is not a Nuremburg tribunal, and the French court is not a subsection of any such tribunal. Croissant should not be the victim of accusations without proof, nor of the current press campaign.

Three things concern us immediately: 1) the possibility that many German leftists, in an organized system of denunciation, will find their lives in Germany increasingly intolerable and will be forced to leave their country; 2) conversely, the possibility that Croissant will be handed over, sent back to Germany, where he risks the worst, or that he will be simply expelled to a country of his "choice" where he would be unwelcome; 3) the possibility that Europe as a whole will fall under the kind of control being called for by Germany.

15

Two Questions on Drugs

I'd just like to ask two questions. Clearly no one knows what to do with drugs, not even the users. But no one knows how to talk about them either. Some people speak of pleasures that are not only difficult to describe, but presuppose the drug. And others evoke overly general, extrinsic causalities to explain drugs (sociological considerations, communication and incommunicability, situation of the youth, etc.). The first question would be: Do drugs have a *specific causality* and can we explore this direction?

Specific does not mean a "metaphysical" or an exclusively scientific (i.e. chemical) causality. It is not an infrastructure on which everything else would depend as on a cause. It implies mapping the territory or contours of a *drug-set*. On the one hand, this set would have an internal relationship to various types of drugs and, on the other, to more general causalities. Let me use a completely different domain as an example: psychoanalysis. Whatever we can say against psychoanalysis, the following fact remains: it attempted to establish the specific causality of a domain, including not only neuroses, but all kinds of psychosocial formations and productions (dreams, myths, etc.). In short, it traced this specific causality by showing how desire invests a system of mnesic traces and affects. The question is not whether this specific causality was right. What matters is the search for this causality, through which psychoanalysis led us out of overly general considerations even if it was only to fall prey to other mystifications. The failure of psychoanalysis in the face of drug phenomena is enough to show that drugs have an entirely different causality. But my question is: Can we conceive of a specific causality of drugs and in what directions? For example, with drugs, there is something very unique where desire *directly invests the system of perception.* That is something completely different. By "perception" I mean both internal and external perceptions, and especially space-time perception. The distinctions between types of drugs are secondary, internal to the system. It seems to me that there was a time when research was heading in this direction: Michaux in France, and in another way, the Beat Generation in America, not to mention Casteneda, etc. They wanted to know how all drugs involve speeds, modifications of speed, thresholds of perception, forms and movements, microperceptions, perception on a molecular level, superhuman or subhuman times, etc. Yes, how desire directly enters into perception, directly invests perception (leading to the phenomenon of the desexualization of drugs). This perspective would help us find the connection to more general external causalities without getting lost. Hence the role of perception, the solicitation of perception in contemporary social systems, which led Phil Glass to say that drugs have in any case changed the problem of perception, even for non-users. This point of view would also lead to a greater appreciation of the importance of chemical research without the risk of falling into a "scientistic" conception. If it is true that some pursued this direction, the *autonomous Desire-Perception system*, why does it seem partially abandoned today? Particularly in France? The discourse on drugs, on drug users and non-users, on doctors as users has lapsed into great confusion. Or is this a false impression? Is there no need to search for a specific causality? What I see as important in the idea of specific causality is that it is neutral and applies to both the use of drugs and to therapeutics.

The second question would be: How do we account for a "turning point" in drugs, how do we determine at what moment this turning point occurs? Does it necessarily happen very quickly, and is the material such that failure or disaster is necessarily part of the drug-plane? It is like an "angled" movement. The drug user creates active lines of flight. But these lines roll up, start to turn into black holes, with each drug user in a hole, as a group or individually, like a periwinkle. Dug in instead of spaced out. Guattari talked about them. *Microperceptions are covered in advance*, depending on the drug in question, by hallucinations, delirium, false perceptions, fantasies, waves of paranoia. Artaud, Michaux, Burroughs—who all knew what they were talking about—hated the "mistaken perceptions," the "bad feelings" which to them seemed both a betrayal and yet an inevitable result. That is also where all control is lost and the system of abject dependence begins, dependence on the product, the hit, the fantasy productions, dependence on a dealer, etc. Two things must be distinguished, abstractly: the domain of vital experimentation, and the domain of deadly experimentation. Vital experimentation occurs when any trial grabs you, takes control of you, establishing more and more connections, and opens you to connections. This kind of experiment can entail a kind of *self-destruction*. It can take place with companion or starter products: tobacco, alcohol, drugs. It is not *suicidal* as long as the destructive flow is not reduced to itself but serves to conjugate other flows, whatever the danger. The suicidal enterprise occurs when everything is reduced to this flow alone: "my" hit, "my" trip, "my" glass. It is the contrary of connection; it is organized disconnection. Instead of a "motif" that serves real themes and activities, it is a simple, flat development like a stereotypical plot where the drug is for the drug's sake. And it makes for a stupid suicide. There is only a single line, whose segments follow alternating rhythms: "I quit drinking—I start drinking again," "I've quit drugs—now I can take them again." Bateson has shown how "I stopped drinking" is strictly part of being an alcoholic, since it is the definitive proof that the person can now have another drink. Like the drug addict who is always quitting, since it proves that he or she is capable of doing more drugs. The addict, in this sense, is perpetually detoxified. Everything is reduced to a dismal suicidal line with two alternative segments, the contrary of connections and multiple intertwining lines. The narcissism, the authoritarianism, the blackmail, the venom—only neurotics equal drug addicts in their efforts to piss off the world, spread their disease, and impose their situation (suddenly, psychoanalysis seems to serve as a mild drug). Why and how is this experience, even when self-destructive, but still vital, transformed into a deadly enterprise of generalized, unilinear dependence? Is it inevitable? If there is a precise point, that is where therapy should intervene.

Maybe my two problems converge. It may be at the level of the specific causality of drugs that we can understand why drugs turn so bad and *alter their own causality*. Once again, desire directly investing perception is something very surprising, very beautiful, a sort of unknown land. But hallucinations, false perceptions, waves of paranoia, and the long list of dependencies —they are all too familiar, even if they are replayed by the addicts, who take themselves to be the experimenters, the knights of the modern world, or the universal providers of bad conscience. What happens to get from one to the other? Would drug addicts try to use the advent of a new desire-perception system to their advantage, or simply for their blackmail? Where do the two problems come in? I have the impression that no progress is currently being made, that good research is not being done. Research. The work to be done is certainly somewhere other than in these two questions, but no one currently understands where it might be. Those who know the problem, the addicts or the doctors, seem to have abandoned their research, for themselves and for others.

16

Making Inaudible Forces Audible

Why us non-musicians?

Pierre Boulez's method led to the selection of these five works of music. The relationships between these works are not filial or dependent. There is no progression or evolution from one work to the others. It is as if the five works were chosen halfway by chance to form a cycle where they begin to react to one another. This weaves a group of virtual relationships from which one could draw a particular profile of musical time applicable to these five works alone. You could easily imagine Boulez choosing four or five other works: you would have had a different cycle, other reactions and relationships and another unique profile of musical time or of a different variable than time. It is not a method for generalization. It is not a question of using works taken as musical examples to reach an abstract concept of time where one could say: "This is musical time." It is a question of taking limited, determined cycles under certain conditions to extract particular profiles of time, and then potentially superposing these profiles to make a veritable cartography of variables. This method concerns music but could just as well be used for a thousand other things.

In the specific case of the cycle chosen by Boulez, the particular time profile had no aims to exhaust the question of musical time in general. We saw a kind of *non-pulsed* time emerging from a *pulsed* time, even though this non-pulsed time could become a new form of *pulsation.* The first work (Ligeti) showed how a non-pulsed time rose from a certain pulsation; the second, third and fourth works developed or showed different aspects of this non-pulsed time; the fifth and last work by Carter showed how a non-pulsed time could lead to a new form of original pulsation, a very particular, very new pulsation.

Pulsed time and non-pulsed time are completely musical, but they are something else as well. The question would be to know what makes up this *non-pulsed time.* This kind of floating time that more or less corresponds to what Proust called "a bit of pure time." The most obvious, the most immediate feature of such a so-called non-pulsed time is duration, time freed from measure, be it a regular or irregular, simple or complex measure. Non-pulsed time puts us first and foremost in the presence of a multiplicity of heterochronous, qualitative, non-coincident, non-communicating durations. The problem is therefore clear: how will these heterochronous, heterogeneous, multiple, non-coincident durations join together since it would appear that this eliminates any recourse to the most general and classic solution that consists in relying on the mind to appose a common measure or a metric cadence to all vital durations. From the start, this solution is blocked.

Turning to a completely different domain, I think that when biologists now speak of rhythms, they have found similar questions. They have also renounced the belief that heterogeneous rhythms are articulated under the domination of a unifying form. They do not seek to explain the articulations between vital rhythms, for example the 24-hour rhythms, in terms of a superior form that would unify them, or even in terms of a regular or irregular sequence of elementary processes. They seek an explanation somewhere completely different, at a sub-vital, infra-vital level in what they call a population of molecular oscillators capable of passing through heterogeneous systems, in oscillating molecules coupled together that then pass through groups and disparate durations. The process of articulation does not depend on a unifiable or unifying form or a meter, cadence or any regular or irregular measure, but on the action of certain molecular couples released through different layers and different rhythmic layers. We are not only using a metaphor to speak of a similar discovery in music: sound molecules rather than pure notes or tones. Sound molecules, coupled together, are capable of passing through totally heterogeneous layers of rhythm and layers of duration. Here lies the first determination of a non-pulsed time.

There is a certain type of individuation that is not reduced to a subject (I) or even to the combination of a form and a material. A landscape, an event, an hour of the day, a life or a fragment of life… proceed in other ways. I have the feeling that the problem of individuation in music, which is surely very, very complicated, is more of the type of the second paradoxical individuations. What do we call the individuation of a phrase, a little phrase in music? I would like to start with the most rudimentary level, the easiest in appearance. A piece of music can remind us of a landscape. Thus the famous case of Swann in Proust's work: the Boulogne woods and Vinteuil's little phrase. Sounds can also evoke colors, either by association or by so-called synaesthetic phenomena. Motifs in operas can finally be connected to people, for example: a Wagnerian motif is supposed to designate a character. Such a mode of listening is not empty or without interest; perhaps at a certain level of relaxation it is even a necessary passage. Yet everyone knows it is not enough. At a higher level of tension, sound does not refer to a landscape, but music itself envelops a distinct sound landscape inside it (as with Liszt). We could say the same about the notion of color and consider that durations, rhythms and timbres all the more so are themselves colors, distinct sound colors that are superimposed on visible colors and that do not have the same speeds or the same passages as visible colors. The same for the third notion, the notion of character. We can consider certain motifs in opera in association with a character. The motifs in Wagner, however, are not only associated with an outside character, they change, have an autonomous life in a non-pulsed floating time where they themselves and by themselves become characters inside the music.

These three different notions of *sound landscapes*, *audible colors* and *rhythmic character* thus appear to be the aspects in which a non-pulsed time produces its very particular individuations.

Every direction leads us, I believe, to stop thinking in terms of substance-form. To such an extent, that we have stopped believing in the hierarchy that moves from the simple to the complex, substance-life-mind, in it in every domain. We even thought that life would be a simplification of matter; one might think that vital rhythms do not find their unification in a spiritual form, but on the contrary in molecular couplings. All of this substance-form hierarchy, with a more or less rudimentary substance and a more or less scholarly sound form, isn't that what we have stopped listening to, what composers have stopped producing? What has formed is a very elaborate sound material, not a rudimentary substance that received a form. And the coupling occurs between this very elaborate sound material and forces which by themselves are not sound, but that become sound or become audible by the material that makes them substantial. Thus Debussy's *Dialogue Between Wind and Sea.* The material is there to make forces audible that are not audible in themselves, such as time, duration and even intensity. The *material-force* couple replaces the *matter-form* couple.

Boulez: *Eclats.* All of the very elaborate sound material, with the extinction of sounds, was done to make sensible and audible two tempos that were not of sound. One was defined as the time of production in general and the other as the time of meditation in general. Therefore, the couple simple substance-sound form informing that the substance was replaced with a coupling between an elaborate material and imperceptible forces that only become perceptible through the material. Music is thus no longer limited to musicians to the extent that sound is not its exclusive and fundamental element. Its element is all the non-sound forces that the sound material elaborated by the composer will make perceptible, in such a way that we can even perceive the differences between these forces, the entire differential play of these forces. We are all faced with somewhat similar tasks. In philosophy, classical philosophy presents itself with a kind of rudimentary substance of thought, a type of flow that one then attempts to submit to concepts or categories. Yet philosophers are increasingly seeking to elaborate a very complex material of thought to make sensible forces that are not thinkable in themselves.

There is no absolute ear; the problem is to have an impossible one—making audible forces that are not audible in themselves. In philosophy, it is a question of an impossible thought, making thinkable through a very complex material of thought forces that are unthinkable.

17

Spoilers of Peace

How could the Palestinians be "genuine partners" in peace talks when they have no country? But how could they have a country when it was taken from them? The Palestinians were never given any choice other than unconditional surrender. All they were offered was death. In the Israeli-Palestinian conflict, the actions of the Israelis are considered legitimate retaliation (even if their attacks do seem disproportionate), whereas the actions of the Palestinians are without fail treated as terrorist crimes. And the death of a Palestinian has neither the same interest nor the same impact as the death of an Israeli.

Since 1969, Israel has unrelentingly bombed and strafed Southern Lebanon. Israel has explicitly said that its recent invasion of Lebanon was not in retaliation for the terrorist attack on Tel-Aviv (eleven terrorists against thirty thousand soldiers);[2] on the contrary, it represents the culmination of a plan, one in a whole series of operations to be initiated at Israel's discretion. For a "final solution" to the Palestinian question, Israel can count on the almost unanimous complicity of other States (with various nuances and restrictions). A people without land, and without a State, the Palestinians are the spoilers of peace for everyone involved. If they have received economic and military aid from certain countries, it has been in vain.

The Palestinians know what they are talking about when they say they are alone.

Palestinian militants are also saying that they have managed to pull off a kind of victory. Left behind in Southern Lebanon were only resistance groups, which seem to have held up quite well under attack. The Israeli invasion, on the other hand, struck blindly at Palestinian refugees and Lebanese farmers, a poor population that lives off the land. Destruction of villages and cities, and the massacre of innocent civilians have been confirmed. Several sources indicate that cluster bombs were used. This population of Southern Lebanon, in perpetual exile, keeps leaving and coming back under Israeli military strikes that one is hard-pressed to distinguish from acts of terrorism. The latest hostilities have ousted more than 200,000 from their homes, now refugees wandering the roads. The State of Israel is using in Southern Lebanon the method which proved so effective in Galilee and elsewhere in 1948: it is "Palestinizing" Southern Lebanon.

Palestinian militants for the most part come from this population of refugees. Israel thinks it will defeat the militants by creating more refugees, thereby surely creating more militants.

It is not merely because we have a relationship with Lebanon that we say: Israel is massacring a fragile and complex country. There is something else. The Israeli-Palestinian conflict is a model that will determine how problems of terrorism will be dealt with elsewhere, even in Europe. The worldwide cooperation of States, and the worldwide organization of police and criminal proceedings, will necessarily lead to a classification extending to more and more people who will be considered virtual "terrorists." This situation is analogous to the Spanish Civil War, when Spain served as an experimental laboratory for a far more terrible future.

Today Israel is conducting an experiment. It has invented a model of repression that, once adapted, will profit other countries. There is great continuity in Israeli politics. Israel believes that the U.N. resolutions verbally condemning Israel in fact put it in the right. Israel has transformed the invitation to leave the occupied territories into the right to establish colonies there. It thinks sending an international peace-keeping force into Southern Lebanon is an excellent idea… provided that this force, in the place of Israeli forces, transforms the region into a police zone, a desert of security. This conflict is a curious kind of blackmail, from which the whole world will never escape unless we lobby for the Palestinians to be recognized for what they are: "genuine partners" in peace talks. They are indeed at war, in a war they did not choose.

18

The Complaint and the Body

Philosopher and psychoanalyst, Pierre Fédida has a new book: *L'Absence*, his third after *Le Concept et la Violence* and *Corps du vide et espace de séance*.[1] *L'Absence* is neither a traditional book, nor a collection of articles. It is more like a selection over the course of a life. Fédida may be young, but this does not mean that he cannot measure his work against the course of a life in progress, as though he were growing in depth, like a tree. Indeed Frédida has written some bizarre pages on the relationship of writing to wood, carpentry, and the table. To the impoverished furniture of psychoanalysis—couch and chair—Fédida has added the table as an active and guiding element.

Fédida's main project, among others, is to elevate psychoanalysis to the current state of the theory and practice of intersubjectivity. This is not a psychology of the psychoanalyst, the patient, and their relationship. He is trying to put together a structure of intersubjectivity which would be something like the condition of possibility of psychoanalysis. And the real innovation of Fédida's book is the invention of all these concepts that are "inter-," thereby designating what is "between." It is neither the "one" nor the "other," but somewhere in the middle, like an intermediary, a messenger, an intermezzo: not the *other* stage, the *other* scene, but in-between two sessions, with the time and space proper to intersubjectivity. If Frédida has been influenced by phenomenology and by existential analysis (not only Husserl, but also Binswanger, Henri Maldiney), it is because he found in them the first major attempt at a theory of intersubjectivity as a transcendental field. And in my view, the inter-concepts which Frédida has created in this book promise to reinvigorate psychoanalytic thought.

Consequently, should we accept this point of departure—intersubjectivity as an originary field, prior with respect to the subjects that populate it and to the objects that furnish it—the task is then to give the object *and* the subject a new status, since this status must follow from a prior intersubjectivity, and not the reverse. This is precisely what Frédida does, constructing a beautiful notion for the purpose: the *objeu* (a word he borrows from Ponge). Secondly, the relations of the subject to the body will themselves follow from the intersubjective; in other words, those problems known as psychosomatic, which in fact trace the variations of those relations, will follow from the hidden problems of intersubjectivity. These troubles are presented in the form of the *complaint*, just regular old complaints. In this sense, Frédida also gives us a picture of the three ancient complaints, which today have assumed overwhelming importance: melancholy, hypochondria, and depression—the scourges of our time. When psychoanalysis is no longer subject to the neurotic regime of demand, but instead the regime of the psychosomatic complaint, including the complaint of the psychoanalyst, the whole field undergoes a transformation. Frédida calls on us to rethink psychoanalysis, from the intersubjective to the psychosomatic, in this exceptional and fascinating book.

19

How Philosophy is Useful to Mathematicians or Musicians

I would like to address a very particular aspect of university teaching. In the traditional arrangement, a professor lectures to students who are acquiring or already possess a certain competence in some discipline. These students are working in other disciplines as well; and let's not forget interdisciplinary studies, even if they are secondary. Generally speaking, then, students are "judged" by their degree in some discipline, abstractly defined.

At Vincennes, the situation is different. A professor, e.g. one who works in philosophy, lectures to a public that includes to varying degrees mathematicians, musicians (trained in classical or pop music), psychologists, historians, etc. The students, however, instead of putting these other disciplines aside to facilitate their access to the discipline they are supposedly being taught, in fact expect philosophy, for example, to be useful to them in some way, to intersect with their other activities. Philosophy will matter to them, not in terms of the degree to which they possess this kind of knowledge, even the zero degree of initiation, but in terms of their immediate concerns, in other words, the other subjects or material which they already possess to whatever degree. Students attend a lecture looking for something they can use for themselves. In this way, what directly orients the teaching of philosophy is the question of how useful it is to mathematicians, or to musicians, etc., even and especially if this philosophy does not discuss mathematics or music. This kind of teaching has nothing to do with general culture; it is practical and experimental, always outside itself, precisely because the students are led to participate in terms of their own needs and competences. In two important respects, therefore, Vincennes differs from other universities: 1) the distinction of years of study, since Vincennes can support the coexistence of students of very different qualifications and ages at the same level of instruction; and 2) the problem of selection, since selection at Vincennes can be subordinated to a method of "triage," where the direction that the instruction takes is constantly guided by the directions the students take.

The presence of numerous workers, as well as numerous foreigners, confirms and reinforces this situation. At this point, the objection is that this kind of teaching does not respect the norm and does not concern the traditional student who legitimately intends to acquire mastery in a single discipline. In my view, this objection is groundless. In fact, it is of the greatest pedagogical importance to encourage *within* each discipline the resonances between different levels and domains of externality. Every student shows up with proper domains already in place, and rather than just ignore such domains, the discipline being taught must "take" on that soil. This resonance is the only way to grasp a subject in itself and from within. Far from being opposed to the norms which the minister demands, the teaching at Vincennes should be an integral part of these norms. Even if we were to limit ourselves to the project of reforming higher education—initiating competitive universities based on the American model—we would have to build three or four Vincennes, not dismantle the one we have. In particular, a Vincennes-inspired faculty of science, with this method of instruction, would be invaluable (many of us would sit in on its classes). This method is in fact connected to Vincennes's specific situation, to its particular history, and no one can dismantle Vincennes without at the same time undermining one of the most important attempts at pedagogical renewal in France. The real problem facing us today is a kind of intellectual lobotomy, the lobotomy of teachers and students, against which Vincennes offers its own particular capacities of resistance.

20

Open Letter to Negri's Judges

There is every reason to fear that recent terrorist attacks may divert our attention from the growing realization in the Negri Affair that the criminal files which originally led to the arrest of Negri and his comrades are empty. The voice on the telephone offers no evidence; the places where Negri was supposed to have been have vanished; Negri's writings are no longer resolutions of the Red Brigades but analyses in which Negri opposes the theses of the Brigades, etc. The judges have postponed the examination of these facts and want to transform the interrogation into an inquisition-style theoretical debate. It is true that time is on their side and the Reale law allows them to imprison a defendant for four years before trial.[1] Ready to engage in theoretical debate, we see three principles at play here, and these three principles concern everyone committed to democracy.

First, justice should conform to a certain principle of identity. Not only the identity of the defendant, but the more profound principle of identity or non-contradiction that should characterize the charges. If other motives for prosecution emerge, the legal action must be changed. In short, an accusation must necessarily possess, in its entirety, a minimum of identifiable consistency. As long as this type of identity exists in the prosecution, one has the possibility to defend oneself.

This is not the case of the Roman warrant. It begins by referring to Moro's kidnapping as if Negri had been there and cites Negri's writing as if, since he was not there, he were therefore all the more responsible. The warrant for arrest jumps from the act to the impetus, from the impetus to the thought, and from the thought to some other action. Such a vacillating and indeterminate warrant for arrest lacks even the most basic legal identity. "You are guilty in any case."

Next, the inquiry and investigation should conform to a certain principle of disjunction or exclusion: it is this or that..., if it is not this, then it is not that, etc. In the Negri affair, however, it seems that they want to preserve every alternative at every juncture. If Negri was not in Rome, we will still keep the phone call by arguing that it was placed in Paris or vice versa. If Negri was not directly involved in Moro's kidnapping, he nevertheless inspired it or conceived it, so it is as if he did it himself. If Negri opposed the Red Brigades in his writings and statements, this is only a mask that proves his alliance with them as their secret leader. These contradictory accusations do not eliminate each other; they are all added together.

As Franco Piperno, an accused fugitive, has said, this is a very strange way to evaluate the impact of political and theoretical texts.[2] The accusers have such a habit of thinking that it is possible to say anything in a political speech that they absolutely cannot understand the situation of a revolutionary intellectual who can only write what he or she thinks. Andreotti or Berlinguer can always hide their thoughts because their thoughts are always opportunistic.[3] Gramsci himself, however, never could do that. Instead of proceeding by alternatives and exclusion, the inquiry is proceeding by inclusion, adding up contradictory terms.

Why are these negations of justice possible today? We believe that the press, with a few rare exceptions, has played and continues to play a major role in the Negri affair. This is not the first time, and yet it may be the first time it has operated in such a systematic and organized manner (and the French press is no less willing and defamatory than the Italians). The justice system would never have been able to abandon its principle of identity, and the inquiry would never have been able to abandon its principle of exclusion, if the press had not given them the means to make them forget their lapses and their abandoning the rules.

In fact, there is a whole other principle that governs the press. Daily or weekly newspapers, as well as radio and television, are governed by a principle of accumulation. Since there is "news" every day, and since yesterday's refutations have no effect on the news of today or tomorrow, the press accumulates everything that is said each day with no concern for contradictions. The use of the "conditional" allows everything to be gathered together and multiplied. Negri can be represented as being in Paris, Rome and Milan on the same day. All three combined. He can be made an active member of the Red Brigades, a secret leader, or on the contrary, a defender of a very different strategy and method: once again, all three combined.

Marcelle Padovani shows this result in a French weekly. Even if Negri does not belong to the Red Brigades, he is an "Autonomous" and "we know about the Autonomous Italians…."[4] Negri deserves what is happening to him in any case. The press has engaged in a fantastical "accumulation of falsehoods" that allow both the courts and the police to hide the emptiness of their files. We have been promised a European legal and justice system that can only function thanks to a European space for the press where all newspapers, from the left to the extreme right, supplement the failures of investigations and laws. A time is fast approaching in Europe when no one will understand the reproach once made against the press when it opposed the imperatives and slogans of the powers that be.

The Italians cannot accuse us this time of meddling in their internal affairs. French people have been under accusation from the very beginning ("the French trail...," "the Parisian branch of the Red Brigades...").[5] Isn't this an awful way to settle scores after the days in Bologna?[6] Negri is a theorist, an important intellectual in France and Italy. The Italians and the French are united by the same problems when confronted with violence and against repression that no longer even needs to seek legal justification since it gets its legitimacy in advance from the press, radio and television.

We are witnessing a veritable "witch hunt" against people who are in prison on the basis of proof that is at the very least vague or yet to be produced. We have no faith whatsoever in this proof which has been promised. We would at least like information on their conditions of detention and isolation. Maybe we have to wait for a disaster in order for the newspapers to say with "definitive" proof that Negri was Pinelli.[7]

21

This Book Is Literal Proof of Innocence

How important is the publication of this book[1] by Negri? Not just in itself, but in relation to Negri's particular situation: he is currently in a special prison.[2]

1) In several Italian newspapers, there has been a curious attempt to disparage Negri, almost in passing: "Negri is not an important thinker. He is mediocre at best, even negligible...." When the fascists imprisoned a theoretician or a thinker, they felt no need to belittle him. They simply said: "We have no use for thinkers! They are a detestable and dangerous lot." But democracy today needs to disparage, because it needs to persuade public opinion that what we have here is a *false thinker*. However, this book by Negri clearly demonstrates what we in France have known all along: Negri is an extremely important Marxist theoretician, both profound and original.

2) Furthermore, Negri has never wanted to be merely a theoretician; his theory and his interpretations are inseparable from a certain kind of practical social struggle. Negri's books describe this field of struggle in terms of what he calls social capital, and in terms of new forms of work in capitalism. One of the most

noteworthy implications of his analysis is that struggles are no longer contained within the simple frame of private enterprise or labor unions. At no time, however, have the kind of practical struggles which Negri analyzes and applies been allied to terrorism; nor can they be confused with the methods favored by the Red Brigades. Therefore, since the Italian judges display such an interest in the style, intentions, and thoughts of Negri, *this book is literal proof of his innocence.* But maybe Negri is two-faced? As a writer, he theorizes a particular social practice; as a secret agent, he practices something else—terrorism. This is a particularly stupid idea, because unless of course he is being bribed by the police, a revolutionary writer *cannot* practice any kind of struggle other than what he values and encourages in his work.

22

Eight Years Later: 1980 Interview

Catherine Clément: *What difference is there between* Anti-Oedipus, *published in 1972, and your latest book,* A Thousand Plateaus, *in 1980?*

Gilles Deleuze: The situation of *Anti-Oedipus* was pretty simple. *Anti-Oedipus* reexamined the unconscious, a field we all know, or at least are familiar with. It sought to replace the familial or theatrical model of the unconscious with a more political model: the factory. It was a kind of Russian "constructivism." Hence the idea of desiring machines, desire as production. *A Thousand Plateaus,* on the other hand, tries to invent its own fields, so it's more complicated. The fields are not pre-existing; they are mapped out by the various parts of the book. It is the sequel to *Anti-Oedipus,* but a sequel in live action, "in vivo." For example, the animal-becoming of human beings, and its connection to music...

But how are the circumstances surrounding the two books different?

Anti-Oedipus came just after May '68, which was a period of upheaval and experimentation. Today a decided reaction has set in. A certain economy of the book, a new politics, is responsible for today's conformity. We see a labor crisis, an organized and deliberate crisis where books are concerned, and in other domains as well. Journalism has appropriated increasing power in literature. And a flood of novels are rediscovering the theme of the family in its most banal form, doing infinite variations on mommy-daddy. It's disconcerting to discover a ready-made, prefabricated novel in one's own family. This year is the year of paternal heritage, and in this sense *Anti-Oedipus* was a total failure. It would take too long to analyze why, but the current situation is especially difficult for young writers, who are suffocating. I can't tell you where these dire feelings come from.

OK, maybe next time. But is A Thousand Plateaus *a work of literature? There are so many fields that you touch on: ethnology, ethology, politics, music, etc. What genre is it?*

It's just plain old philosophy. When people ask: What is painting? the answer is relatively simple. A painter is someone who creates lines and colors (even if lines and colors already exist in nature). Well, a philosopher is no different. It's someone who creates concepts, someone who invents new concepts. Of course, thought already exists outside of philosophy, but not in this special form: the concept. Concepts are singularities that have an impact on ordinary life, on the flows of ordinary or day-to-day thinking. *A Thousand Plateaus* tries to invent numerous concepts: rhizome, smooth space, haecceity, animal-becoming, abstract machine, diagram, etc. Guattari is always inventing concepts, and my conception of philosophy is the same.

If there is no single field to act as a foundation, what is the unity of A Thousand Plateaus?

I think it is the idea of an assemblage (which replaces the idea of desiring machines). There are various kinds of assemblages, and various component parts. On the one hand, we are trying to substitute the idea of assemblage for the idea of behavior: whence the importance of ethology, and the analysis of animal assemblages, e.g. territorial assemblages. The chapter on the Ritornello, for example, simultaneously examines animal assemblages and more properly musical assemblages: this is what we call a "plateau," establishing a continuity between the ritornellos of birds and Schumann's ritornellos. On the other hand, the analysis of assemblages, broken down into their component parts, opens up the way to a general logic: Guattari and I have only begun, and completing this logic will undoubtedly occupy us in the future. Guattari calls it "diagrammatism." In assemblages you find states of things, bodies, various combinations of bodies, hodgepodges; but you also find utterances, modes of expression, and whole regimes of signs. The relations between the two are pretty complex. For example, a society is defined not by productive forces and ideology, but by "hodgepodges" and "verdicts." Hodgepodges are combinations of interpenetrating bodies. These combinations are well-known and accepted (incest, for example, is a forbidden combination). Verdicts are collective utterances, that is, instantaneous and incorporeal transformations which have currency in a society (for example, "from now on you are no longer a child"...).

These assemblages which you are describing, seems to me to have value judgments attached to them. Is this correct? Does A Thousand Plateaus *have an ethical dimension?*

Assemblages exist, but they indeed have component parts that serve as criteria and allow the various assemblages to be qualified. Just as in painting, assemblages are a bunch of lines. But there are all kinds of lines. Some lines are segments, or segmented; some lines get caught in a rut, or disappear into "black holes"; some are destructive, sketching death; and some lines are vital and creative. These creative and vital lines open up an assemblage, rather than close it down. The idea of an "abstract" line is particularly complex. A line may very well represent nothing at all, be purely geometrical, but it is not yet abstract as long as it traces an outline. An abstract line is a line with no outlines, a line that passes *between* things, a line in mutation. Pollock's line has been called abstract. In this sense, an abstract line is not a geometrical line. It is very much alive, living and creative. Real abstraction is non-organic life. This idea of non-organic life is everywhere in *A Thousand Plateaus*, and this is precisely the life of the concept. An assemblage is carried along by its abstract lines, when it is able to have or trace abstract lines. You know, it's curious, today we are witnessing the revenge of silicon. Biologists have often asked themselves why life was "channeled" through carbon rather than silicon. But the life of modern machines, a genuine non-organic life, totally distinct from the organic life of carbon, is channeled through silicon. This is the sense in which we speak of a silicon-assemblage. In the most diverse fields, one has to consider the component parts of assemblages, the nature of the lines, the mode of life, the mode of utterance...

In reading your work, one gets the feeling that those distinctions which are traditionally most important have disappeared: for instance, the distinction between nature and culture; or what about epistemological distinctions?

There are two ways to suppress or attenuate the distinction between nature and culture. The first is to liken animal behavior to human behavior (Lorenz tried it, with disquieting political implications). But what we are saying is that the idea of assemblage can replace the idea of behavior, and thus with respect to the idea of assemblage, the nature-culture distinction no longer matters. In a certain way, behavior is still a contour. But an assemblage is first and foremost what keeps very heterogeneous elements together: e.g. a sound, a gesture, a position, etc., both natural and artificial elements. The problem is one of "consistency" or "coherence," and it is prior to the problem of behavior. How do things take on consistency? How do they cohere? Even among very different things, an intensive continuity can be found. We have borrowed the word "plateau" from Bateson precisely to designate these zones of intensive continuity.

Where did you get this idea of intensity which governs the "plateau"?

Pierre Klossowski. He is responsible for refurnishing intensities with philosophical and theological depth. He developed a whole semiology out of them. The notion was still active in medieval physics and philosophy, but it was more or less obscured by the privilege given to extensive quantities and the geometry of extended space. But physics in its own way keeps rediscovering the paradoxes of intensive quantities; mathematics has confronted non-extended spaces; and biology, embryology, and genetics have discovered a whole realm of "gradients." In these cases, as in the case of an assemblage, scientific or epistemological moves are difficult to isolate. Intensities are about modes of life, and experimental practical reason. This is what constitutes non-organic life.

Perhaps A Thousand Plateaus *will make for difficult reading...*

The book demanded an enormous amount of work from us, and it will demand work from the reader. But a section which seemed difficult to us may seem easy to someone else, and vice versa. Aside from the quality of this book, or lack thereof, *A Thousand Plateaus* is precisely the kind of book being threatened today. That's why it feels like we're doing politics even when we're discussing music, trees, or faces. The question facing every writer is whether or not people have some use, however small, to make of the book, in their own work, in their life, and their projects.

23

Painting Sets Writing Ablaze

Hervé Guibert: *Before this text came about, what shape did your appreciation of Bacon take?é*

Gilles Deleuze: For most people, Bacon causes a shock. He says himself that his work is making images, and these are shock-images. The meaning of this shock does not refer to something "sensational" (which is represented), but depends on sensation, on lines and colors.

You are confronted with the intense presence of figures, sometimes solitary figures, sometimes with several bodies, suspended in a plane, in an eternity of colors. So you wonder how this mystery is possible. You start to think about the place of such a painter in contemporary painting, and more generally in the history of art (Egyptian art, for example). It seemed to me that current painting offered three broad directions that had to be defined materially and genetically rather than formally: abstraction, expressionism, and what Lyotard calls the Figural, which is something other than figurative, precisely a production of Figures. Bacon goes farthest in the latter direction.

At one point, you establish a link between Kafka's characters and those in Bacon. Writing about Bacon after writing about Sacher-Masoch, Proust and then Kafka, isn't there also a connection?

The connections are multiple. They are authors of Figures. Several levels need to be distinguished. First, they present us with unfathomable suffering and profound anguish. Then you recognize a certain "mannerism," in the artistic sense of the word, *à la* Michelangelo, full of force and humor. And you notice that far from being excessive complication, it comes from pure simplicity. What first appears to be torture or contortion refers to very natural postures. Bacon seems to make tortured characters, many say the same of Kafka, and we could have mentioned Beckett, but you only have to look long enough at someone who is forced to sit for a long time, like a child at school, to see his or her body simply take the most "economical" posture depending on the forces acting on it. Kafka was obsessed with a roof weighing down on someone's head: either their chin will be horribly crushed into their chest or the top of their skull will break through the roof.... In short, there are two very different things: the violence of the situations, which is figurative, but also the incredible violence of the poses, which is "figural" and much harder to grasp.

How do you write a book on painting? By calling on the things or beings of literature, in this case Kafka, Proust, Beckett?

What in literature is called a style also exists in painting: an assemblage of lines and colors. And a writer is recognized by his or her way of enveloping, unfurling or breaking a line in "his" or "her" sentences. The secret of great literature is to move towards increasing sobriety. To mention an author I like, a Kerouac sentence ends like a line from a Japanese drawing, hardly touching the paper. A Ginsberg poem is like a fractured expressionist line. We can therefore imagine a common or comparable world between painters and writers. And that is precisely the aim of calligraphy.

Did you find any special pleasure in writing about painting?

It frightened me. It seemed genuinely difficult. There are two dangers: either you describe the painting, and then a real painting is no longer necessary (with their genius, Robbe-Grillet and Claude Simon succeeded in describing paintings that did not need to exist). Or you fall into indeterminacy, emotional gushing or applied metaphysics. The problem specific to painting is found in lines and colors. It is hard to extract scientific concepts that are not mathematical or physical, and that are not just literature superimposed on painting either, but that are almost carved in and through painting.

Wasn't it also an occasion to shake up critical vocabulary, to resuscitate it?

Writing has its own heat, but thinking about painting is the best way to grasp the line and color of a sentence, as if a painting could communicate something to the words (sentences)… I have rarely had more pleasure in writing a book. When dealing with a colorist like Bacon, the confrontation with color is overwhelming.

When you speak of the ambient clichés that preexist the canvas, aren't you also dealing with the problem of the writer?

A canvas is not a blank surface. It is already heavy with clichés, even if we do not see them. The painter's work consists in destroying them: the painter must go through a moment when he or she no longer sees anything thanks to a collapse of visual coordinates. That is why I say that painting includes a catastrophe, one that is the crux of the painting. This is already obvious in Cézanne and

Van Gogh. In the case of other arts, the conflict with clichés is very important, but it mostly remains outside the work although it is inside the author. Except in the case of Artaud, for whom the collapse of ordinary linguistic coordinates are part of the work. In painting, however, it is a rule: the painting comes from an optical catastrophe that remains present in the painting itself.

Did you have the paintings in front of you as you wrote?

I had reproductions in front of me when I was writing and in doing so I was following Bacon's method: when he thinks of a painting, he doesn't go look at it. He has color photos or even black and white photos. I went back to see the paintings in between writing or afterwards.

Did you sometimes need to separate yourself from the work, to forget it?

I didn't need to forget it. There was a moment when the reproduction was no longer useful because what it had given me already referred to another reproduction. Let me give you an example: I was looking at the triptychs and had the feeling that there was a certain internal law, forcing me to jump from one reproduction to the other to compare them. Secondly, I had the impression that if this law existed, it had to be found secretly even in the single paintings. It was an idea floating around that came to me between the triptychs.

Thirdly, while flipping through the reproductions of single paintings, I ran across one called *Man and Child*, which seemed to me to have an obvious triptych construction. It represents an odd little girl with large feet looking stern with her arms crossed who is looking at a man, like those Bacon does, sitting on an adjustable stool that may be going up or down. The organization of this painting makes it obvious that it is an enveloped triptych instead of a developed one. The reproductions sent me back and forth from one to the other, but the idea of looking at a third reproduction generally comes between two others…

To what extent did David Sylvester's interviews with Bacon serve as a starting point for your work, one that was different from the paintings?[1]

They were a necessary foundation. First of all, the interviews are excellent and Bacon says a great deal. In general, when artists talk about what they do, they have extraordinary modesty, self-imposed rigor, and great strength. They are the first to suggest strongly the nature of the concepts and affects emanating from their work. A painter's texts therefore operate much differently than his or her paintings. When you read the interviews, you always want to ask further questions, and since you know you won't be able to ask them, you have to get by on your own.

You never met Bacon?

Yes, afterwards, after the book. You can sense power and violence in him along with great charm. As soon as he sits more than an hour, he twists in every direction; he really looks like a Bacon. But his posture is always simple, given a sensation that he might feel. Bacon distinguishes between the violence of spectacle, which does not interest him, and the violence of sensation as an object of painting. He says, "I started by painting horror, bullfights and crucifixions, but that was still too dramatic. It is important to paint the cry." Horror is too figurative, and by moving from horror to the cry, there is a significant increase in sobriety and the ease of figuration falls away. The most beautiful Bacons are of characters sleeping or a man seen from the rear as he shaves.

Beyond its role as an homage, is your book intended to increase the reputation of Bacon's paintings?

If it were successful, it would necessarily have this effect. But I believe it has a higher aspiration, something everyone dreams of: to reach something like a common supply of words, of lines and colors, and even of sounds. Writing about painting or writing about music always implies this aspiration.

The second volume of the book (the reproductions of paintings) is not chronological in terms of Bacon's work. Is it the history of your attachment to Bacon, a way to reconstitute an order of viewing?

In the margins of the text, in fact, there are numbers that refer to the reproduced paintings. This order of appearance is somewhat rearranged for technical reasons (the role of the triptychs). But their succession does not refer to Bacon's chronology. It proceeds logically from relatively simple aspects to relatively complex ones. A painting can therefore reappear when more complex elements are found in it.

As for the chronology, Sylvester distinguishes three periods for Bacon and defines them very clearly. But Bacon has recently started a new period, given the artist's power of renewal. To my knowledge, there are only three paintings so far: a fountain of water, a fountain of grass and a fountain of sand. It is entirely new. All "figures" have disappeared. When I met Bacon, he said that he dreamed of painting a wave but did not dare believe such an undertaking could be successful. It is a lesson in painting: a major painter who has come to say, "If only I could catch a little wave…" It is very Proustian. Or Cézanne: "Ah! If only I could paint a little apple!"

You describe the work, you try to describe its systems, but at no point do you say "I"?

Emotion does not say "I". You said it yourself: you are beside yourself. Emotion is not of the order of the ego but of the event. It is very difficult to grasp an event, but I do not believe that this grasp implies the first person. It would be better to use the third person like Maurice Blanchot when he says that there is more intensity in the sentence "he suffers" than "I suffer."

24

Manfred: an Extraordinary Renewal

An artist's power lies in renewal. Carmelo Bene is a perfect example. *Thanks* to everything he has done, he can *break* with what he did. He is currently blazing a new trail for himself. And for the rest of us, he is constructing a new, active relationship with music.

First of all, every image in principal contains visual and sound elements. And for a long time, while "doing" theater or cinema, Carmelo Bene treated both elements at once (décor colors, visual organization of the staging, characters seen and heard at the same time). He is now increasingly interested in sound alone. He turns sound into a *point* that draws the entire image; the entire image becomes sound. Instead of the characters speaking, sound becomes a character, a sound element becomes a character. Carmelo Bene is thus continuing his project to be a "protagonist" or *operator* more than an actor, but he is pursuing it under new conditions. Voices no longer whisper, yell or bellow depending on the emotion to express, but whispering becomes *a voice*, cries become *a voice*. At the same time, the corresponding emotions (affects) become *vocal modes*. And all of these voices and modes communicate from inside. This leads to a renewed role for changes in speed and even for play-back. Play-back has never been a quick fix for Carmelo Bene; it is an instrument of creation.

Secondly, the question is not only to extract sound from vision, but also to extract all the musical power from the spoken voice. These new powers are not to be confused with song. They can in fact accompany singing, collaborate with it, but without forming a song or even a *sprechgesang*: they create a *modalized voice*, a filtered voice. His invention may be as important as the invention of the *sprechgesang* itself but is essentially different. It means at one and the same time capturing, creating or modifying the basic color of a sound (or group of sounds) and making it vary or evolve over time, changing its physiological curve. Carmelo Bene is renewing all of his research into vocal addition and subtraction, and this research increasingly confronts him in the power of the synthesizer.

Carmelo Bene's *Manfred* is the first product of a vast undertaking and a new step in his creative work. In *Manfred*, this voice, these voices of Carmelo Bene slide between the singing choirs and the music, conspire with them, augmenting or diminishing them. It would be a mistake to say that Carmelo Bene favored Byron over Schumann. Carmelo Bene did not choose Schumann by chance but out of love. Schumann's music opened many new possibilities for the voice and led to new vocal instrumentation. There could be no doubt of this at La Scala in Milan. Carmelo Bene inserted the text that had become sound between song and music, made it coexist with them, react to them. He did it in such a way that we heard the combination for the first time in a profound alliance between song and musical element, on the one hand, and the invented, created, vocal element that made itself necessary on the other. Yes, what an extraordinary success, this inauguration of Carmelo Bene's new research.

25

Preface to *The Savage Anomaly*

Negri's book on Spinoza, written in prison, is a major book that in many ways renews our understanding of Spinozism. I would like to concentrate on two of the main arguments he develops.

1. Spinoza's Anti-Legalism

Spinoza's fundamental idea is the spontaneous development of forces, at least virtually. In other words, there is no need for mediation in principle to establish the relationships that correspond to forces.

On the contrary, the idea of a necessary mediation belongs essentially to the legal conception of the world found in Hobbes, Rousseau and Hegel. This conception implies: 1) that forces have an individual or private origin; 2) that they must be socialized to bring about adequate relationships corresponding to them; 3) that there is thus mediation of a Power ("Potestas"); and 4) that the horizon is inseparable from crisis, war or antagonism that Power proposes to solve, though an "antagonist solution."

Spinoza is often presented as belonging to this legal lineage between Hobbes and Rousseau. Not according to Negri. For Spinoza, forces are inseparable from a spontaneity and productivity that make possible their development without mediation or their *composition.* They are elements of socialization in themselves. Spinoza immediately thinks in terms of "multitudes" and not individuals. His entire philosophy is a philosophy of "potentia" against "potestas." It takes its place in an anti-legalist tradition that includes Machiavelli and leads to Marx. It is a conception of ontological "constitution" or of a physical and dynamic "composition" that conflicts with the legal *contract.*[1] In Spinoza, the ontological perspective of an immediate production conflicts with any call to a Should-Be, a mediation or a finality ("with Hobbes the crisis connotes the ontological horizon and subsumes it; with Spinoza the crisis is subsumed under the ontological horizon").

Although one can sense the importance and newness of Negri's argument, the reader might shrink from the utopian atmosphere it exudes. Thus Negri is careful to point out the special character of the Dutch milieu that that made Spinoza's position possible. Against the Orange family that represented a "potestas" in accordance with European monarchy, the Holland of the De Witt brothers could attempt to promote the market as a spontaneity of productive forces, or capitalism as an immediate form of the socialization of forces. Spinozist anomalies and Dutch anomalies... But in each case, isn't it the same *utopia*? This is where the strong second point of Negri's analysis comes into play.

2) Spinoza's Evolution

The first Spinoza, the Spinoza of the *Short Treatise* and of the beginning of the *Ethics*, retains the utopian perspective. He renews them, however, by ensuring that forces have maximum expansion by attaining an *ontological constitution* of substance and of modes through substance (pantheism). Yet precisely because of the spontaneity of the operation or the absence of mediation, the *material composition* of concrete reality is not made manifest as a power as such, and knowledge and thought still must turn back into themselves, subjected to a solely ideal productivity of Being instead of opening to the world.

That is why the second Spinoza as he appears in the *Theological-Political Treatise* and as he asserts himself in the *Ethics* is recognizable in two fundamental themes: on the one hand, the power of substance is reduced to the modes for which it serves as horizon; on the other hand, thought opens to the world and establishes itself as material imagination. Utopia then comes to an end in favor of the premises of revolutionary materialism. Not that antagonism and mediation are restored. The horizon of Being subsists immediately but as the *place* of political constitution and not as the *utopia* of ideal and substantial constitution.

Bodies (and souls) are forces. As such they are not only defined by their chance encounters and collisions (state of crisis). They are defined by relationships between an infinite number of parts that compose each body and that already characterize it as a "multitude." There are therefore *processes* of composition and decomposition of bodies, depending on whether their characteristic relationships suit them or not. Two or several bodies will form a whole, in other words, another body, if they compose their respective relationships in concrete circumstances. And it is the highest exercise of the imagination, the point where it inspires understanding, to have bodies (and souls) meet according to composable relationships. Thus the importance of the Spinoza's theory of *common notions* which is a cornerstone of the *Ethics*, from Book II to Book V. The material imagination seals its alliance with the understanding by ensuring, under the horizon of Being, both the physical composition of bodies and the political constitution of humans.

What Negri did so profoundly for Marx in terms of the *Grundrisse*, he now does for Spinoza: a complete reevaluation of the respective place of the *Short Treatise*, and the *Theological-Political Treatise*, in Spinoza's work. Negri does this to suggest an evolution in Spinoza: from *progressive utopia* to *revolutionary materialism*. Negri is certainly the first to give a full, philosophical meaning to the anecdote that tells of how Spinoza drew himself as Masaniello, the Neapolitan revolutionary (cf. what Nietzsche says on the importance of "anecdotes" fitting "thought, in the life of a thinker.").

I have given an extremely rudimentary presentation of Negri's two arguments. I do not think that it is appropriate to discuss these arguments and to reject or confirm them too hastily. These arguments have the obvious merit of accounting for the exceptional situation of Spinoza in the history of thought. The theses are profoundly new, but what they make us see are, first of all, the newness of Spinoza himself, in the sense of a "future philosophy." They show the central role of politics in Spinoza's philosophy. Our first task should be to appreciate the scope of these arguments and to understand what Negri found in Spinoza, how he is authentically and profoundly Spinozist.

26

The Indians of Palestine

Gilles Deleuze: It seems like something has come of age in the Palestinian camp. A new tone is apparent, as though they had overcome the first stage of their crisis, as though they had reached a place of certainty or serenity, with a new sense of their "rights." This would seem to indicate a new consciousness. The new tone seems to enable them to speak in a new way, neither aggressively nor defensively, but as "equals" with the world. How do you explain this, since the Palestinians have yet to achieve their political objectives?

Elias Sanbar: We had a sense of this right after the publication of our first issue. Many concerned with the struggle said, "Hey, now the Palestinians have their own journal," and it seems to have shaken up a long-standing image of Palestinians in the eyes of the world. Let's not forget that, in the eyes of many, the image of the Palestinian combatant—the one which we are trying to promote—had remained very abstract. In other words, before we imposed the reality of our presence, we were thought of only as refugees. When our resistance movement made clear that our struggle could not be ignored, we were again reduced to a clichéd image: we were seen as pure and simple militarists. This image was isolated and reproduced ad infinitum. We were perceived as standing for nothing else. It is to rid ourselves of the militarist image in the strict sense, that we prefer this other image of the combatant.

I believe the surprise which our journal has elicited also comes from the fact that some people must be telling themselves that Palestinians actually exist, and not merely for the sake of calling abstract principles to mind. Although the journal is Palestinian, it nonetheless constitutes a terrain where many different preoccupations can be expressed, a place where not only Palestinian voices can be heard, but also Arab, Jewish, and European voices.

Some people must also be realizing that this kind of work, coming as it does from various horizons, points to the existence of many different Palestinians in the various sectors of Palestinian society: painters, sculptors, workers, farmers, novelists, bankers, actors, business men, professors, etc. In short, they realize that a whole society exists behind this journal.

Palestine is not only a people, but a land. Palestine is what links this people to a land which has been pillaged and plundered. It is a place where exile and an immense desire to return are at work, a unique place, made up of all the expulsions which our people have suffered since 1948. When we study Palestine, scrutinize it, follow its least movements, and keep track of the changes that affect it, we have an image of Palestine in our eyes. And we never lose that from sight.

Gilles Deleuze: Many of the articles in your journal refer to, and analyze in a new way, the methods that have been used to chase Palestinians from their territory. This is crucial because Palestinians do not find themselves in a typical colonial situation. They are not so much colonized as they are cleared away, chased off. In your book, you compare the Palestinians to American Indians.[1] There are indeed two distinct movements in capitalism. In the first, a people is maintained on its land and made to work, exploited to accumulate a surplus. This is what we usually mean by "colony." But in the second, a territory is emptied of its people. Capitalism thus makes a giant leap in a single bound, even if that means importing workers and manual labor. The history of Zionism, the history of Israel, and the history of the United States have all gone that route: how does one create a vacuum, how does one empty out a territory?

Yassir Arafat in an interview has pointed out the limits of the comparison,[2] and this limit comprises the horizon of your journal: he says the difference is the Arab world, whereas the American Indians, having been expulsed from their territory, had no one to whom they could turn for economic or military support.

Elias Sanbar: As exiles, we are rather particular because we were expulsed not to some foreign country, but to the outer reaches of our "homeland." We were exiled to Arab countries where it never crossed anyone's mind to disband us. I am thinking of the hypocrisy of some Israelis who assert that the Arabs are at fault for not "integrating" us—which in Israeli-speak means "making us disappear." Those who expulsed us are suddenly concerned about some supposed Arab racism against us. Does that mean we did not encounter difficult situations in certain Arab countries? Of course not. We certainly did. But these difficulties did not come from our being Arab. They were unavoidable because we were and still are an armed revolution. But to our Jewish colonizers we are indeed the Indians of Palestine. All we were to do was disappear from view. In this sense, the history of the establishment of Israel is a repeat of the process that gave birth to the United States of America. Therein probably lies one of the essential ingredients in their mutual solidarity.

In this, moreover, you see elements that illustrate how during the period of the British Trust[3] we were not subjected to a "classic" colonization, where colonizers and colonized live side by side. The French, the English, etc., wanted to establish areas whose very condition of existence depended on the presence of indigenous people. For any domination to take effect, there had to be a people to be dominated. This created, perhaps unintentionally, common areas, that is, networks or sectors or aspects of social life where the "encounter" between colonizer and colonized took place. That this encounter was unbearable, exploitative, crushing, or oppressive does not change the fact that the "foreign colonizer" had first to be "in contact" with "the locals" in order to exert his domination.

Then Zionism comes along, but its assumptions are the opposite: *our absence* is a necessity, and what is more, as Ilan Halevi has shown,[4] the cornerstone of our rejection, our displacement, our "transfer" and substitution is a specific feature of Zionists, namely their belonging to the Jewish community. In this way, a whole new breed of colonizer was born, "an unknown," arriving amidst the mass of what I just called "foreign colonizers." This new colonizer proceeds by making of his own characteristics the basis for the total rejection of the Other.

Furthermore, in some ways, our country was not just colonized in 1948—it "disappeared." In any event, that is how the Jewish colonizers who had become "Israelis" must have experienced it. The Zionist movement mobilized the Jewish community in Palestine not with the idea that the Palestinians would one day leave, but with the idea that the country was "empty." There were other Jews, of course, who having arrived, saw how untrue it was and wrote about it! But the majority of the Jewish community acted like the people with whom they came face to face every day, living and working, were not there. This blindness, however, was not physical. No one was fooled to that degree. But everyone understood that the people living in their midst were "in the process of disappearing." And they realized that if this disappearance was going to succeed, from the outset they had to act as though it had already happened, by "never seeing" the existence of the Other, who was nonetheless unmistakably present. Emptying the territory, if it were to succeed, had to begin by emptying "the Other" from the head of the colonizer.

One of the ways Zionism succeeded was by playing the race card, making Judaism the very basis for the expulsion, the rejection of the Other. The racist persecutions in Europe were extremely helpful in this respect, since they provided Zionism with a confirmation of the steps it had to take. We believe that Zionism has imprisoned Jews, holding them captive to the vision I just described. I want to emphasize that it still holds them captive. It is not true merely of one particular historical moment. I say this because Zionism's rationale changed after the Holocaust. Zionism mutated, positing a pseudo-"eternal principle" that Jews everywhere were from time immemorial the "Other" in whatever society they lived. However, no people, no community can claim to occupy this position of the marginalized, the cursed "Other" in a way that is permanent and inalterable. And luckily this is true, especially for the Jews.

Today in the Middle East, the Other is the Arab, and the Palestinian. The disappearance of this Other is now the order of the day, and the fact that it is from this Other, who is in danger of disappearing, that the Western powers ask for assurances is the height of hypocrisy and cynicism. We are the ones who need assurances, if we are to be protected from the madness of the Israeli military leaders.

In any event, the PLO, our unique and only representative, has proposed a solution to the conflict: a democratic state in Palestine, a state where the walls that exist between inhabitants, whoever they are, would be demolished.

Gilles Deleuze: The opening pages of the first issue of your journal contain a manifesto: we are "a people like any other people." The sense of this declaration is multiple. In the first place, it is a reminder, or a cry. The Palestinians are constantly reproached with refusing to recognize Israel. Look, say the Israelis, they want to destroy us. But for more than 50 years now, the Palestinians have been struggling for recognition as a people. In the second place, the declaration marks an opposition with the manifesto of Israel, which says "we are not a people like any other people" because of our transcendence and the enormity of our persecutions. Hence, in the second issue, the importance of two texts by Israeli writers on the Holocaust and the significance which this event has assumed in Israel, especially with respect to the Palestinians and the Arab world, untouched by such a catastrophe. By demanding "to be treated as a people with an exceptional status," the State of Israel maintains an economic and financial dependence on the West in a way that no other State ever has (Boaz Evron).[5] This dependence on the West explains why the Palestinians are so adamant about the contrary declaration: they want to become what they are, that is, a people with an "unexceptional" status. As opposed to history as apocalypse, there is a sense of history as possibility, the multiplicity of what is possible, the profusion of multiple possibilities at every moment. Is this not what your journal hopes to make apparent in its analyses?

Elias Sanbar: Absolutely. The idea of a cry to remind the world of our existence is deeply meaningful, but it is also quite simple. It is the kind of truth which, once it has been recognized, will make things very difficult for anyone still counting on the disappearance of the Palestinian people. In the end, what this truth says is that every people has "a right to its rights," so to speak. This is self-evident, but so powerful that it represents the point of departure and the destination of every political struggle. Look at the Zionists: What do they have to say on the subject? You will never hear them say: "the Palestinian people have a right to nothing." No amount of force can maintain such a position, and they know it. But you will hear them say: "there is no Palestinian people." This is why the affirmation of the existence of the Palestinian people is so very powerful, much more so than it might at first appear.

27

Letter to Uno on Language

Dear Friend,

Thank you for your very fine letter. You ask a great many questions, and as usual, the only person truly able to provide an answer is the one who is asking the questions. However, I believe we are close enough for me to tell you how I see the problem of narrative.

First, language has no self-sufficiency, at least that is my view. It follows that language has no significance of its own. It is composed of signs, but signs are inseparable from a whole other element, a non-linguistic element, which could be called "the state of things" or, better yet, "images." As Bergson has convincingly shown, images have an existence independently of us. What I call an "assemblage of utterance" is thus composed of images and signs, moving and circulating in the world.

Second, utterance does not refer to a subject. There is no expressing subject, i.e. subject of utterance, but only assemblages. This means that, in any assemblage, there exist "processes of subjectivation" which assign various subjects: some are images, and some are signs. This is why what in European languages is known as "free indirect discourse" seems so crucial: it is an utterance contained in a statement which itself depends on another utterance. For example: "She gathers her strength, she would rather die than betray...." In my view, every utterance is of this type and is composed of several voices. In the last few years, metaphor has been elevated into an operation coextensive with language. In my view, metaphors do not exist. What I mean is that free indirect discourse is the only "figure," the only one coextensive with language. I don't know whether Japanese has free indirect discourse (you will have to let me know). If not, perhaps it is simply because free indirect discourse is a form consubstantial with Japanese, so there is no reason to single it out.

Third, language is never a homogeneous system, nor does it contain such systems. Linguists, whether Jakobson or Chomsky, believe in such systems because they would be out of a job without them. But a language is always a heterogeneous system, or as physicists say, a system far from equilibrium. Labov is a linguist who makes this claim quite convincingly, thereby renewing the field of linguistics. And this fact is what has made literature possible from the beginning: literature is writing far from equilibrium, writing in one's own language as "in a foreign language" (Proust and French, Kafka and German, etc.).

All this explains why I am working on cinema at the moment. Cinema is an assemblage of images and signs (even silent movies used to contain types of utterance). I would like to create a classification of images and signs. For example, there would be the movement-image, which would then be subdivided into the perception-image, the affection-image, and the action-image. And to each type of image there would correspond signs or voices, various forms of utterance. An immense table of images could be compiled in this way, since every author has his or her own preferences. In this respect, Japanese cinema has been a marvelous discovery for me.

28

Preface to the American Edition of *Nietzsche and Philosophy*

To Hugh Tomlinson

For a French book, it has always been an enviable proposition to be translated into English. Such an occasion, after so many years, inspires an author with dreams of how he would like to be received by the proposed reader, with whom he feels at once very close and yet all too distant.

Two ambiguities have plagued the posthumous reception of Nietzsche: Did his work prefigure fascist thought? And was his thought even philosophy? Or was it just violent poetry, capricious aphorisms, and pathological fragments, all of it too excessive? These misunderstandings may have culminated in England. Tomlinson suggests that the principal themes Nietzsche confronts, and that Nietzsche's philosophy combats, e.g. French rationalism or German dialectic, never had much appreciable influence on English thought to begin with. The English already possessed their own theoretical pragmatism and empiricism that made any detour through Nietzsche totally unnecessary. They simply had no use for that brand of Nietzschean pragmatism and empiricism which had been turned against common sense. Nietzsche's influence in England, therefore, has been limited to novelists, poets, and playwrights—an influence more practical, more affective than philosophical, more lyrical than theoretical…

However, Nietzsche was one of the great nineteenth-century thinkers, who radically altered both the theory and the practice of philosophy. He compared the thinker to an arrow shot from Nature's bow: wherever it lands, another thinker comes and picks it up, to shoot it in another direction. For Nietzsche, the thinker is neither eternal nor historical, but "untimely," always untimely. Nietzsche's predecessors are few. Aside from the pre-Socratics, there is only Spinoza.

Nietzsche's philosophy can be organized along two axes. The first has to do with force, or forces, and constitutes a general semiology. For Nietzsche, phenomena, things, organisms, societies, consciousnesses, spirits, are signs or rather symptoms, and as such refer to a state of forces. Hence his conception of the philosopher as "physiologist and doctor." For any given thing, what state of forces, both internal and external, must we presuppose? Nietzsche invented a typology of forces which distinguishes active forces from reactive forces (those which are acted on) and analyzes their various combinations. Designating a type of force which is properly reactive is one of the most original points of Nietzsche's thought. This book on Nietzsche tries to define and analyze these different forces. Such a general semiology includes linguistics, or rather philology as one of its departments. This is because a proposition is itself a group of symptoms expressing a speaker's way of being or mode of existence, the state of forces someone maintains, or tries to maintain, with himself and others (conjunctions have a role to play here). In this sense, a proposition always refers to a mode of existence, a "type." For any given proposition, what is the mode of existence of the person who pronounces it? And what mode of existence is necessary in order to have the power to pronounce it? A mode of existence is a state of forces that constitutes a type expressible through signs or symptoms.

Resentment and bad conscience, the two great reactive human concepts, at least as Nietzsche "diagnoses" them, express the triumph of negative forces in humankind, and even constitute the human, i.e. the human-slave. This shows precisely to what extent the Nietzschean conception of slave does not necessarily designate someone who is dominated, whether by destiny or by social condition, but characterizes both dominant and dominated, ruler and ruled, whenever a regime of domination works through reactive forces rather than active ones. In this sense, totalitarian regimes are the regimes of slaves, not only in terms of the peoples they subjugate, but especially the "leaders" they foster. A universal history of resentment and bad conscience, as it is found in the Jewish priest, and the Christian priest, all the way down to the secular priest of today, is essential in Nietzsche's historical perspectivism (Nietzsche's alleged anti-Semetic texts in fact deal with this original type of priest).

The second axis has to do with power, and constitutes an ethics and an ontology. All misunderstanding of Nietzsche culminates in his notion of power. Interpreting the Will to Power as "wanting or seeking Power" is merely the worst platitude, which has nothing to do with Nietzsche's thought. If it is true that any given thing refers to a state of forces, then Power designates the element, or rather the differential relation, of the forces at work. This relation is expressed in the dynamic qualities of the "affirmation," "negation" type. Power is thus not what the will wants, but what wants in the will. And "wanting or seeking Power" is merely the lowest degree of the will to power, its negative form, or the aspect it assumes when negative forces triumph in the state of things. One of the most original characteristics of Nietzsche's philosophy is having transformed the question *What is it?* into *Who is it?* For example, for any given proposition, *who* is capable of uttering it? Still, we must do away with all "personalist" references. "Who" does not refer to an individual or a person, but to an event, to relational forces in a proposition or a phenomenon, as well as to a genetic relation that determines these forces (power). "Who" is always Dionysos, an aspect or a mask of Dionysos, a flash of lightning.

Misunderstanding has plagued the Eternal Return no less than the Will to Power. Whenever one understands the Eternal Return as the return of a combination (after all the other combinations have been tried), whenever one interprets the Eternal Return as the return of the Identical or the Same, one again substitutes puerile hypotheses for Nietzsche's thought. No one has taken the critique of identity farther than Nietzsche. In two passages of *Zarathustra*, Nietzsche explicitly denies that the Eternal Return is a circle that brings back the Same. The Eternal Return is strictly the opposite, since it is inseparable from a selection, a twofold selection. First, it is the selection of will or thought (Nietzsche's ethics): to will only those things whose eternal return we also will (to eliminate all half-willing, what we will when we say "just this once, only once"). Second, it is the selection of Being (Nietzsche's ontology): what returns, or is apt to return, is only that which *becomes* in the fullest sense of the word. Only action and affirmation return: Being belongs to becoming and only to becoming. Whatever is opposed to becoming—the Same or the Identical—is not, rigorously speaking. The negative as the lowest degree of power, the reactive as the lowest degree of form, these do not return, because they are the opposite of becoming, and becoming constitutes the only Being. One can see how the Eternal Return is tied not to a repetition of the Same, but to a transmutation. The Eternal Return is the instant or the eternity of becoming eliminating whatever offers resistance. It brings out, or better yet, it creates the active, the pure active, and pure affirmation. The overman has no other meaning: it is what the Will to Power and the Eternal Return, Dionysos and Ariadne, produce together. This is why Nietzsche says that the Will to Power has nothing to do with wanting, coveting, or seeking, but only "giving," "creating." The primary focus of this book is the analysis of what Nietzsche calls Becoming.

The Nietzsche question, however, involves more than conceptual analyses. It involves practical evaluations that elicit a whole climate, all kinds of affective dispositions on the part of the reader. Like Spinoza, Nietzsche always posited the most profound relationship between concept and affect. Conceptual analyses are indispensable, and Nietzsche takes them farther than anyone else. But they remain ineffectual as long as the reader continues to grasp them in a climate other than Nietzsche's. As long as the reader obstinately insists 1) on seeing in the "Nietzschean" slave someone who is dominated by a master, and who deserves it; 2) on understanding the will to power as a will that wants and seeks power; 3) on conceptualizing the Eternal Return as the meticulous return of the same; 4) on imagining the overman as a race of masters—there can be no positive relationship between Nietzsche and his reader. Nietzsche will look like a nihilist, or worse a fascist; at best, he will seem an obscure and terrifying prophet. Nietzsche knew this. He was well aware of the destiny awaiting him. He gave Zarathustra a double in the "monkey" and the "clown," predicting that

Zarathustra would be confused with his monkey (a prophet, a fascist, a madman...). Hence a book on Nietzsche must attempt to rectify any practical and affective incomprehension while at the same time renewing his conceptual analyses.

It is true that Nietzsche diagnosed nihilism as the movement which overtakes history. No one has given a better analysis of nihilism—Nietzsche invented the concept. But he defined it precisely as the triumph of reactive forces, or as the negative in the will to power. His opposition to the negative and the reactive was unwavering. He proposed instead transmutation or becoming, which is the only action of force and the only affirmation of power, the transhistoric element of humanity, the Overman (and not the superman). The overman is the focal point where the reactive (resentment and bad conscience) is overcome, and where the negative gives way to affirmation. At whatever point we grasp him, Nietzsche remains inseparable from future forces, those forces to come, which he is hoping and praying for, which his thought sketches and his art prefigures. Not only did he diagnose, as Kafka says, the diabolic forces already knocking at the door, but he also chases them away by erecting the last Power capable of doing battle with them, against them, and rooting out the reactive forces within us and outside us. An "aphorism" in Nietzsche's hands is not a simple fragment, a snippet of thought: it is a proposition which makes sense only in relation to the state of forces which it expresses, and whose sense changes—whose sense must change—according to the new forces which it is "able" (has the power) to elicit.

Undoubtedly, what is most important in Nietzsche's philosophy is to have transformed the image of thought which we have made for ourselves. Nietzsche wrests thought from the element of truth and falsehood. He makes it into an interpretation and an evaluation, an interpretation of forces, and an evaluation of power—it is a thought-movement. In this sense, not only does Nietzsche want to reconcile thought and concrete movement, but thought itself must produce extraordinary movements, speeds, and decelerations (here again the aphorism has a role to play, with its variable speeds and its projectile-like movement). It follows that philosophy assumes a new relationship to theater, dance, music, the arts of movement. Nietzsche never contents himself with discursive writing, the dissertation (logos), as the expression of philosophical thought, even if he did write some very fine dissertations, especially *The Genealogy of Morals*, to which all modern ethnology owes an inexhaustible "debt." But a book like *Zarathustra* can be read only as a modern opera—viewed and heard, I should say. Not that Nietzsche writes a philosophical opera or allegorical theater. Rather, he creates a theater or an opera which directly expresses thought as experience and movement. And when Nietzsche says that the overman resembles Borgia more than Parsifal, or that the overman belongs both to the Jesuit order and to the Prussian officer corps, we are mistaken to see prefascist declarations in such remarks. They should instead be seen as director's notes indicating how the Overman should be "played" (like Kierkegaard saying the knight of faith resembles a bourgeois in his Sunday best). Nietzsche's greatest teaching is that thinking is creating. Thinking is a roll of the dice... This is the meaning of the Eternal Return.

29

Cinema-I, Premiere

You are wondering why so many people write about cinema. I ask myself the same question. It seems to me to be because cinema contains a lot of ideas. What I call Ideas are images that make one think. From one art to another, the nature of images varies and is inseparable from the techniques used: colors and lines for painting, sound for music, verbal descriptions for novels, movement-images for cinema, etc. And in each case, the thoughts are inseparable from the images; they are completely immanent to the images. There are no abstract thoughts realized indifferently in one image or another, but concrete images that only exist through these images and their means. Drawing out cinematic ideas means extracting thoughts without abstracting them, grasping them in their internal relationship with the movement-images. That is why people write "about" cinema. The great cinematic authors are thinkers just as much as painters, musicians, novelists and philosophers (philosophy has no special privilege).

Cinema and the other arts sometimes intersect; they can reach similar thoughts. But this is never because there is some abstract thought indifferent to its means of expression. It is because images and means of expression can create a thought that is repeated or taken up again from one art to another, autonomous and complete in each case. Take your favorite example: Kurosawa. In Dostoyevsky, there are always characters caught up in very urgent situations that require immediate answers. Then, all of a sudden, the character stops and seems to waste time for no reason: he or she has the impression that they have not yet found the hidden "problem" that is more urgent than the situation. It is like someone being chased by a mad dog and suddenly stopping to say: "Wait, there is a problem here. What is the problem?" This is precisely what Dostoyevsky calls the Idea. We can see the exact same type of Ideas in Kurosawa. Kurosawa's characters constantly move from the "fact" of a very urgent situation to the "fact" of an even more urgent question hidden in the situation. What I call a thought is not the content of a question, which can be abstract and banal (where are we going, where do we come from?). It is the formal passage from a situation to a hidden question, the metamorphosis of the facts. Kurosawa does not adapt Dostoyevsky, but his art of movement-images and the means available to him led him to create a thought that existed once before in the art of Dostoyevsky's verbal descriptions. Whether he adapts Dostoyevsky or not becomes entirely secondary.

You yourself, for example, distinguish different types of images in cinema. You speak of a deep image, where there is always something hiding something else. Then there is the flat image where everything is visible; then combinations of images where each one slides over the others or fits into them. It is obvious that these are not solely technical resources. You also have to take the acting into consideration. Different types of images require very different acting. For example, the crisis of the action-image imposed a new genre of actors who are not non-professional actors but on the contrary professional non-actors, actors who "dabble" like Jean-Pierre

Léaud, Bulle Ogier and Juliet Berto in France. Here again, the actors are not only technique but thought. Actors do not always think, but they are thoughts. An image is only worth the thoughts it creates. In your classification of images, the flat image is inseparable from a thought reacting to it. The thought varies depending on the director: for Dreyer, the suppression of depth as the third dimension is inseparable from a fourth and fifth dimensions, as he said himself (and the actors act accordingly). For Welles, depth is not the deep image you mention. It is tied to the discovery of "layers of the past" and it doubles the movement-image with an exploration of the past that a flashback alone would be incapable of producing. It is a major cinematographic creation, the construction of a time-image that leads to new functions of thought.

The state of cinematographic critique seems strong in books and magazines. There are several very beautiful books. Maybe it is due to the recent and rapid character of cinema: its recentness and its speed. In cinema, people are not yet in the habit of disconnecting the classical (what has been done and is the object of overly confident university critics) from the modern (what is being done now and is judged haughtily). This disassociation between an art and its history is always ruinous. If it happens to cinema it will be ruined as well. For the moment, a task is already underway: the search for cinematographic Ideas. It is both the most intimate research within cinema and a comparative search because it establishes a comparison with painting, music, philosophy and even science.

30

Portrait of the Philosopher as a Moviegoer

Hervé Guibert: *Your last book was a monograph on Francis Bacon: How did you make the leap from painting to film? Did you already have the inkling of a project that would entail such a leap?*

Gilles Deleuze: I didn't make a leap from painting to film. I don't think of philosophy as a reflection on one thing or another—painting or film. Philosophy is about concepts. It produces concepts, it creates them. Painting creates one kind of image: lines and colors. Film creates another kind: movement-images and time-images. But concepts themselves are already images; they are images of thought. It is no more difficult, nor any easier, to understand a concept than it is to look at an image.

So, it's not a matter of reflecting on film. It almost goes without saying that the concepts which philosophy produces would resonate with pictorial images today, or with cinematographic images, etc. For example, film constructs very particular spaces: empty spaces, or a space whose pieces have no fixed connection. But philosophy is also in the business of constructing spatial concepts, and these correspond to the spaces of film, or those of the other arts, or even science... There may even be a zone of indiscerpibility, where the same thing could be expressed by a pictorial image, a scientific model, a cinematographic image, or a philosophical concept. And yet the practitioner of each discipline experiences a movement, methods, and problems specific to each.

You are progressively—perhaps provisionally—leaving behind the traditional objects which a philosopher studies in favor of other kinds of material: Are these more modern? Are they overlooked? Or are they more interesting, more desirable?

I don't know. Philosophy's own material is already interesting and desirable. I don't believe in the death of philosophy. Concepts are not austere or ancient things. They are modern entities with a life. Let's take an example. Maurice Blanchot says an event has two dimensions that coexist and are inseparable. On the one hand, there is that which plunges into bodies and finds its fulfillment in bodies; and on the other, there is an inexhaustible potentiality that exceeds every actualization. This is the concept of an event that *he* constructs.

But an actor might decide "to play" an event precisely in these terms. Or one might apply to film the old Zen formula: "the visual reserve of things in their exactitude." What I find so interesting in philosophy is how it chooses to divide things up: it groups under one concept things which you would have thought were very different, or it separates things you would have thought belonged together. As for film, it also divides things up, proposing distinct groups of visual and sonorous images. And distinct modes of grouping visual and sonorous images can and do compete with one another.

Do you prefer the movie theater to the library?

Libraries are necessary, but you don't feel so great inside them. Movie theaters are intended to be pleasurable. I'm not a big fan of the small movie theater where you find a great many films, with each showing only once at a particular hour. For me, film is inseparable from a notion which it invented: the permanent spectacle. On the other hand, I do like specialized movie theaters: exclusively musicals, exclusively French film, or exclusively Soviet film, or action flicks... You will recall that it was the Mac-Mahon that made Losey famous.

Do you write in the dark, sitting in front of the screen?

I don't write while I'm watching the film—that would be too weird. But I take notes as soon as I can afterwards. I'm what you call a naïve moviegoer. I'm especially hostile to the notion of different levels: a first, a second, and a third level of meaning, understanding or appreciation. What works on the second level already works on the first. What fails on the first level remains a failure on every level. Every image is literal and must be taken literally. When an image is flat, you must not impart to it, even in thought, a depth that would disfigure it. What is most difficult is grasping images how they are presented, in their immediacy. And when a film-maker says, "Hey, folks, it's only a film," this is yet another dimension of the image which we must take literally. As Vertov used to say, there are several distinct lives that must be considered together: a life for the film, a life in the film, a life of the film itself, etc. In any case, an image does not represent some prior reality; it has its own reality.

Do you ever cry at the movies?

Crying, or causing tears to flow, and provoking laughter are the functions of certain images. You can cry because it's too beautiful or too intense. The only thing that bugs me is the knowing laughter of the cinephiles. This kind of laughter is supposedly on some higher level, a second level. I'd rather see the whole house in tears. How could you not cry at Griffith's *Broken Blossoms*?

Your book contains twenty references, the majority of which refer to other works on cinema. Did you not at least momentarily feel like you were writing an original work? Were you not seduced into thinking you were the first spectator, almost alone with the image, writing blindly, as it were, or seeing with clairvoyance?

A film is inseparable not only from the history of cinema as a whole, but also from the history of what has been written on cinema. Saying what you have figured out how to see is already an important aspect of writing. There is no original spectator. There is no beginning, there is no end. We always begin in the middle of something. And we only create in the middle by extending lines that already exist in a new direction or branching off from them.

What you call "seeing with clairvoyance" is not just a quality of the spectator; it is a possible quality of the image itself. For example, a film can present us with sensory-motor images: a character reacting to a situation. That's the visible. But sometimes the character is in a situation that exceeds any possible reaction, because it's too beautiful, too powerful, almost unbearable: e.g. Rosselini's heroine in *Stromboli*. In this case, you "see with clairvoyance," but it is a function of the image, it is already in the image itself. The clairvoyant is Rosselini or Godard, not the spectator.

Some images, moreover, are presented not only as visible, but as readable, though they remain pure images. Every sort of visual communication exists between the visual and the readable. It is the images themselves that impose a specific use of eyes and ears on the spectator. But the spectator will be left only with empty intuitions if he or she does not know how to appreciate the originality of an image, a series, or a film. And this originality of a type of image necessarily goes hand in hand with everything that has come before.

How precisely do you understand the value of originality?

Originality is the sole criterion of a work. If you don't feel you have seen something new, or have something new to say, why write, why paint, why shoot a film? Similarly, in philosophy, if you're not going to invent new concepts, why would you want to do philosophy? There are only two dangers: 1) repeating what has been said or done a thousand times already, and 2) seeking out the new for itself, for the mere pleasure of novelty, in an empty way. In both cases, you are copying. You are copying the old or whatever is in fashion. You can copy Joyce, Céline, or Artaud, and you may even believe you're better than the original. However, the new in fact cannot be separated from something that you show, that you say, that you articulate, that you cause to emerge and that begins to exist on its own account. In this sense, the new is always unexpected, but it is also what becomes immediately eternal and necessary. Doing it over again, copying it, what's the point?

A great film is always new, and this makes it unforgettable. It goes without saying that cinematographic images are signed. The great auteurs in cinema have their own lighting, their own space, their own themes. The space in Kurosawa's films is hard to confuse with the space in Mizoguchi's films. The violence in Losey's films cannot be mistaken for the violence in Kazan's films (the first is a static, immobile violence, whereas the second is an acting-out). The red in Nicholas Ray's film is not the same red as in Godard's films...

You often speak of "problems" when it comes to lighting or the depth of a shot: in what way are these problems?

Lighting and depth are the givens of an image. It is precisely in terms of a "given" that problems are discussed, and it is in virtue of such givens that a problem has various solutions. Originality, or the new, is precisely how problems are resolved differently, but most especially because an author figured out how to pose the problem in a new way. No one way is better than another. It's all about creation. Take the example of lighting. Some film-makers have posed the problem of light in terms of shadow. And, to be sure, they did it in various ways, in the form of two halves, striations, or a chiaroscuro effect. They displayed enough unity among themselves to merit the label of cinematic "expressionism." And don't forget that this kind of light-shadow image is connected to a philosophical concept, an image of thought: the battle or the conflict between good and evil.

Of course, the problem totally changes if you consider, and are aiming for, light in terms of white light instead of shadow. From this perspective, you have a whole other world; shadow is only one result. There is no less harshness or even cruelty in this solution, but now everything is light. However, there are two kinds of light: the light of the sun, and the light of the moon. In terms of concepts, moreover, the theme of battle or conflict will be replaced by that of alternation and alternative. It is a "new" way to deal with lighting. But this is because the nature of the problem has changed. One creative path is followed, and then an author or a movement comes along and maps out another path. Sometimes the first path has been exhausted, but sometimes the other path shows up while the first is still going strong.

Do you go to the movies very often? At what point did you decide to write about film? How did you construct your book?

Before the war I was an infant, but when I was about ten years old, I started going to the movies all the time, more so than my peers. I still have fond memories of the actors and films of that era. I loved Danielle Darrieux, and I got a kick out of Saturnin Fabre because he scared me and made me laugh. He had a diction all his own. But after the war, I rediscovered the movies long after everyone else. It wasn't until very late that the obviousness of film as art or creation in its own right struck me. By then I thought of myself only as a philosopher. What led me to start writing about film was that I had been wrestling with a problem of signs for some time. Linguistics did not seem particularly apt to deal with it. I turned to film almost by accident because it is made of movement-images and thus engenders the proliferation of all kinds of strange signs. Film seemed to demand a classification of signs that exceeds linguistics in every respect. And yet film was no pretext or field of application. Philosophy is not in a state of exterior reflection on other fields or disciplines, but in a state of active and interior alliance with them. It is no more abstract than they are, nor any more difficult.

I didn't imagine that I was doing philosophy on cinema. I considered cinema for itself through a classification of signs. This classification is flexible and can be altered. Its only value resides in what it allows you to see. The book may have a complicated organization, but this is because the material itself is difficult. What I had hoped to do was to invent sentences that function like images, that "show" the great works of film. My argument is simple: the great auteurs of film are thinking, thought exists in their work, and making a film is creative, living thought.

There is no list of the different filmmakers at the end of the book... How far along are you in the second volume? Are there any new names in it?

The first volume, *The Movement-Image*, should have the feel of a complete work, but it should also leave the reader asking for more. The sequel is the time-image, but not as an opposition to the movement-image. Rather, the movement-image implies in itself only an indirect image of time, one that is produced by the editing. The second volume must therefore examine the kinds of images that have a direct impact on time, or those which reverse the relation between movement and time. For example: Welles, or Resnais. You won't find a word on these authors in the first volume, or on Renoir, or Ophüls, and several others. Nor will you find anything on the video-image. Neo-realism, French New Wave, Godard, Rivette—they're barely mentioned. An index of authors and works is certainly necessary, but I want to wait until I'm finished.

Has your perception of film changed since you began writing your book?

Of course. I still take the same pleasure in film as before, even if I still don't go all that often. But now the conditions are different. Sometimes they seem more pure, sometimes less. It does happen that I feel like I "absolutely need" to see some film or other, and that if I don't, I won't be able to continue the work. And then I give up—I'm forced to do without it; or it reappears, having been re-released. It also happens that when I go see a film, if it seems really beautiful, I know I will want to write about it. This changes the writing conditions, which is not always desirable.

Now that the book is finished, in the interval between its printing and release, which necessarily excludes you, have you seen anything this summer or fall that has made you want to revisit it?

Have I seen anything good recently? Besides films like *Ludwig*, *Passion*, or *L'Argent*, I saw a great film by Caroline Roboh, *Clémentine tango*, and on television I saw an INA production by Michèle Rosier, *le 31 juillet*, which takes place in a train station at the start of summer vacation. There was also a film made for television—absolutely perfect, really amazing—a sequence from Kafka's *Amerika*, by Benoît Jacquot. But I've definitely missed a bunch of films. I would like to see Chéreau, Woody Allen... The life of cinema relies on an accelerated temporality, it goes so fast, that's its power. You have to have the time to go. But the saddest thing about movies is not the long lines for really bad films; it's when film-makers like Bresson or Rivette can draw only a handful of people. It's disconcerting, both in itself and for the future, especially for up-and-coming film-makers.

31

Pacifism Today

LES NOUVELLES: *People are talking about possible world war. In your view, does the installation of the Pershing missiles seem to have any other consequences?*

Gilles Deleuze and Jean-Pierre Bamberger: World war is certainly a possibility. In the short term, however, the installation represents a significant move in the cold war and a new escalation in the arms race. It is well known that no equilibrium is possible in an arms race. The most important factors in missile technology are speed, distance, accuracy, and the multiplicity of warheads (which only continues to increase). This latest episode in the arms race is disastrous in several respects. It is disastrous for a Europe in crisis: the pressure is growing on Europe to assume at least some of the costs associated with "its own defense." The U.S. has been frank about the costs of the "double decision,"[1] about how much it will cost each European country. Even France will be forced to accelerate the modernization of its "deterrent" nuclear arsenal. But it is disastrous in another way for the Third World: the current over-armament implies maximum exploitation of strategic materials and minerals, and therefore the permanence of repressive regimes, while the crafting of new policies to deal with the problems of oppression and famine has been put on hold until some time in the future. It will be smooth-sailing for South Africa. And in Mitterrand's latest interview, we see that a comprehensive Third World policy is decidedly off the table.[2] Finally, it is disastrous for the Soviets: any acceleration in the arms race will further destabilize the Soviet economy. This is most likely the primary rationale behind the installation of the Pershing missiles in the mind of Reagan and his new advisors. They want to provoke responses which the Soviet economy will increasingly be unable to sustain. Only the U.S. is in a position to withstand the burden of a new cycle of armament without serious damage.

Is it such a bad thing to "destabilize" a country widely identified with the gulag?

The real question is: What is the best way to do it? It is too easy to make fun of the pacifists, who supposedly want unilateral disarmament, and who are supposedly stupid enough to believe that "example" alone would persuade the Soviet Union to disarm. Pacifism is a political philosophy. It demands partial or global negotiations among the U.S., the U.S.S.R., and Europe—and not merely technical negotiations. For example, when Mitterrand begins his interview by saying that "no one wants war, neither the East nor the West, but the real question is whether the responsible authorities will lose control of the situation, which is worsening every day," and that we therefore need "an equilibrium of deployed forces to avoid war," it becomes apparent that any problems or questions of politics have been effectively bracketed. Pacifism wants technical negotiations to be linked in some way to political problems and political modifications: for example, progressively neutral zones in Europe. Pacifism supports those movements which are in favor of German reunification in the East and the West. But reunification can work only if there is neutrality. Pacifism also relies on the support of any contemporary elements likely to increase the autonomy of countries in the Eastern Bloc. The recent declaration by Romania, taking its distance from the Soviets as well as from the Americans, is crucial in this respect.[3] The political foundations and declarations of pacifism are well formulated: the 1961 plan of the U.N., in which an accord was reached between the U.S. and the U.S.S.R.;[4] the Palme plan; and contemporary local arrangements such as the negotiations among Greece, Romania, Bulgaria, and Yugoslavia.[5] It makes no sense to pit pacifism in the West against missiles in the East. The politics of pacifism is at work in the East, too. As Sean MacBride has said, pacifism is a counter-force in international politics (*Les Nouvelles*, November 2). We don't see any reason why pacifism should not have its own observers present at international negotiations. As a popular movement, pacifism cannot and does not want to separate technical (quantitative) problems from political modifications.

If we must "destabilize" the Soviet Union, this is a better way than the arms race. We know already that one of the Soviet responses to these measures by NATO will be to extend its missiles into the Eastern Bloc. And the gulag will surely be expanded and reinforced. As Edward Thompson[6] recently reminded us in *Le Monde* (November 27): "Each new missile in the West locks the door of a prison in the East by shoring up the hawks and validating their security concerns." The U.S.S.R. will be unable to allow the least elements of autonomy to exist in its sphere of influence. This spells a death sentence for Poland, sooner or later. Whatever movements are stirring in East Germany, in Hungary, will be stifled. The

Greek initiative will be torpedoed. Clearly, the arms race cannot be presented as a struggle against the gulag. The arms race has precisely the opposite effect. Even in Western Europe, it will entail an increased police and military presence. Only pacifism, which has its own demands, can relax the grip of the gulag.

Did you support an unarmed Europe in the face of Soviet missiles?

That's not the question. Pacifism wants monitored technical and political negotiations between governments. A purely technological equilibrium is pure fantasy. We want negotiations on intercontinental weapons, where the U.S. has a clear advantage (in the essential area of sea-to-land ballistic missiles). We don't believe that the U.S.S.R. must first catch up. And we want negotiations on continental weapons, where the U.S.S.R. has the advantage: Why should the U.S. first have to catch up? This is all the more true, given that Europe is not disarmed, and that NATO has nuclear submarines that can be adapted to continental or intercontinental uses. Antoine Sanguinetti says as much in a recent interview: "When the Americans withdrew their land-based missiles early in the 60s, they didn't leave Europe with nothing. NATO has nuclear submarines at its service somewhere in the Mediterranean, with warheads comparable to the SS-20s. Their accuracy is about the same, but their range is superior. These warheads have been in place since 1965, but no one ever talks about them" (*Lui*, June 1983).

The continental missiles in Europe are part of a long story. Both the Soviets and the Americans used to have them. Kennedy decided to withdraw them, for two reasons: 1) as compensation to the U.S.S.R., whose allies did not want the threat of continental American missiles next door, just as the Americans refused to tolerate the threat of Soviet missiles in Cuba; and 2) because Kennedy thought that American intercontinental missiles were technologically advanced enough. This was an important moment for the end of the Cold War. But Chancellor Schmidt demanded the reinstallation of American missiles in 1977, citing the technological progress of the new Soviet missiles (always the same old technological argument). Thus Reagan seems like he's doing something long-expected. It just so happens, however, that the missiles which were going to be installed could not reach the Soviet Union. But the new missiles have been improved, and thus their function has been modified, as former English Minister David Owen makes clear (*Le Monde*, November 22). How can the pundits refer to a "fully lucid" decision on Reagan's part? The U.S.S.R. might very well interpret it as a breach of the implicit pact with Kennedy, or worse, an intensification of the project of 1979[7] and of the aggressive character of NATO.

Reagan thinks the time is right for a new Cold War because the Soviet Union is in political and economic straights. He thinks it's a good idea to run the Soviets through another round of armaments. This will put the Soviet economy to the test, and it will force the Soviets to spread their resources: the more the Soviets increase their presence in Europe, the more the U.S. will control the Pacific. Andropov's reply should come as no surprise: of course the U.S.S.R. will install its continental missiles in Eastern Europe (even with all the consequences such a move entails), but it will be busy working on the other aspect of the equation, i.e. developing its intercontinental capability "in the oceans and seas of the world." The West is in such bad faith that we are told we should have expected as much, and yet poor Reagan is "saddened" by this attitude from the Soviets.

But why did the Soviets continue developing missiles while the Americans had withdrawn their own? How could Western Europe not feel exposed to possible Soviet aggression?

No one thinks that the Soviets want to destroy Western Europe, let alone conquer it. Western Europe lacks natural resources vital to the Soviets, and many Europeans are openly hostile to the Soviet regime. Why would the U.S.S.R. want a dozen monkeys worse than Poland on its back? And what about the 300,000 American soldiers stationed in Europe? The Soviet Union would have to go head to head with the U.S. in a continental war. Only Chancellor Kohl talks seriously about avoiding a new Munich. The analogy between Nazi expansion and Soviet imperialism does not hold. Russo-Soviet imperialism has always advertised its directions: toward East Asia, toward the Balkans, and toward the Indian Ocean. Soviet expansion after the war has followed this same pattern. Its significance has been essentially strategic. Unfortunately, it remains in force and is constantly being renewed, to the detriment of Eastern Europe (though Yugoslavia and Albania have managed to extricate themselves).

We're not forgetting the wealth of Western Europe, nor the large group of processing industries located here. The U.S. in fact controls much of it (for example, there are more than 1,000 American companies in West Germany). Since WWII, the U.S.S.R. has a deep-seated fear of Germany, but this fear has been adapted to the new conditions. *The U.S.S.R. is afraid that the U.S. may one day reconcile its isolationism and its imperialism* by expanding the boundaries of Europe and pushing Germany into a limited first-strike war on the continent. Schlesinger officially formulated this hypothesis during the Nixon years.[8] As Europeans, we might think such an hypothesis totally absurd. But it is no more absurd than our own hypothesis of the Soviets waging war against Europe. Just as French missiles are a "deterrent," so the Soviets claim their missiles are "defensive." This is why the reunification of Germany, once each side has become neutral, is so important to pacifism. It would have a calming effect on these mutual fears.

This is indeed one of the goals of pacifism, but this is not the goal of the U.S.S.R. (cf. the declarations of Proektor in *Libération*, November 3, 1981).[9] The real stakes of the debate have been obscured. The Soviets' problem is the hold which the U.S. has over Western Europe. The hold which the Soviets have over Eastern Europe is much more stringent politically, but much less effective economically. The arms race, over-armament, indeed fosters war. But it also has another significance.

For the U.S., the arms race is a kind of label or tag signifying their dominance over Western Europe, which does not have a genuinely autonomous economy, nor will it ever. *In this respect, the decision to install the Pershing missiles is an important one for Western Europe, since it shows that Western Europe has decided to remain not only under the military protection of the United States, but within its narrow economic orbit.* The pretext for this political choice is the desire not to become a "satellite" of the U.S.S.R., but the choice confirms Western Europe as an economic satellite of the U.S. The Soviets need an economically free Western Europe, even if it remains within NATO and the Atlantic Alliance (only Papandreou and the European Left want more). Today, one of the main efforts of the U.S.S.R. is to reestablish an equilibrium in the balance of payments, not only in Eastern Europe, but also within its own borders. Unlike the arms race, the notion of balance makes sense here: the debt of Eastern European countries is slowly diminishing, thereby offering favorable conditions for expanding trade with the West. The

U.S.S.R. has taken extreme measures by greatly diminishing its internal purchasing power (that was the occasion for the beginning of the Polish movement). But Western Europe, including even the socialist governments, is facing a similar problem and will take similar measures, though it will proceed more cautiously. It is not even clear that Western Europe will avoid Poland's predicament. American economic dominance is responsible for putting both Europes at risk and increasing the chances of a confrontation between them.

Thus the arms race, over-armament, has another dimension beyond the military and the political. The arms race is an indirect means for the U.S. to keep Western Europe under strict economic dependence. It is also how the U.S.S.R. keeps Eastern Europe within its sphere of influence (indeed, as Edward Thompson says: "the SS-20 missiles are also aimed at internal dissidence in Eastern Europe"); it is the Soviets' answer to an Americanized Western Europe. Any move toward economic independence in Western Europe is thus a move toward peace, because the U.S.S.R. and its satellites have the same problems as the West; it is the same crisis in two different forms, and can be dealt with only through disarmament.

All the talk lately about the arms race, the whole discussion leaves to one side what is most important. Granted, we are being led to war, but the underlying economic problems have been overlooked. These problem are not even underlying, they're in plain sight. Do you want to know something crazy: What is the flipside of the arms race? It's the domination of the dollar, the way the Americans use it to dominate the world and *to block any progress in the relationship between Eastern and Western Europe*. Everyone knows it, we all agree. But only pacifism acts on it. In any event, maybe the crisis of the summit in Athens will lead some countries, such as France, to a new political strategy in Europe.[10]

French public opinion seems indifferent to pacifism, and the press and even some books have harshly criticized it…

Yes, it is true that in France we have not had terrorists since 1968, but we have penitents and reactionaries. Pacifism has even been accused of promoting anti-Semitism. It's all in print. The argument is far-fetched; it goes something like this:

1) Auschwitz is absolute evil;

2) The gulag is absolute evil;

3) There cannot be two "absolute evils," so Auschwitz and the gulag are the same thing;

4) The threat of nuclear war is a dizzying thought, it is thinking on the brink, it is the new philosophy. The possibility of a planetary Hiroshima is the price we must pay to avoid repeating Auschwitz and to escape the gulag. This is where the "new philosophy" has led us. Pascal's wager is in the hands of the military, and Reagan is the new Pascal. This new philosophy is distressing, and a little stale.[11] Chancellor Kohl refers more modestly to an "intellectual watershed." The idea of an absolute evil is a religious, not an historical idea. The horror of Auschwitz and the horror of the gulag derive from not confusing the one with the other, as they take their place in long series: Auschwitz, the gulag, Hiroshima, the Third World, the security state being prepared for us… It was painful enough to see Auschwitz serve as justification for Sabra and Chatila; now it justifies Reaganism. Edward Thompson in his interview explains why certain French intellectuals want people to believe there is an opposition to pacifism and human rights. Because they discovered the gulag so late, he says, they are all the more bellicose, calling for a new Cold War. They don't want to acknowledge the fact that over-armament is in fact the ideal

condition for the continuation of the gulag. And then Sartre is no longer around. His presence alone would have kept them from talking such nonsense.

French public opinion is another question altogether. It didn't require any metaphysical underpinning. People are not concerned about the Pershing missiles because they're not on our soil. Mitterrand's position seems to mirror the state of public opinion. Unfortunately, consensus favors the Right. But we don't think the French will long remain indifferent to pacifism as a growing popular movement. But we think pacifism will gradually come to be the number one issue on everyone's mind.

But how would you explain the current state of French politics?

Perhaps there are two aspects to the legacy of de Gaulle. First, Mitterrand didn't just push the other Europeans to accept the Pershing missiles, even if he had to break with the social-democrats and ally himself with the conservatives; he demonstrated, in word and action, that he is not interested in continental weapons. What he wants is to be a world player, with a seat at the negotiating table of intercontinental weapons. But we don't quite see what sort of weight France can bring to the negotiating table, especially if it means France will be cut off from the rest of Europe, opposed to the pacifist movement, and will have given up on a new Third-World politics. France, by playing its hand in a way that reflects its particular situation in Europe (belonging to the Atlantic Alliance but not to NATO), actually increases its dependence on the U.S. in terms of any eventual negotiation. Second, Mitterrand has fully embraced the Euro-African "vision" of France, while the other European nations could care less about it. The hegemonic idea of a Mediterranean-African Europe is not easily reconciled with the idea of neutrality, the reunification of Germany, etc. And certainly, rethinking policy in Africa should be one of the main planks of a new Socialist platform in France. A whole new political climate is needed... Well, as far as the Third World is concerned, France today is facing the same situation that its previous governments faced. They say that France's preventive weaponry is credible in the eyes of the Soviet Union only if the world believes the president is capable of pushing the button in an emergency. But the only way to convince the world of this is to conduct limited operations which are supposed to display our determination. These operations impact the Third World and only serve to alienate us all the more (e.g. the unconditional support for the Falklands War, our equivocal situation in Lebanon, the raid on Baalbek, the military support of Hissene Habre in Chad, the arming of Iraq, etc.).

The two faces of over-armament keep coming back. One of its faces is turned to the East, and the other face to the South. It clearly increases the threat of war with the Soviet Union, but it also necessitates an increased control over the Third World. Antoine Sanguinetti says, for example, that the American missiles to be installed in Sicily cannot reach the Soviet Union, but could easily reach Egypt, Algeria, or Morocco. On the other hand, our deterrent force is put to the test in Africa, though being of no service, because Africa is where the depth of our determination is measured. Certainly, France is always open to negotiations. However, when France cuts itself off from the pacifist movement in Europe, and from Third-World movements all over the globe, it condemns itself to a narrowly technical form of negotiation emptied of political content and real objectives for change. But, it bears repeating, the crisis in Europe could change the assumptions of French politics.

32

May '68 Did Not Take Place

In historical phenomena such as the revolution of 1789, the Commune, the revolution of 1917, there is always one part of the *event* that is irreducible to any social determinism, or to causal chains. Historians are not very fond of this aspect: they restore causality after the fact. Yet the event is itself a splitting off from, or a breaking with causality; it is a bifurcation, a deviation with respect to laws, an unstable condition which opens up a new field of the possible. Ilya Prigogine spoke of such states in which, even in physics, the slightest differences persist rather than cancel themselves out, and where completely independent phenomena resonate with each other. In this sense, an event can be turned around, repressed, coopted, betrayed, but there still is something there that cannot be outdated. Only renegades would say: it's outdated. But even if the event is ancient, it can never be outdated: it is an opening onto the possible. It passes as much into the interior of individuals as into the depths of a society.

And again, the historical phenomena that we are invoking were themselves accompanied by determinisms or causalities, even if they were of a different nature. May '68 is more of the order of a pure event, free of all normal, or normative causality. Its history is a "series of amplified instabilities and fluctuations." There were a lot of agitations, gesticulations, slogans, idiocies, illusions in '68, but this is not what counts. What counts is what amounted to a visionary phenomenon, as if a society suddenly saw what was intolerable in it and also saw the possibility for something else. It is a collective phenomenon in the form of: "Give me the possible, or else I'll suffocate..." The possible does not pre-exist, it is created by the event. It is a question of life. The event creates a new existence, it produces a new subjectivity (new relations with the body, with time, sexuality, the immediate surroundings, with culture, work...).

When a social mutation appears, it is not enough to draw the consequences or effects according to lines of economic or political causality. Society must be capable of forming collective agencies of enunciation that match the new subjectivity, in such a way that it desires the mutation. That's what it is, a veritable redeployment. The American *New Deal* and the Japanese boom corresponded to two very different examples of subjective redeployment, with all sorts of ambiguities and even reactionary structures, but also with enough initiative and creativity to provide a new social state capable of responding to the demands of the event. Following '68 in France, on the contrary, the authorities did not stop living with the idea that "things will settle down." And indeed, things did settle down, but under catastrophic conditions. May '68 was not the result of a crisis, nor was it a reaction to a crisis. It is rather the opposite. It is the current crisis, the impasses of the current crisis in France that stem directly from the inability of French society to assimilate May '68. French society has shown a radical incapacity to create a subjective redeployment on the collective level, which is what '68 demands; in light of this, how could it now trigger an economic redeployment that would satisfy the expectations of the "Left?" French society never came up with anything for the people: not at school nor at work. Everything that was new has been marginalized or turned into a caricature. Today we see the population of Longwy cling to their steel, the dairy farmers to their cows, etc.: what else could they do? Every collective enunciation by a new existence, by a new collective subjectivity, was crushed in advance by the reaction against '68, on the left almost as much as on the right? Even by the "free radio stations." Each time the possible was closed off.

The children of May '68, you can run into them all over the place, even if they are not aware who they are, and each country produces them in its own way. Their situation is not great. These are not young executives. They are strangely indifferent, and for that very reason they are in the right frame of mind. They have stopped being demanding or narcissistic, but they know perfectly well that there is nothing today that corresponds to their subjectivity, to their potential of energy. They even know that all current reforms are rather directed against them. They are determined to mind to their own business as much as they can. They keep it open, hang on to something possible. It is Coppola who created their poetized portrait in *Rumble Fish*; the actor Mickey Rourke explained: "The character is at the end of his rope, on the edge. He's not the Hell's Angel type. He's got brains and he's got good sense. But he hasn't got any university degree. And it is this combination that makes him go crazy. He knows that there's no job for him because he is smarter than any guy willing to hire him..." (*Libération*, February 15, 1984).

This is true of the entire world. What we institutionalize in unemployment, in retirement, or in school, are controlled "situations of abandonment," for which the handicapped are the model. The only subjective redeployment actually occurring on a collective level are those of an unbridled American-style capitalism or even of a Muslim fundamentalism like in Iran, or of Afro-American religions like in Brazil: they are the reversed figures of a new orthodoxy (one should add here European neo-Papism). Europe has nothing to suggest, and France seems to no longer have any other ambition than to assume the leadership of an Americanized and over-armed Europe that would impose from above the necessary economic redeployment. Yet the field of the possible lies elsewhere: *along the East-West axis,* in pacifism, insofar as it intends to break up relations of conflict, of over-armament, but also of complicity and distribution between the United States and the Soviet Union. *Along the North-South axis,* in a new internationalism that no longer relies solely on an alliance with the Third-World, but on the phenomena of third-worldification in the rich countries themselves (for example, the evolution of metropolises, the decline of the inner-cities, the rise of a European third-world, such as Paul Virilio has theorized them). There can only be a creative solution. These are the creative redeployments that would contribute to a resolution of the current crisis and that would take over where a generalized May '68, an amplified bifurcation or fluctuation, left off.

33

Letter to Uno: How Félix and I Worked Together

Dear Kuniichi Uno,

You wanted to know how Félix and I met and how we worked together. I can only give you my point of view; Félix would probably have a different take on it. One thing is certain, there is no recipe or general formula for working together.

It was not long after 1968 in France. We didn't know each other but a mutual friend wanted us to meet. And yet, on the surface, we didn't seem to have much in common. Félix has always possessed multiple dimensions; he participates in many different activities, both psychiatric and political; he does a lot of group work. He is an "intersection" of groups, like a star. Or perhaps I should compare him to the sea: he always seems to be in motion, sparkling with light. He can jump from one activity to another. He doesn't sleep much, he travels, he never stops. He never *ceases.* He has extraordinary speeds. I am more like a hill: I don't move much, I can't manage two projects at once, I obsess over my ideas, and the few movements I do have are internal. I like to write alone, and I don't like to talk much, except during my seminars, when talking serves another purpose. Together, Félix and I would have made a good Sumo wrestler.

However, when you examine Félix more closely, you realize how alone he really is. Between two activities, or in the midst of people, he can plunge into the deepest solitude. He disappears to play piano, to read, to write. I have never met anyone who is so creative, or who produces more ideas. And he never stops tinkering with his ideas, fine-tuning them, changing their terms. Sometimes he gets bored with them, he even forgets about them, only to rework and reshuffle them later. His ideas are like drawings, or even diagrams. Concepts are what interests me. It seems like concepts have their own existence. They are alive, like invisible creatures. But we have to create them. For me philosophy is an art of creation, much like music or painting. Philosophy creates concepts, which are neither generalities nor truths. They are more along the lines of the Singular, the Important, the New. *Concepts* are inseparable from *affects*, i.e. from the powerful effects they exert on our life, and *percepts*, i.e. the new ways of seeing or perceiving they provoke in us.

Between Félix with his diagrams and me with my articulated concepts, we wanted to work together, but we didn't know how. We began by reading a lot: ethnology, economics, linguistics, etc. That was our raw material. I was fascinated by what Félix took from it, and I think he was interested in the philosophy I tried to inject in it. We knew pretty quickly what *Anti-Oedipus* was going to be about: a new presentation of the unconscious as a machine, a factory; and a new conception of delirium as indexed on the historical, political, and social world. But how should we go about it? We began with long, disorderly letters. They were interminable. Then we started meeting, just the two of us, for several days or weeks at a time. You have to understand: it was exhausting work, but we laughed a lot too. We worked independently, each one at his desk, developing this or that point in different directions; we swapped drafts, and we coined terms whenever we needed them. The book at times took on a powerful coherence that could not be assigned to either one of us.

Our differences worked against us, but they worked for us even more. We never had the same rhythm. Félix would sometimes complain that I didn't respond to the long letters he would send me: it's because I wasn't up to it, not at that moment. I was only able to use them later, after a month or two, when Félix had already moved on. And during our meetings, we didn't dialogue: one of us would speak, and the other would listen. I refused to let Félix go, even when he had had enough, and Félix kept after me, even when I was exhausted. Gradually, a concept would acquire an autonomous existence, which sometimes we continued to understand differently (for example, we never did understand "the organless body" in quite the same way). Working together was never a homogenization, but a proliferation, an accumulation of bifurcations, a rhizome. I could tell you who came up with this particular theme or that particular idea, but from my perspective, Félix had these brainstorms, and I was like a lighting rod. Whatever I grounded would leap up again, changed, and then Félix would start again, etc., and that is how we progressed.

The experience of *A Thousand Plateaus* was entirely different. The book has a more complex composition, and the disciplines we deal with are much more varied, but Félix and I had developed such a good working relationship that the one could guess where the other was headed. Our conversations now were full of ellipses, and we were able to establish various resonances, not between us, but among the various disciplines that we were traversing. The best moments of the book while we were writing it were: music and the ritornello, the war-machine and nomads, and animal-becoming. In these instances, under Félix's spell, I felt I could perceive unknown territories where strange concepts dwelt. The book has been a source of happiness for me, and as far as I'm concerned, it's inexhaustible. Please don't see any vanity in such a statement. I'm speaking for myself, not for the reader. Finally, Félix and I, we each had to return to our own work, so we could catch our breath. But I feel certain that we will work together again.

There you have it, my dear Uno, I hope I have answered at least some of your questions. All the best…

34

Michel Foucault's Main Concepts

For Daniel Defert

Foucault refers to his work as "studies in history," though he does not see it as "the work of an historian." He does the work of a philosopher, but he does not work on the philosophy of history. What does it mean to think? Foucault has never dealt with any other problem (hence his debt to Heidegger). And the historical? It is formations which are stratified, made up of strata. But to think is to reach a non-stratified material, somewhere between the layers, in the interstices. Thinking has an essential relation to history, but it is no more historical than it is eternal. It is closer to what Nietzsche calls the Untimely: to think the past *against* the present—which would be nothing more than a common place, pure nostalgia, some kind of return, if he did not immediately add: "*in favor*, I hope, of a time to come." There is a becoming of thought which passes through historical formations, like their twin, but which does not resemble them. Thinking must come from the outside of thought, and yet at the same time be engendered from within—beneath the strata and beyond them. "To what extent the task of thought thinking its own history can liberate thought from what it thinks in silence and enable it to think differently."[1] "Thinking differently" informs the work of Foucault along three different axes, discovered one after the other: 1) strata as historical formations (archeology), 2) the outside as beyond (strategy), and 3) the inside as a substratum (genealogy). Foucault often took pleasure in underlining the turning-points and the ruptures in his own work. But these changes in direction rightfully belong to this kind of work, just as the ruptures belong to the method, in the construction of the three axes, i.e. the creation of new coordinates.

1. Strata or historical formations: the visible and the utterable (Savoir)

Strata are historical formations, both empirical and positive. They are made of words and things, seeing and speaking, the visible and the utterable, planes of visibility and fields of legibility—content and expression. These last terms we may borrow from Hjelmslev, provided we do not confuse content with the signified, nor expression with the signifier. Content has its own form and substance: for example, the prison and its inmates. Expression also has a form and a substance: for example, criminal law and "delinquency." Just as criminal law as a form of expression defines a field of utterability (the propositions of delinquency), so the prison as a form of content defines a place of visibility ("panoptics," the surveillance of everything at every moment without being seen). This example is drawn from the last major analysis of strata which Foucault conducted in *Discipline and Punish*. But such an analysis was already present in *The History of Madness*: the asylum as a place of visibility, and the medicine of psychology as a field of utterances. In the meantime, Foucault writes *Raymond Roussel* and *Birth of the Clinic*, more or less together. The first shows how the work of Roussel is divided into two parts: inventions of visibility by machines, and productions of utterances through "procedures." The second shows how the clinic and then pathological anatomy lead to variable partitions between the visible and the utterable. Foucault will draw his conclusions in *The Archeology of Knowledge*, where we find a general theory of the two elements of stratification: the forms of content, or non-discursive formations; and the forms of expression, or discursive formations. In this sense, that which is stratified constitutes Knowledge (the lesson of things and the lesson of grammar) and is subject to archeology. Archeology does not necessarily refer to the past, but to strata, such that our present has an archeology of its own. Present or past, the visible is like the utterable: it is the object not of phenomenology, but of epistemology.

To be sure, words (*mots*) and things (*choses*) are rather vague terms to designate the two poles of knowledge, and Foucault will admit that the title *Les Mots et les choses* [English translation: *The Order of Things*] should be taken ironically. The task of archeology is to discover a genuine form of expression which cannot be confused with linguistic units, no matter what they are: words, phrases, propositions, or speech-acts. As we know, Foucault will discover this form in a totally original conception of the "utterance," defined as a function that intersects diverse units. But an analogous operation holds for the form of content: the visible, or units of visibility, is not to be confused with visual elements, whether qualities, things, objects, or amalgams of action and reaction. In this respect, Foucault constructs a function which is no less original than his "utterance." Units of visibility are not the forms of objects, nor even those forms which would be revealed in the contact between light and things. Instead, they are forms of the luminous, luminous forms, created by light itself, allowing things and objects to subsist only as flashes, reflections, or sparkles (*Raymond Roussel*, but maybe

Manet as well). Thus the task of archeology is twofold: to "extract," from words and language, "utterances" that correspond to each stratum, but also to "extract" from things and vision, units of visibility, the visible. Of course, from the beginning, Foucault singles out the primacy of utterances, and we will see why. Furthermore, in *The Archeology of Knowledge*, the planes of visibility will receive only a negative definition, "non-discursive formations," situated in a space that is merely complimentary to the field of utterances. Nevertheless, despite the primacy of utterances, the visible remains irreducibly distinct from it. Knowledge has two irreducible poles, and there also exists an "archeology of seeing." The primacy of one in no way implies a reduction. When we neglect his theory of the visible, we mutilate the conception which Foucault had of history, and we mutilate his thought, the conception he had of thinking. Foucault never stopped being fascinated by what he saw, just as he was by what he heard or read. Archeology in his conception is an audiovisual archive (beginning with the history of science). And in our own time, the joy Foucault secretly takes in the utterance is necessarily linked to his passion for seeing. Voice and Eyes.

This is because utterances are never directly legible or even utterable, although they are not hidden. They become legible and utterable only in relation to certain conditions which make them so, and which constitutes their inscription on an "enunciative support." The condition is that "there be some (a little) language," that is, a mode of being of language on each stratum, a variable way in which language is, is full, and is gathered (*The Order of Things*). Words must thus be pried open, split apart, either phrases or propositions, to grasp the way in which language appears in each stratum, understood as the dimension which provides "some" language and which conditions the utterances. If we cannot rise to the level of this condition, we will not find utterances, but will instead bump up against the words, phrases, and propositions which seem to conceal them (so it is with sexuality, in *Volonté de savoir*). On the other hand, if we can rise to this condition, we understand that every age says all it can say, hides nothing, silences nothing, in terms of the language at its disposal: even in politics, but especially in politics, even in sexuality, but especially in sexuality—in the most cynical or the crudest language. The same goes for the visible. The units of visibility are never hidden, but they too have conditions without which they remain invisible, although in plain sight. Hence one of Foucault's themes: the visible invisible. In this instance, the condition is light, that "there be" some light, variable according to each stratum or historical formation: a way of being of light, which causes the units of visibility to emerge as flashes and sparkles, a "second light" (*Raymond Roussel*, but also *Birth of the Clinic*). Things and objects must now in turn be pried open to grasp the way in which light appears on each stratum and conditions the visible: this is the second aspect of the work of Raymond Roussel, and more generally, the second pole of epistemology. An age sees only what it can see, but sees all it can, independently of any censorship and repression, in terms of the conditions of visibility, just as an age utters all it can. There are no secrects whatsoever, although nothing is immediately visible, nor immediately legible.

This research into conditions constitutes a kind of neo-Kantianism in Foucault—but with two differences which Foucault formulates in *The Order of Things*: 1) the conditions are those of real experience and not of possible experience, thus being on the side of the "object," not on the side of a universal "subject"; and 2) they have to do with historical formations or strata as *a posteriori* syntheses, and not with the *a priori* syntheses of all possible experience.

But Foucault's neo-Kantianism lies in a Receptivity constituted by the units of visibility along with their conditions, as well as a Spontaneity constituted in turn by the units of utterablity along with their own conditions. The spontaneity of language, and the receptivity of light. Receptive here does not mean passive, since there is just as much action and passion in what light makes visible. Nor does spontaneous mean active, but rather the activity of an "Other" that acts on the receptive form (so it is in Kant, where the spontaneity of "I think" acts on the receptive beings which represent this spontaneity to themselves as other). In Foucault, the spontaneity of the understanding, the cogito, is replaced by the spontaneity of language (the "being there" of language), whereas the receptivity of intuition is replaced by the receptivity of light (space-time). Now the primacy of utterance over the visible is easily explained: *The Archeology of Knowledge* indeed lays claim to a "determinant" role for utterances as discursive formations. But the units of visibility are no less irreducible, because they refer to a form of the "determinable," which will not allow itself to be reduced to a form of determination. This was Kant's great problem: the mutual adaptation of two forms, or two sorts of conditions, different by nature.

In his transformation of Kant, Foucault makes some essential claims, one of which I believe is this: from the beginning, there exists a *difference of nature* between the visible and the utterable, although they are inserted in one another and ceaselessly interpenetrate one another as they compose each stratum or knowledge. It is perhaps this aspect, this first aspect which attracts Foucault to Blanchot: "speaking is not seeing." But whereas Blanchot insists on the primacy of speaking as determinant, Foucault (despite hasty first impressions) maintains the specificity of seeing as determinable. Between speaking and seeing, there is no isomorphism, and no conformity, although there exists a mutual presupposition, and the uttterable has primacy of the visible. *The Archeology of Knowledge* indeed insists on this primacy, but will add: "In vain do we say what we see; *what we see never resides in what we say*, and we vainly try to make others see, through imagery, through metaphor and comparison, what we are seeing; the place where imagery, metaphor, and comparison shine in all their radiance is not the place which our eyes unfold; it is rather the place defined by the successions of syntax."[2] The two forms do not have the same formation, the same "genealogy," in the archeological sense of the word *Gestaltung*. *Discipline and Punish* will provide the final great demonstration of this difference between seeing and speaking: an encounter occurs between the utterances of "delinquency," which depend on a new regime of penal utterances, and the prison as the form of content which depends on a new regime of visibility; the two are different by nature, they do not have the same genesis, nor the same history, although they encounter one another on the same stratum, helping and reinforcing one another, though their alliance can be broken at certain moments. Here we see Foucault's method assume its historical meaning and development: the "play of truth" between what we see and what we say, delinquency as utterance, the prison as visibility. But early on in his work, as I mentioned, Foucault had done a similar analysis in a different case (*The History of Madness*): the asylum as a place of visibility, mental illness as an object of utterance, and the two having different geneses, indeed a radical heterogeneity, but enjoying a mutual presupposition on the same stratum, even if they should be forced to brake their alliance on some other stratum.

On each strata, or in each historical formation, certain phenomena of capturing and holding can be found: series of utterances and segments of the visibility are inserted in one another. Forms of content like the prison, like the asylum, engender secondary utterances which produce or reproduce delinquancy and mental illness; but also, forms of expression like delinquancy engender secondary contents which are vehicles of the prison (*Discipline and Punish*). Between the visible and its luminous condition, utterances slip in; between the utterable and its language condition, the visible works its way in (*Raymond Roussel*). This is because each condition has something in common: each constitutes a space of "rarity," of "dissemination," littered with interstices. Thus the particular way in which language is *gathered* on a stratum (its "being there") is at the same time a space of *dispersion* for those utterances stratified in language. Similarly, the particular way in which light is gathered is at the same time a space of dispersion for the units of visibility, the "flashes," the "glimpses," of a second light. It is a mistake to think that Foucault is primarily interested in imprisonment. Such environments merely perform the conditions of visibility in a certain historical formation; they didn't exist before, and they won't exist after. Imprisonment or not, these spaces are forms of exteriority, either language or light, in which utterances are disseminated and the visible dispersed. This is why utterances can slip in to the interstices of seeing, and the visible, in to the interstices of speaking. We speak, we see and make see, at the same time, although they are not the same thing and the two differ in nature (*Raymond Roussel*). And from one stratum to another, the visible and the utterable are transformed at the same time, although not according to the same rules (*Birth of the Clinic*). In short, each stratum, each historical formation, each positivity, is made up of the interweaving of determinant utterances and determinable units of visibility, in as much as they are heterogeneous, though this heterogeneity does not prevent their mutual insertion.

2. Strategies or the non-stratified (Power): Thinking the outside

The coadaptation of the two forms is in no way impeded, but that is not enough. Coadaptation must be positively engendered, through a moment comparable to what Kant called "schematism." We are now on a new axis. This new axis has to do with power, and no longer with knowledge. The preceding determinations are found on this new axis, only now it is a mutual presupposition between power and knowledge, a difference of nature between them, and the primacy of power. But it is no longer a question of the relation between two forms, as it was with knowledge. Now it is a question of *power relations*. The essence of force is to be sought in its relation to other forces: form affects other forms, and is affected by them. Consequently, Power (with a capital 'P') does not express the dominance of a class, and does not depend on a State apparatus, but "is produced at every point, or rather in every relation from point to point."[3] Power flows through the ruling class no less than through those who are ruled, in such a way that classes result from it, and not the reverse. The State or Law merely effects the integration of power. Classes and the State are not forces, but subjects which align forces, integrate them globally, and perform the relation of forces, on and in the strata. These agents of stratification presuppose power relations prior to any subject and object. This is why power is exercised before being possessed: it is a question of strategy, "anonymous strategies," "almost mute," and blind. One cannot say that a social field is self-structuring, or that it is self-contradictory. A social field strategizes, it is self-strategizing (hence a sociology of strategies, as in the work of Pierre Bordieu). This is also why power introduces us to a realm of "microphysics," or presents itself as a complex of micro-powers. Therefore, we should distinguish the strategy of forces from the stratification of forms which flows from it. But from one to the other, there is no enlargement, or inversely, miniaturization: there is heterogeneity.

In this celebrated Foucaltian thesis, can we not see a kind of return to natural law? But with this one difference: it has nothing to do with law, a too global notion, nor with Nature, another global term too heavily freighted. Rather, a Nietzschean inspiration is behind this thesis, as Foucault's article on Nietzsche demonstrates. And later on, if Foucault opposes every manifestation of what he considered facile and hasty conceptions of repressive power, it is because power relations are not so easily determined by simple violence. The relation of one force to another consists in the way in which one force affects the others, and is affected by them; in which case, we can draw up a list of "functions": sample and subtract, enumerate and control, compose and increase, etc. Force itself is defined by a double capacity, to affect and be affected, hence it is inseparable from its relation to other forces which, on every occasion, determine or fulfill these capacities. We thus see something like a receptivity of force (a capacity to be affected) and a spontaneity of force (a capacity to affect). Now, however, receptivity and spontaneity no longer have the same meaning as they did a while ago with respect to the strata. On the strata, seeing and speaking were each composed of already formed substances and already formalized functions: prisoners, students, soldiers, and workers were not the same "substance," precisely because locking up, teaching, fighting, and laboring were not the same function. Power relations, however, mix and blend non-formed materials and non-formalized functions: for example, some body, or some population, over which is exercised a general function of control and sectorization (independently of the concrete forms which the strata impart to them).

In this sense, Foucault can say, or at least he does so once in a crucial passage of *Discipline and Punish*, that a "diagram" expresses a relation of force or power: "a functioning abstracted from any obstacle, resistance, or friction… and which should be detached from any specific use."[4] For example, a disciplinary diagram that defines modern societies. But other diagrams act on societies with other stratifications: the diagram of sovereignty, which functions by means of sampling rather than sectorization; or the pastoral diagram, which has to do with a "flock" and assumes "grazing" as its function… One of the more original aspects of the diagram is its being a place of mutations. The diagram is not exactly outside the strata, but *it is the outside of the strata*. It is between two strata as the place of mutations which enables the passage from one stratum to the other. Thus power relations constitute the power in a diagram, whereas the relations of forms define the knowledge in an archive. Foucault's genealogy is no longer a simple archeology of forms that appear in a stratum; it now becomes a strategy of forces on which the stratum itself depends.

His study of stratified relationships of knowledge culminates in the *Archeology*. The study of strategic relations of forces or power begins in earnest in *Discipline and Punish* and is further developed in *The Will to Knowledge*. Between the two, there is both irreducibility, reciprocal presupposition and a certain predominance of the latter. "Diagrammatism" will play a role similar to Kant's schematism but in a completely different way: the receptive spontaneity of forces accounts for the receptivity of visible forms, the spontaneity of utterable statements and their correlation. The relationships between forces *occur* in the strata, which would have nothing to embody or actualize without them. Inversely, without the strata actualizing them, the relationships of forces would remain transitive, unstable, fleeting, almost virtual, and would not take shape. We can understand this by referring to *The Archeology of Knowledge*, which already suggested "regularity" was a property of the utterance. Regularity for Foucault does not designate frequency or probability but a curve connecting singular points. The relationships of forces indeed determine singular points, singularities as affects, such that a diagram is always a discharge of singularities. It is like in mathematics where the determination of singularities (nodes of force, focal points, method of steepest descent, etc.) is distinguished from the slope of the curve passing nearby. The curve initiates the relationships of force by regularizing them, aligning them, making the series converge, tracing a "general line of force" connecting singular points. When he defines the utterance as a regularity, Foucault notes that curves or graphs are utterances and that utterances are the equivalent of curves and graphs. Thus the utterance is essentially related to "something else," something of a different nature that cannot be reduced to the meaning of the sentence or the referent of the clause: they are the singular points of the diagram next to which the *curve-utterance* is traced in language and becomes regular or legible. And maybe the same should be said of visibilities. In that case, *paintings* organize the singularities from the point of view of receptivity, by tracing lines of light that make them visible. Not only Foucault's thought but his style proceed by curve-utterances and painting-descriptions (*Las Meninas* or the description of the Panopticon; all of the remarkable descriptions Foucault introduced into his texts). Thus a theory of descriptions is just as crucial for him as a theory of utterances. And these two elements result from the diagram of forces that is actualized in them.

We could present things in the following way: if a force is always in relation to other forces, the forces necessarily refer to an irreducible Outside made up of indivisible distances through which one force acts on another or is acted on by another. Only from the outside, does a force confer on others or receive from other forces the variable affectations that only exist at a certain distance or in a certain relationship. Forces are therefore in a perpetual becoming that doubles history or rather envelops it, according to a Nietzschian conception: "emergence designates a place of confrontation," states the article on Nietzsche, "not a closed field where a struggle takes place," but "a non-place, a pure distance" that only acts in the interstices.[5] An outside more distant than any external world and even farther than any form of exteriority. The diagram is such a non-place, constantly disturbed by changes in distance or by changes in the forces in relation. It is only a place for mutation. While seeing and speaking are forms of exteriority, each exterior to the other, then thinking addresses an outside that no longer has any form. Thinking means reaching non-stratification. Seeing is thinking, speaking is thinking, but thinking takes place in the gap, in the disjunction between seeing and speaking. This is Foucault's second meeting point with Blanchot: thinking belongs to the Outside to the extent that the latter, this "abstract storm," surges into the interstice between seeing and speaking. Blanchot's article takes up where the Nietzsche article leaves off. The call of the outside is a constant theme for Foucault and means that thinking is not the innate exercise of a faculty but must happen to thought. Thinking does not depend on an interiority uniting the visible and the utterable but takes place under the intrusion of the outside that carves the interval: "*thought of the outside*" as a roll of the dice, as a discharge of singularities.[6] Between two diagrams, between two states of diagrams, there are mutations, reworkings of the relationships of forces. Not because anything can connect to anything else. It is more like successive drawings of cards, each one operating on chance but under external conditions determined by the previous draw. It is a combination of randomness and dependency like in a Markov chain. The component is not transformed, but the composing forces transform when they enter into relation with new forces. The connection therefore does not take place by continuity or interiorization but by re-connection over the breaks and discontinuities. The formula of the outside is the one from Nietzsche quoted by Foucault: "the iron hand of necessity shaking the cup of chance."[7]

The theme of the "death of man" in *The Order of Things* can be explained in this way. Not only does the concept of man disappear, and not because man "surpasses" himself, but the component forces of man enter into new combinations. They did not always compose man, but for a long time, during the classical period, they were in relationship with other forces in such a way as to compose God and not man, such that the infinite was first in relation to the finite and thought was thought of the infinite. Then they composed man, but to the extent that they entered into relationship with another type of forces, obscure forces of organization of "life," "production" of wealth, "filiation" of language that were able to reduce man to his own finiteness and to give him a History to make his own. But when these forces appear at a third draw, new compositions must arise and the death of man connects to the death of God to make room for other flashes or other utterances. In short, man only exists on a stratum depending on the relationships of forces taking place on it. Thus the outside is always the opening of a future where nothing ends because nothing has started, but everything changes. *The diagram as the determination of a group of relationships of force* does not exhaust forces, which can enter into other relationships and other compositions. The diagram comes from the outside but the outside is not to be confused with any diagram as it constantly "draws" new ones. Force in this sense possesses a potential in relation to the diagram in which it is caught, like a third power distinct from its power to affect or be affected. This third power is *resistance.* In fact, a diagram of forces presents, alongside the singularities of power corresponding to its relationships, singularities of resistance, "points, nodes, foci" that in turn act on the strata in order to make change possible. Moreover, the last word in the theory of power is that resistance comes first, since it has a direct relationship with the outside. Thus a social field resists more than it strategizes and the thought of the outside is a thought of resistance (*The Will to Knowledge*).

3. The folds or the inside of thought (Desire)

We must therefore distinguish between the formalized relationships on the strata (Knowledge), the relationships of forces at the diagram level (Power), and the relationship with the Outside, the absolute relationship, as Blanchot says, which is also a non-relationship (Thought). Does that mean there is no inside? Foucault subjects interiority to constant and radical critique. But what of an inside that is deeper than any internal world just as the outside is farther than any external world? Foucault often returns to the theme of the *double.* The double for him is not a projection of the interior but on the contrary a fold of the outside, like in embryology for the invagination of tissue. For Foucault—and for Raymond Roussel—the double is always a "*doublure*" in every sense of the word.[8] If thought continues to "hold" onto the outside, how could the outside not appear inside as what it does not think or cannot think: an unthought in thought, says *The Order of Things*. This unthought is the infinite for the classical age, but starting in the 19th century, the dimensions of finiteness begin to fold the outside and develop a "depth," a "thickness pulled back into itself," an inside of life, work and language. Foucault takes up the Heideggerian theme of the Fold, the Crease in his own way. He sends it in a completely different direction. A crease in the outside, be it the fold of the infinite or the folds of finiteness, imposes a curve on the strata and forms their inside. Becoming the doubling [*doublure*] of the outside or, as it was already put in the *History of Madness*, being "inside the outside."[9]

Perhaps there is not the rupture between recent books by Foucault and his earlier work as many have said and he himself suggested. There is instead a reevaluation of them all according to this axis or dimension: the inside. *The Order of Things* already asked the question of the unthought as well as the question of the subject: "What do I have to be, me who thinks and who follows my thought, to be what I do not think, for my thought to be what I am not?"[10] The inside is an outside operation; it is a *subjectivation* (which does not necessarily mean an interiorization). If the outside is a relationship, the absolute of relationships, then the inside is also a relationship, the relationship becoming subject. *The Use of Pleasure* gives it its name: "the relationship of self to self." If force receives a dual power from the outside, the power to affect (other forces) and to be affected (by other forces), how could there not ensue a relationship between force and itself? Perhaps this is the element of "resistance." At this point, Foucault rediscovers the affection of self by self as the greatest paradox of thought: the relationship with oneself forms an inside that is constantly derived from the outside.

Here again, it is necessary to show how the relationship with the outside comes first and yet how the relationship to self is irreducible and takes places along a specific axis. The subject is always constituted, the product of a subjectivation, but it appears in a dimension that opposes all stratification or codification. Consider the historical formation of the Greeks: using the light that was their own and with the utterances they invented, they actualized the relationships of force of their diagram and it led to the city-state, the family, but also eloquence, games, everywhere where at that moment the domination of one over another could take place. At first glance, the domination of self by self, or Virtue as morality is only another example: "Ensuring the direction of one's self, managing one's house, participating in the government of the city-state are three practices of the same type."[11] And yet the relationship to the self *does not let itself be aligned* according to the concrete forms of power or be subsumed in an abstract diagrammatic function. One might say that it only develops by *detaching itself* from relationships with others, by "disconnecting itself" both from the forms of power and the functions of virtue. It is as if the relationships of the outside folded to make a double [*doublure*] and allow a relationship to the self to arise that develops according to a new dimension. *Enkrateia* is "a power exercised over oneself *in* the power one exercises over others"[12] (how could one claim to govern others if one could not govern oneself?), to such an extent that the relationship to the self becomes the primary internal regulator in relation to the constitutive powers of politics, the family, eloquence or games, and even virtue itself. Government of others is reflected, doubled or submits in a government of the self that relates force to itself and not to another force. Maybe the Greeks invented this dimension, at least as a partially autonomous dimension (an aesthetic conception of existence).

Foucault's thesis seems to be this: among the Greeks, the relationship to self found the opportunity to occur in sexuality. This is because the sexual relationship or affect is inseparable from the two poles that constitute its terms: spontaneity-receptivity, determinant-determinable, active-passive, masculine role-feminine role. But because of its violence and expenditure, sexual activity will only exercise its determinant role if it is able to regulate itself, to affect itself. Thus sexuality is the matter and test of the relationship to self. From this point of view, the relationship to self occurs in three forms: a simple relationship with the body as a Dietetics of pleasures or affects (governing oneself sexually to be able to govern others); a developed relationship, with the spouse, as the Economy of the household (governing oneself to be able to govern the spouse, for the wife to attain good receptivity); finally a *redoubled* relationship with the young man as the Erotics of homosexuality or pederasty (not only governing oneself, but making the boy govern himself by resisting the power of others). What seems essential to me in this presentation of the Greeks is that there is no necessary connection, only an historical encounter between the relationship to self, which would more likely tend towards the food model, and sexual relations, which provides the terms and the material. Therein lies the difficulty Foucault had to surmount: he started, he says, by writing a book on sexuality, *The Will to Knowledge*, but without reaching the Self. Then he wrote a book on the relationship to self but it did not arrive at sexuality. He had to reach the point or the moment when the two notions were balanced, with the Greeks. From there, the entire history of the Inside could be developed: how the connection between the relation to self and sexual relations became increasingly "necessary" on the condition that the value of the relationship to self, the terms of sexual relations, the nature of the ordeal and the quality of the material changed. This led to Christianity with the substitution of flesh for the body, desire for pleasure… The Greeks certainly did not lack either individuality or interiority. But it is a long history, the history of modes of subjectivation as they formed the constantly reworked genealogy of the desiring subject.

The inside takes on many figures and modes depending on the way the folds are formed. Desire. Isn't desire the inside in general, or the mobile connection between the inside and the two other features, the outside and the strata? If it is true that the inside is formed by a crease in the outside, then there is a *topological relationship* between them. The relationship to self is homologous to the relationship with the outside and all the contents of the inside are in relation with the outside. "The interior of the exterior, and vice versa," said *Madness and Civilization. The Use of Pleasure* speaks of isomorphism. Everything is done through the strata, which are relatively exterior settings and therefore relatively interior. The stratified formations place the absolute outside and inside derived from it in contact; or inversely, they unfold the inside on the outside. The entire inside is actively present for the outside at the edge of the strata. Thinking combines the three axes; it is a constantly changing unity. There are three types of problems here or three figures of time. The strata delve into the past in vain; they only extract successive presents from it, they are in the present (what is one seeing, what is one saying at this moment?). But the relationship with the outside is the future, possible futures depending on the chances for transformation. The inside, for its part, condenses the past in modes that are not necessarily continuous (for example, Greek subjectivity, Christian subjectivity...). *The Archeology of Knowledge* raised the problem of long and short durations, but Foucault seemed to consider primarily relatively short durations in the domain of knowledge and power. With *The Use of Pleasure* he discovered long durations, starting with the Greeks and the Fathers of the Church. The reason for this is simple: we do not save the knowledge that is no longer useful for us or power that is no longer exercised, but we continue to serve moralities in which we no longer believe. In each moment, the past accumulates in the relationship to self while the strata carry the changing present and the future comes into play in the relationship to the outside. Thinking means taking residence in the strata in the present which serves as a limit. But it is thinking the past as it is condensed in the inside, in the relationship with the self. Thinking the past against the present, resisting the present, not for a return, the return to the Greeks for example, but "in favor, I hope, of a time to come." Foucault's work was created by inventing a topology that actively puts the inside and outside in contact on the stratified formations of history. It is up to the strata to produce layers that show and tell something new; but it is also up to the relationship of the outside to call the powers in place into question, and it is up to the relationship with the self to inspire new modes of subjectivization. Foucault work abruptly stops at this final point. Foucault's interviews are a full part of his work because each one is a topological operation that involves us in our current problems. His work has led thought to discover an entirely new system of previously unknown coordinates. It paints the most beautiful paintings of light in philosophy and traces unprecedented curves of utterances. It reconnects with the great works that have changed what thinking means for us. Its transformation of philosophy has only begun.

35

Zones of Immanence

A whole Platonic, neo-Platonic, and Medieval tradition is behind the idea of the universe as a "great chain of being," as we have often been told. It is a universe suspended from the One as transcendent principle, unfolding in a series of emanations and hierarchical conversions. Entities have more or less being, more or less reality, according to their distance from, or proximity to the transcendent principle. At the same time, however, a whole other inspiration traverses this cosmos. Zones of immanence seemingly proliferate at the various stages or levels, even establishing connections between levels. In these zones, Being is univocal, equal. In other words, every entity is equally being, in the sense that each actualizes its power in immediate vicinity with the first cause. The distant cause is no more: rocks, flowers, animals, and humans equally celebrate the glory of God in a kind of sovereign an-archy. The emanations and conversions of the successive levels are replaced by the coexistence of two movements in immanence—*complication* and *explication*—where God "complicates each thing" while "each thing explicates" God. The multiple is in the one which complicates it, just as the one is in the multiple which explicates it.

To be sure, theory will never finish reconciling these two aspects or these two universes, and most important, subordinating immanence to transcendence and measuring the Being of immanence by the Unity of transcendence. Whatever the theoretical compromises, something in the proliferations of immanence tends to overtake the vertical world, to reverse it, as if the hierarchy bred a particular anarchy, and the love of God, an internal atheism proper to it. Heresy is flirted with every time. And the Renaissance will tirelessly develop and extend this immanent world, which can be reconciled with transcendence only at the cost of threatening to inundate it anew.

This seems to me the most important aspect of Maurice de Gandillac's historical research: this play of immanence and transcendence, the proliferations of the Earth into the celestial hierarchies—he was responsible for bringing these themes the attention they deserve. What a shame that his greatest book, *La Philosophie de Nicolas de Cues*,[1] is now so hard to find, not having been reprinted. In its pages we watch a group of concepts being born, both logical and ontological, that will characterize "modern" philosophy through Leibniz and the German Romantics. One such concept is the notion of *Possest*, which expresses the immanent identity of act and power. And this flirtation with immanence, this competition between immanence and transcendence, already traverses the work of Eckhart, as well as the work of the Rhine mystics, and in another way, Petrarch's work, too. Moreover, Gandillac stresses that the seeds and the mirrors of immanence are already present in the early stages of neo-Platonism. In his book on Plotinus, one of the finest on this philosopher, Gandillac shows how Being proceeds from the One and yet nonetheless complicates each entity in itself, at the same time that it is explicated in each.[2] Immanence of the image in the mirror, immanence of the tree in the seed—these two ideas are the basis for an expressionist philosophy. Even in the pseudo-Denys, the rigor of the hierarchies reserves a virtual place for zones of equality, univocity, and anarchy.

Philosophical concepts are also modes of life and modes of activity for the one who invents them, or knows how to tease them out, giving them consistency. The mode of life emblematic of Maurice de Gandillac is precisely this ability to recognize the world of hierarchies at the same time that he conveys a sense of the zones of immanence within these hierarchies, which destabilizes them more effectively than a frontal attack. There is a kind of Renaissance man in Gandillac. His lively sense of humor is apparent in his fabric of immanence: complicating the most diverse things and persons in the self-same tapestry, at the same time that each thing, each person, explicates the whole. Tolstoy once said that the secret of feeling joyful was to ensnare as in a spider web, however you could (there is no rule), "an old woman, a child, a woman, and a police officer." An art of living and thinking is what Gandillac has always practiced, and what he has reinvented. This is embodied in his concrete sense of friendship.[3] We find it also in another one of Gandillac's activities: he is a skillful "debater." He and Geneviève de Gandillac have breathed new life into the conferences at Cerisy. In one conference after another, which Gandillac organizes like successive terraces, he has inspired the kind of debate which points out zones of immanence, like the various parts of the self-same tapestry. The explicit contributions of Gandillac are brief and to the point, but they display a remarkable wealth of content, to such an extent that they should be gathered together in a volume. This wealth of content is often due to the *philological* nature of his remarks, and here we touch on another aspect of Gandillac's activity: if he is steeped in philology, being a

Germanic scholar and translator, it is because the original thought of an author must somehow include both the source text and the target text, at the same time that the target text explains, in its own way, the source text (though without any additional commentary). Gandillac's translations, most notably his *Zarathustra*,[4] may continue to provoke heated debate, but the very power of his versions implies a new theory and conception of translation, which to this day Gandillac has only hinted at. Philosopher, historian, professor, translator, friend—these pursuits are one and the same enterprise for Gandillac.

36

He Was a Group Star

Something he said at the very end, just before he went to the hospital, has stayed with me because it says a lot. He said, "My illness is becoming too hard to manage." François could not have said it better, and I cannot think of a more noble death. Over the last few months, it had become too difficult to manage, and managing an illness means something. It was a minute and daily sickness. In a certain way, he never stopped knowing how to manage. In my oldest memories, I see François as a sort of center of attraction. As a student (we were students together at the end of the war), François was like a star in a group. He was always a star, not a "celebrity" but a constellation. There were so many people who gravitated around him, both students and professors.

A certain mystery shrouds François' life because he was so discreet. There were little breaks that only appeared years later. I think, for example, that much of his prestige came from his immense knowledge of formal logic. He was considered even by his professors to be a promising logician with a great future before him, someone who would replace the loss of Cavaillès or Lautman. And then that disappeared completely.

A first break: his conversion to the philosophy of history. And I think this conversion was influenced by someone who was very important for him: Eric Weil, with the extension of Kojève that such a conversion entailed. Eric Weil was his introduction to Hegel, the return to a sort of neo-Hegelianism that could correctly be called a conservative neo-Hegelianism. But François, while absolutely recognizing the influence of Eric Weil, did *leftist* neo-Hegelianism.

This was very important and it led to two things: 1) his major book on *La Naissance de l'histoire* [The Birth of History],[1] and 2) his joining the Communist Party. But his adhesion to the party did not follow the usual scenarios: enthusiasm and deception, or deception and departure. His involvement in the Party was a segment, and a thousand things led to his departure.

The final period of his work is directed more towards a questioning of logos; it was a new political philosophy that, instead of being a return to Hegel, or a return to logos, was a new type of critique: François was doing a critique of logos and of historical or political rationality. I say there is something mysterious about François because the other aspect of this man (whose life and work were constantly associated) involves the publication of a major novel that went unnoticed at the time.

Maybe people will now reread *Les Années de démolition* [The Demolition Years].[2] I will read it again with him in mind. It is an excellent novel that in my opinion is only equaled by Fitzgerald's work. There is an entire Fitzgeraldian side to François; and I can say this because, for me, Fitzgerald is one of the greatest authors their ever was. And *Les Années de demolition* is a major novel on the idea that any creative life is also a process of self-destruction with the theme of fatigue as a vital process. I should mention that he connected with Blanchot's themes on thought and fatigue, and the novel is really a commentary on the relationships between life and self-destruction. It is an extremely beautiful and moving book.

François' work, I believe, is truly a significant body of work. It was read perhaps less frequently or not quite as well as it should be because François did what all of us say we want to do but have not done. We all said, starting with Foucault, that the "author" was a function, not a name, and in the end it was not the only function. In the creative domains, we said that there was something other than the author function, which derives in part from cinema: there is the producer function, the director function, and many other functions. In François' final words—"this illness is becoming too difficult to manage"—managing is really a function. Just as leading is a function. For me, he was an excellent producer in the cinematic sense of the word. Not those who finance a film, but something else. It is a distinct function.

He was also a great negotiator in combination with his keen political sense. Negotiation for him was anything but an art of compromise. To my knowledge, he is a man who never compromised in the least, but he knew how to lead a negotiation. You could even see it in the little things. He held the Philosophy Department at Paris VIII together. He was the one who managed this challenging department and his political sense was always expressed through his sense of tough negotiation, with no compromises.

While he was at the crossroads of several functions (author, because he was an author, negotiator, producer, manager, etc.), I think he was above all, fundamentally, an author-producer. He excelled in directing work and in the end, the creative act, for him, was less the production of his own books than directing collective work in new directions. Some have said he was a great pedagogue.

Most remarkable of all are not simply his pedagogical concerns and tastes. He was definitely a great professor, but it was more important for him that this collective work allowed him to move in new directions. He did not do history. In fact, he was truly blazing new trails. In this light, I think we can only judge his recent work by connecting it to a renewal of political philosophy. What is this renewal? I think we have to connect the two ends.

François' starting point was an excellent book in the philosophy of history, *La Naissance de l'histoire* [The Birth of History], in Greece, which is an essential book and was his first. It later became a classic subject, but he was the one who first set off in the direction of thinking about history as the Greeks did and then had a major following. Afterwards, no one referred to this major book, but it was a major book. If we take the other end (I mean each time François intervened), what is, for example, the best book on Marxist atheism and Marx? It is François' article.[3] Concerning his final work, I think, to use Debray's title, it was in the Kantian sense a *Critique of Political Reason*. It was as if François had come back from his adhesion to logos and had to do a critique of political logos, a critique of political rationality, a critique of historical rationality. And his endeavors for this new critique were joined—this was the collective work direction—by a vast work comparable to the linguists: a vast political vocabulary. That was his producer-creator side. He was able to lead the critique of political reason, but it was inseparable from the collective work for a vast political vocabulary, a vocabulary of political institutions. The importance of his thought and his work is absolutely fundamental. It is the work of a creator; not only an illustrious professor, but a creator who creates with production and management.

37

Preface to the American Edition of *The Movement-Image*

This book stems from a desire not to recount a history of cinema, but to bring certain cinematographic concepts to light. These concepts are not of a technical nature (e.g. the various shots or the different camera movements), nor of a critical nature (e.g. the major genres, such as Westerns, cop movies, period films, etc.). Nor are these concepts linguistic, in the sense that cinema is said to be a universal language, or that it is said to be a particular language. My own view is that cinema is a composition of images and signs, an intelligible preverbal material (pure semiotics), whereas the semiology inspired by linguistics abolishes the image and tends to do away with the sign. What I am calling cinematographic concepts are types of images and the signs which correspond to each type. Since the image of cinema is "automatic," and is given first and foremost as a movement-image, I wanted to know under what conditions the different types of the image could be specified. The primary types are the perception-image, the affection-image, and the action-image. Their distribution surely determines a certain representation of time, but we cannot forget that time remains the object of an indirect representation to the extent that it depends on the editing and comes from the movement-images.

One can argue that a direct time-image has been created and imposed on cinema since the war. My claim is not that there is more movement, but just as in philosophy, there has been a reversal in the relationship between time and movement: time is no longer traced back to movement—the anomalies of movement depend on time. Instead of an indirect representation of time that comes out of movement, the direct time-image of time comes out of movement, and the direct time-image governs false movement. Why did the war make this reversal possible, this emergence of a cinema of time, in Welles, in neo-realism, in the French New Wave? Again, we will want to examine what type of images correspond to the new time-image, and which signs are combined with these types. Perhaps the whole thing emerges in the explosion of the sensory-motor schema. This schema, which binds perceptions, affections, and actions together, cannot undergo a profound crisis without altering the general regime of cinema. In any event, this mutation in cinema has been far more important than what cinema experienced with the invention of talkies.

It would be pointless to claim that the modern cinema of the time-image is "better" than the classic cinema of the movement-image. Here I deal exclusively with cinematic masterpieces which do not allow any such hierarchy of evaluation. Cinema is always perfect, as perfect as it can be, given the images and signs it invents and uses at any particular moment. Hence this study must weave concrete analyses of images and signs with monographs on the great cinematic auteurs who have created or renewed them.

Volume 1 focuses on the movement-image, and volume 2, on the time-image. At the end of this first book, I attempt to grasp the importance of Hitchcock, one of England's greatest filmmakers, simply because he seems to have invented an extraordinary type of image: the image of mental relations. Relations, as exterior to their terms, have always occupied the English philosophers. When a relation disappears, or changes, what happens to the terms? Similarly, in a minor comedy *Mr. and Mrs. Smith*, Hitchcock asks: what happens to a man and a woman when they suddenly learn that their marriage is illegal, and thus they have never been married? Hitchcock's cinema of relations is just like the English philosophy of relations. Perhaps, in this sense, he is situated at the cusp of two different cinemas: the classic cinema he perfects, and the modern cinema he prepares. In this light, the great auteurs of cinema must be compared and contrasted with more than painters, architects, or musicians—they should be placed alongside great thinkers. A crisis in cinema is often mentioned, due to the pressure exerted by television, and now the electronic image. But their creative capacities are already inseparable from what the great auteurs of cinema have been able to contribute. Not unlike Varèse in music, the great auteurs are calling for the new technologies and new materials that the future will make possible.

38

Foucault and Prison

HISTORY OF THE PRESENT: *Before moving to more general questions on intellectuals and the political arena, could you explain your relationship to Foucault and the GIP?*[1]

Gilles Deleuze: So you want to begin with the GIP. You will have to double-check what I tell you. I have no memory; it is like trying to describe a dream, it's rather vague. After '68, there were many groups, very different groups, but necessarily compact ones. It was post-'68. They survived, they all had a past. Foucault insisted on the fact that '68 had no importance for him. He already had a history as an important philosopher, but he was not burdened with a history from '68. That is probably what allowed him to form such a new type of group. And this group gave him a kind of equality with other groups. He would never have let himself be taken in. The GIP allowed him to maintain his independence from other groups like the Proletarian Left. There were constant meetings, exchanges, but he always preserved the complete independence of the GIP. In my opinion, Foucault was not the only one to outlive a past, but he was the only one to invent something new, at every level. It was very precise, like Foucault himself. The GIP was a reflection of Foucault, a Foucault-Defert invention. It was one case where their collaboration was close and fantastic. In France, it was the first time this type of group had been formed, one that had nothing to do with a party (there were some scary parties, like the Proletarian Left) nor with an enterprise (like the attempts to revamp psychiatry).

The idea was to make a "Prison Information Group." It was obviously more than just information. It was a kind of thought-experiment. There is a part of Foucault that always considered the process of thinking to be an experiment. It's his Nietzschean heritage. The idea was not to experiment on prisons but to take prison as a place where prisoners have a certain experience and that intellectuals, as Foucault saw them, should also think about. The GIP almost had the beauty of one of Foucault's books. I joined wholeheartedly because I was fascinated. When the two of them started, it was like stepping out into the darkness. They had seen something, but what you see is always in darkness. What do you do? I think that is how it started: Defert began distributing tracts among the families waiting in lines during visiting hours. Several people would go, and Foucault was sometimes with them. They were quickly singled out as "agitators." What they wanted was not at all to agitate, but to establish a questionnaire that families and prisoners could complete. I remember that in the first questionnaires, there were questions about food and medical care. Foucault must have been very reassured, very motivated, and very shocked by the results. We found something much worse, notably the constant humiliation. Foucault the observer then passed the mantle to Foucault the thinker.

The GIP was, I think, a forum for experimentation until *Discipline and Punish.* He was immediately sensible to the great difference between the theoretical and the legal status of prisons, between prison as a loss of freedom and the social uses of prison, which is something else altogether, since not only do they deprive an individual of his or her freedom, which is already huge, but there is systemic humiliation—the system is used to break people, and that is separate from taking away one's freedom. We discovered, as everyone knew, that there was a form of justice with no supervision that had taken shape in prison ever since the creation of a prison within the prison, a prison behind the prison, known as the "*mitard*" [solitary confinement]. The QHS[2] did not yet exist. Prisoners could be sentenced to solitary without any possibility of defending themselves. We learned a great deal. The GIP worked alongside the prisoners' families and former inmates. Like everything special, there were some very funny moments, like the time we first met with former inmates and each one wanted to be more of a prisoner than the others. Each one had always experienced something worse than the others.

What was the group's relationship to politics?

Foucault had a keen political intuition, which was something very important for me. Political intuition, for me, is the feeling that something is going to happen and happen *here*, not somewhere else. A political intuition is a very rare occurrence. Foucault sensed that there were little movements, small disturbances in the prisons. He was not trying to take advantage of them or cause them. He *saw* something. For him, thinking was always an experimental process up until death. In a way, he was a kind of *seer*. And what he saw was actually intolerable. He was a fantastic seer. It was the way he saw people, the way he saw everything, in its comedy and misery. His power of sight was equivalent to his power to write. When you see something and see it very profoundly, what you see is intolerable.

These are not the words he used in conversation, but it is in his thinking. For Foucault, to think was to react to the intolerable, the intolerable things one experienced. It was never something visible. That was also part of his genius. The two parts complement each other: thinking as experimentation and thinking as vision, as capturing the intolerable.

A kind of ethics?

I think it served as an ethics for him. The intolerable was not part of his ethics. His ethics was to see or grasp something as intolerable. He did not do it in the name of morality. It was his way of thinking. If thinking did not reach the intolerable, there was no need for thinking. Thinking was always thinking at something's limit.

People say it is intolerable because it is unjust.

Foucault did not say that. It was intolerable, not because it was unjust, but because no one saw it, because it was imperceptible. But everyone knew it. It was not a secret. Everyone knew about this prison in the prison, but no one saw it. Foucault *saw* it. That never stopped him from turning the intolerable into humor. Once again, we laughed a lot. It was not indignation. We were not indignant. It was two things: seeing something unseen and thinking something that was almost at a limit.

How did you become a part of the GIP?

I was completely convinced from the start that he was right and that he had found the only new type of group. It was new because it was so specific. And like everything Foucault did, the more specific it was, the more influence it had. It was like an opportunity that he knew not to miss. There were completely unexpected people involved who had nothing to do with prisons. I am thinking, for example, of Paul Eluard's widow who helped us a great deal at one point for no special reason. There were very consistent people like Claude Mauriac, who was very close to Foucault. When we made connections at the time of the Jackson affair and problems in American prisons, Genet stepped forward.[3] He was great. It was very lively. A movement inside the prisons was formed. Revolts took shape. Outside, things were going in every direction, with prison psychiatrists, prison doctors, the families of inmates. We had to make pamphlets. Foucault and Defert took on endless tasks. They were the ones with the ideas. We followed them. We followed them with a passion. I remember a crazy day, typical for the GIP, where the good and tragic moments came one after the other. We had gone to Nancy, I think. We were busy from morning to night. The morning started with a delegation to the prefecture, then we had to go to the prison, then we had to hold a press conference. Some things took place at the prison, and then we ended the day with a demonstration. At the start of the day, I told myself I would never make it. I never had Foucault's energy or his strength. Foucault had an enormous life force.

How did the GIP disband?

Foucault did what everyone else was contemplating: after a while, he disbanded the GIP. I remember Foucault was seeing the Livrozets frequently. Livrozet was a former inmate. He wrote a book for which Foucault did a beautiful preface.[4] Mrs. Livrozet was also very active. When the GIP disbanded, they continued its work with the CAP, the "Comité d'Action des Prisonniers" [Prisoners' Action Committee] that was going to be run by former inmates. I think Foucault only remembered the fact that he had lost; he did not see in what way he had won. He was always very modest from a certain point of view. He thought he had lost because everything closed down again. He had the impression that it had been useless. Foucault said it was not repression but worse: someone speaks but it is as if nothing was said. Three or four years later, things returned to exactly the way they were.

At the same time, he must have known what an impact he had made. The GIP accomplished many things; the prisoners' movements were formed. Foucault had the right to think that something had changed, even if it was not fundamental. It's an oversimplification, but the goal of the GIP was for the inmates themselves and their families to be able to speak, to speak for themselves. That was not the case before. Whenever there was a show on prisons, you had representatives of all those who dealt closely with prisons: judges, lawyers, prison guards, volunteers, philanthropists, anyone except inmates themselves or even former inmates. Like when you do a conference on elementary school and everyone is there except the children, even though they have something to say. The goal of the GIP was less to make them talk than to design a place where people would be forced to listen to them, a place that was not reduced to a riot on the prison roof, but would ensure that what they had to say came through. What needed to be said is exactly what Foucault brought out, namely: we are deprived of freedom, which is one thing, but the things happening to us are something else altogether. They own us. Everyone knows it, but everyone lets it happen.

Wasn't one of the functions of the intellectual for Foucault to open a space where others could speak?

In France, it was something very new. That was the main difference between Sartre and Foucault. Foucault had a notion, a way of living the political position of the intellectual that was very different from Sartre's, one that was not theoretical. Sartre, no matter what his force and brilliance, had a classical conception of the intellectual. He took action in the name of superior values: the Good, the Just and the True. I see a common thread that runs from Voltaire to Zola to Sartre. It ended with Sartre. The intellectual taking action in the name of the values of truth and justice. Foucault was much more functional; he always was a functionalist. But he invented his own functionalism. His functionalism was seeing and speaking. What is there to see here? What is there to say or think? It was not the intellectual as a guarantor of certain values.

I know that he later discussed his conception of truth, but that was different. "Information" was not the right word finally. It was not about finding the truth about prison, but to produce statements about prison, once it was said that neither the prisoners nor the people outside prison had been able to produce any themselves. They knew how to make speeches about prison, etc. but not produce them. Here as well, if there was any communication between his actions and his philosophical work, it was that he lived like that. What was so exceptional about Foucault's sentences when he spoke? There is only one man in the world I have ever heard speak like that. Everything he said was *decisive*, but not in the authoritarian sense. When he entered a room, it was already decisive; it changed thc atmosphere. When he spoke, his words were decisive. Foucault considered a statement to be something very particular.

Not just any discourse or sentence makes a statement. Two dimensions are necessary: seeing and speaking. It is more or less words and things. Words are the production of statements; things are the seeing, the visible formations. The idea is to see something imperceptible in the visible.

Does producing statements mean letting someone speak?

In part, but that is not all. We said—it was the theme—like the others, we said: others must be allowed to speak, but that was not the question. Here is a political example. For me, one of the most fundamentally important things about Lenin was that he produced new statements before and after the Russian Revolution. They were like signed statements, they were Leninist statements. Can we talk about a new type of statement or one that emerges in a certain space or under certain circumstances that are Leninist statements? It was a new type of statement. The question is not to seek the truth like Sartre, but to produce new conditions for statements. 1968 produced new statements. They were a type of statement that no one had used before. New statements can be diabolical and very annoying and everyone is drawn to fight them. Hitler was a great producer of new statements.

Did you find that politically sufficient at the time?

Was it enough to keep us occupied? Certainly. Our days were completely full. Foucault brought with him a type of practice that had two fundamentally new aspects. How could that not have been sufficient? Your question is too harsh in a way. Foucault would have said that it was not sufficient because in one sense, it failed. It did not change the status of the prisons. I would say the opposite. It was doubly sufficient. It had a lot of resonance. The main echoes were the movement in the prisons. The movement in the prisons was not inspired by either Foucault or Defert. The GIP amplified the movement because we also wrote articles and spent our time hassling the people in the Ministry of Justice and the Interior Ministry. Now there is a type of utterance on prisons that is regularly made by inmates and non-inmates that would not have been imaginable before. It was successful in this way.

You have a much more fluid view of the social world than Foucault. I am thinking of A Thousand Plateaus. *Foucault uses more architectural metaphors. Do you agree with this description?*

Completely. Unfortunately, in the final years of his life, I did not see him much, and of course I now regret it deeply, because he was one of the men I liked and admired the most. I remember we talked about it when he published *The Will to Knowledge*. We did not have the same conception of society. For me, a society is something that is constantly escaping in every direction. When you say I am more fluid, you are completely right. It flows monetarily; it flows ideologically. It is really made up of lines of flight. So much so that the problem for a society is how to stop it from flowing. For me, the powers come later. What surprised Foucault was that faced with all of these powers, all of their deviousness and hypocrisy, we can still resist. My surprise is the opposite. It is flowing everywhere and governments are able to block it. We approached the problem from opposite directions. You are right to say that society is a fluid, or even worse, a gas. For Foucault, it is an architecture.

You spoke with him about this?

I remember that at the time of *The Will to Knowledge*, which was, I think, the start of a kind of intellectual crisis, he was asking himself many questions. He was in a kind of melancholy and at the time, we spoke a great while about his way of viewing society.

What were your conclusions? Did you grow apart...

I always had enormous admiration and affection for Foucault. Not only did I admire him, but he made me laugh. He was very funny. I only resemble him in one way: either I am working, or I am saying insignificant things. There are very few people in the world with whom one can say insignificant things. Spending two hours with someone without saying a thing is the height of friendship. You can only speak of trifles with very good friends. With Foucault, it was more like a sentence here or there. One day during a conversation, he said: I really like Péguy because he is a madman. I asked: Why do think he is a madman? He replied: Just look at the way he writes. That was also very interesting about Foucault. It meant that someone who could invent a new style, produce new statements, was a madman. We worked separately, on our own. I am sure he read what I wrote. I read what he wrote with a passion. But we did not talk very often. I had the feeling, with no sadness, that in the end I needed him and he did not need me. Foucault was a very, very mysterious man.

39

The Brain Is The Screen

CAHIERS DU CINÉMA: *How did cinema come into your life, as a spectator, but especially as a philosopher? When did your love affair with it begin? And when did you first think it merited philosophical consideration?*

Gilles Deleuze: I feel very privileged to have experienced cinema in two discrete periods of my life. When I was a kid, I used to go to the movies all the time. There were these family plans, I think, where you could get a subscription to a particular movie house, like the Pleyel, and people sent their kids there. I couldn't choose what I wanted to see. But I saw Harold Lloyd and Buster Keaton. I remember *Les Croix de bois* [Wooden Crosses] gave me nightmares, and *Fantômas* really scared me when they released it again. I would be curious to know which movie houses in a particular neighborhood disappeared after the war. New movie houses have sprung up, but many have disappeared.

And then after the war, I started going to the movies again, but this time I was a philosophy student. I wasn't naïve enough to want to do a philosophy of cinema, but what made an impression on me was a certain intersection or encounter: the philosophical authors I preferred were those who demanded that movement be introduced into thought, "real" movement (they criticized the Hegelian dialectic as abstract movement). How could I not encounter the sort of cinema which introduced "real" movement into the image? It was not a matter of applying philosophy to cinema. I just went straight from philosophy to cinema and back again, from cinema to philosophy. There was something strange about cinema. What struck me, and I hadn't expected this, was how well it manifested not behavior, but spiritual life (including aberrant behaviors). Spiritual life is not dream or fantasy (these have always been dead-ends in cinema), but the realm of clear-headed decision making, a kind of absolute stubbornness, the choice of existence. How is it that cinema is so apt for mining the riches of spiritual life? This can be a recipe for the worst: the most vulgar cliché, an insipid Catholicism proper to cinema. Or it can be a recipe for the best: Dreyer, Sternberg, Bresson, Rosselini, Rohmer, etc. It is fascinating how Rohmer uses his films to study certain spheres of existence. *La Collectionneuse* [The Collector] is a study of esthetic existence, *Beau mariage* [A Good Marriage] is a study of ethical existence, and *Ma nuit chez Maud* [My Night at Maud's] is a study of religious existence. It is very much like Kierkegaard who long before cinema felt the need to write using strange synopses. Cinema puts movement not just in the image; it puts it in the mind. Spiritual life is the movement of the mind. It is perfectly natural to go from philosophy to cinema, and from cinema to philosophy.

The unity here is the brain. The brain is the screen. I don't think psychoanalysis or linguistics have much to offer cinema. But molecular biology, the biology of the brain—that's a different story. Thought is molecular. We are slow beings, constituted by certain molecular speeds. Michaux says: "Man is a slow being, made possible only through fantastic speeds."[1] Cerebral circuits and connections do not preexist the stimuli, the corpuscles, or particles that trace them. Cinema is not theater: it composes its bodies using particles. The chains of connections in cinema are often paradoxical and cannot be reduced to the simple association of images. There is always something left over. Because cinema puts the image in motion, or endows the image with self-movement, it is forever tracing and retracing cerebral circuits. Again, this can be for better or worse. The screen, in other words, we ourselves, can be the deficient idiot brain, as well as the brain of creative genius. The power of early cinematic clips resided in new speeds, new connections and re-connections. But before they could even develop this power, they sank into lousy tics and grimaces, and haphazard cuts. Bad cinema always works with the ready-made circuits of the lower brain: a representation of mere violence and sexuality, combining gratuitous cruelty with organized stupidity. Real cinema breaks through to a different violence, a different sexuality, which are molecular and not localizable. Losey's characters, for example, are these little bundles of static violence, which are all the more violent for being still. The various speeds of thought—acceleration or petrifaction—are inseparable from the movement-image. Take the speed of Lubitsch's films: his images are genuine arguments, lightning bolts, the life of the mind.

It is not when one discipline begins to reflect on another that they come into contact. Contact can be made only when one discipline realizes that another discipline has already posed a similar problem, and so the one reaches out to the other to resolve this problem, but on its own terms and for its own needs. We can imagine similar problems which, at different moments, in different circumstances, and under different conditions, send shock waves through various fields: painting, music, philosophy, literature, and cinema. The tremors are the same, but the fields are different. All criticism is comparative (and cinematic criticism is at its worst when it limits itself to cinema as though it were a ghetto) because every work in whatever field is already self-comparing. Godard confronts painting in *Passion* and music in *Prénom Carmen* [First Name: Carmen]. He makes a serial cinema, but he also makes a cinema of catastrophe in a sense very close to the mathematical conception of René Thom. Every work has its beginning or its consequence in the other arts. I was able to write on cinema not because I have some right to reflect on it, but because certain philosophical problems pushed me to seek out the solutions in cinema, even if this only serves to raise more problems. All research, scholarly or creative, participates in such a relay system.

What stands out in your two books on cinema is something that can be found in your other books, though not to the same extent: taxonomy, the love of classification. Have you always been so inclined to classification, or did it come about in the course of your research? Does classification have a particular connection to cinema?

Yes, there is nothing quite so amusing as classifications and tables. A classification scheme is like the skeleton of a book; it's like a vocabulary or a dictionary. It's not what is most essential, but it is a necessary first step. Balzac's work is built on some astonishing classifications. In Borges there is a Chinese taxonomy of animals that amused Foucault: animals belonging to the emperor, stuffed animals, tame animals, sirens, suckling pigs, etc. Every classification is similar: they are flexible, their criteria vary according to the cases presented, they have a retroactive effect, and they can be infinitely refined or reorganized. Some compartments are crowded, and others are empty. In any classification scheme, some things which seem very different are brought closer together, and others which seem very close are separated. This is how concepts are formed. You hear people say that categories like "classic," "romantic," "nouveau roman," or "neo-realism" are mere abstractions. I think they're perfectly fine, provided that they're grounded in singular signs or symptoms, and not general forms. A classification scheme is essentially a symptomology, and signs are what you class in order to extract a concept, not as abstract essence, but as event. In this respect, different disciplines or fields are signal-materials, materials of signaling. Classifications will vary in terms of the material, but they will also reinforce one another in terms of the various affinities in different materials. Cinema, because it animates and temporalizes the image, is both a very particular material, and a material that shows a high degree of affinity with other materials: pictorial, musical, literary, etc. Cinema should be understood not as a language, but as a signal-material.

For example, I will try out a classification of cinematic lighting. You have one kind of light that presents a composite physical environment, and whose composition gives you white light, a Newtonian light that can be found in American cinema, and perhaps in Antonioni's films, though in a different way. Then you have a Goethe-light, an indestructible force that slams into shadows and picks things out (expressionism, but Ford and Welles are in this group, no?). You have another kind of light defined by its contrast not with shadow, but with shades of white, opacity being a total white out (this is another aspect of Goethe, and Sternberg as well). You have also a kind of light no longer defined either by composition or by contrast, but by alternation and the production of lunar figures (this is the light of the pre-war French school, particularly Epstein and Grémillon, and maybe Rivette today; it is very close to the conceptualization and practice of Delaunay). The list could go on forever, because new lighting events can always be created, like what Godard does in his film *Passion*. And you can do the same thing for cinematic spaces. You have organic or surrounding spaces (the Western, but Kurosawa gives an immense amplitude to surrounding space). There are functional universe-lines (the neo-Western, but also Mizoguchi). Or Losey's flat spaces: terraces, cliffs, plateaus—which led him to discover Japanese spaces in his last two films. Or Bresson's disconnected spaces, whose links are non-determined. You have empty spaces in the manner of Ozu and Antonioni. There are stratigraphic spaces, whose importance derives from what they cover, such that you have to "read" them, as in the Straubs' films. Or Resnais's topological spaces... The classification is open-ended. There are as many kinds of space as there are inventors. And light and space can be combined in a variety of ways. In each case, we see how the classifications of luminous or spatial signs are proper to cinema, and yet refer to other disciplines in the sciences and the arts—Newton or Delaunay. In these other disciplines, the signs have a different order, different contexts and relations, and different divisions.

There has been a crisis of the auteur in cinema. The current state of the debate seems to be: "There are no more auteurs, everyone is an auteur, and whoever is an auteur bores us to death."

There are many different forces at work today trying to level the differences between commercial and creative work. By denying the difference between them, people think they're clever, cutting-edge, sophisticated. In reality, all that is being expressed is one of the demands of capitalism: a rapid turn-over. Those who work in advertising call it today's modern poetry, but this shameless proposition forgets that no art ever aims to introduce or sell a product that responds to a public demand. Advertising can be shocking, intentionally or not, but it still responds to a supposed demand. On the other hand, art necessarily produces the unexpected, the unrecognizable, and the unacceptable. There is no such thing as commercial art. It's a contradiction in terms. Of course, there is popular art. Some art indeed requires financial investment, and there is such a thing as an art market, but there is no such thing as commercial art. What makes things so confusing is that commercial and creative work use the same form. You see this already with the form of the book: Harlequin and Tolstoy use the same form. You can always compare airport reading and great novels, and the airport reading, the best-seller, will beat the great novels in a market place governed by quick turnover—or worse, the best-sellers lay claim to the qualities of great works and effectively take them hostage. This is what is happening on TV, where esthetic judgment becomes "delicious," like a good meal, or "unbelievable," like a home run. This is promotion according to the lowest common denominator, modeling literature on mass consumption. "Auteur" is a function that refers to a work of art (and in a different context, to a crime). There are other terms, just as respectable, for those who make these other products: producers, directors, editors, programmers, etc. The people who say there are no auteurs today would have been incapable of recognizing the auteurs of yesterday when they were still making names for themselves. It's pure vanity. To thrive, all art needs the distinction between these two sectors, the commercial and the creative.

The *Cahiers* is largely responsible for introducing this distinction into cinema and for defining what it means to be an auteur in cinema (even if movie-making includes producers, editors, commercial agents, etc.). Païni has recently said some interesting things on these topics.[2] People today think they're being clever when they erase the distinction between the creative and the commercial: that's because they have an interest in doing so. It is hard to create a work; it is much easier to discover criteria. Every work, even a short one, implies a major undertaking or a long internal duration (for example, recounting the memories of one's family is not a major undertaking). A work is always the creation of a new space-time (it's not a question of telling a story situated in a determined space and time; the rhythms, the lighting, the space-time must themselves become the real characters). A work is supposed to bring out problems and questions in which we find ourselves caught, and not to provide answers. A work is a new syntax, which is much more important than diction. It carves out a foreign language in the language. In cinema, syntax is the connecting and the re-connecting of chains of images, as well as the relation between the visual image and sound (there is an intimate connection between these two aspects). If you had to define culture, you could say that it is not about mastering a difficult or abstract domain, but realizing that works of art are much more concrete, funny, and moving than commercial products. In creative works, you find a multiplication of emotion, a liberation of emotion, the invention of new emotions, which are to be distinguished from the prefabricated models of emotions you find in commerce. Bresson and Dreyer are totally unique in this respect: they are the masters of a new humor. This whole question of the cinematic author is certainly about ensuring the distribution of films that could not stand up against the competition from commercial films, since creative work solicits a whole other temporality, but it is also about keeping open the possibility of creating films that do not yet exist. Maybe cinema is not yet capitalist enough. There are circuits of money with very different durations: short-term, mid-term, and long-term cinematic investment should be recognized and encouraged. In science, capitalism does now and then rediscover the interest in doing fundamental research.

In your book there is one thesis that has the makings of a scandal. This thesis goes against everything that has been written on cinema, and it has to do with the time-image. Filmographic analysis has always maintained that in a film, despite the presence of flashbacks, dreams, memories, or even prefiguations, whatever time-frame is being evoked, it is always in the present, in front of the spectator, that movement occurs. But you maintain that the cinematographic image is not in the present.

That's strange, because it seems obvious to me that the image is not in the present. What is in the present is whatever the image "represents," but not the image itself. The image itself is a bunch of temporal relations from which the present unfolds, either as a common multiplier, or a common denominator. Temporal relations are never seen in ordinary perception, but they can be seen in the image, provided the image is creative. The image renders visible, and creative, the temporal relations which cannot be reduced to the present. For example, an image shows a man walking along a river, in mountainous terrain: in this case, you have at least three "coexisting" durations in the image, which are not to be confused with the present of what the image represents. This is what Tarkovsky means when he rejects the distinction between montage and shot, because he defines cinema by "the pressure of time" in the shot.[3] It will be clearer if we look at some examples: an Ozu still-life, a Visconti traveling-shot, and a Welles deep-focus shot. If you stick to what is represented, you have a motionless bicycle, or a mountain; you have a car, or a man, traveling across a space. But from the perspective of the image, Ozu's still-life is that form of time which does not change although everything in it changes (the relation of what is in time to time). Similarly, in Visconti's film, Sandra's car is driving into the past even as it traverses a space in the present. This has nothing to do with flashback, nor with memory, because memory is only a former present, whereas a character in the image literally goes deeper into the past or emerges from the past. Generally speaking, when space stops being "Euclidian," when space is created the way Ozu, Antonioni, or Bresson does it, then space no longer accounts for those characteristics that call on temporal relations. Certainly, Resnais is one of the auteurs whose image is least in the present, because his image is entirely founded in the coexistence of heterogeneous durations. The variation of temporal relations is the very subject of *Je t'aime je t'aime*, independent of any flashback. What is a "false sync," or the disjunction between sight and sound, as in the Straubs' films or Marguerite Duras' films, or the feather-brushed look of Resnais's screen, or Garrel's black and white cuts? In every case, it is "a piece of pure time," and not a present. Cinema does not reproduce bodies, it produces them with particles, and these are particles of time. It is particularly stupid to talk about the death of cinema, because cinema is just beginning to explore the relations between sound and image, which are temporal relations, and it is totally reinventing its relation to music. The inferiority of TV is that it sticks with images in the present, it makes everything present, unless TV becomes the medium of a great film-maker. Only mediocre or commercial works are characterized by the idea of images in the present. It's a received idea, a false idea, the very example of false appearances. To my knowledge, only Robbe-Grillet still works with it. But if he does, it is out of malice, a diabolical malice. He is one of the only authors to produce images in the present, but by means of complex temporal relations that are all his own. He is living proof that such images are difficult to create, if you care to go beyond what is represented, and that the present is not a natural given of the image.

40

Occupy Without Counting: Boulez, Proust and Time

Boulez has often raised the question of his relationship to writers and poets: Michaux, Char, Mallarmé... If it is true that a cut is not the contrary of continuity, if continuity is defined by the cut, then the same gesture establishes the continuity of a literary text and a musical text and places the cuts between them. There is no general solution: each time, the relationships must be measured according to varying and often irregular measures. Yet now Boulez has an entirely different relationship to Proust. Not a more profound one, but a relationship of a different nature, tacit, implicit (even though he often cites Proust in his writings). It is as if he knew him by "heart," by will and by chance. Boulez defined an important alternative: count to occupy space-time, or occupy without counting.[1] Measure to generate relationships, or implement relationships without measure. Wouldn't his connection to Proust be of this second type: haunt or be haunted ("What do you want from me?"), occupy or be occupied without counting, without measure?

The first thing Boulez grasped in Proust is how sounds and noises detach from the characters, places and names to which they are first attached to make independent "motifs" that constantly change over time, growing or shrinking, cutting or adding, varying their speed or slowness. The motif is at first associated with a landscape or a character like a signpost but it then becomes the sole varying landscape or the sole changing character. Proust necessarily evokes the little phrase and Vinteuil's music to account for the alchemy that is present throughout the *Search* and he pays homage for it to Wagner (even though Vinteuil is supposedly very different from Wagner). Boulez in turn pays homage to Proust for having a deep understanding of the independent life of the Wagnerian motif to the extent that it undergoes changing speeds, moves through free modifications, and enters a continuous variation that presupposes a new form of time for "musical beings."[2] All of Proust's work is made this way: the successive loves, jealousies, slumbers, etc., all detach from the characters so well that they themselves become infinitely changing characters, individuations without identity, Jealousy I, Jealousy II, Jealousy III... This type of variable developing in the independent dimension of time is called a "block of duration," an "endlessly variable sound block." And the independent, non-preexisting dimension that is traced along with the block's variations is called *diagonal* to indicate that it cannot be reduced to either the harmonic vertical or the melodic horizontal as preexisting coordinates.[3] The epitome of the musical act for Boulez consists in the diagonal, each time under different conditions, from polyphonic combinations, through the resolutions of Beethoven, the fusions of harmony and melody in Wagner up to Webern abolishing the frontier between vertical and horizontal, producing sound blocks in the series, moving them along a diagonal as a temporal function distributing the entire work.[4] Each time, the diagonal is like a vector-block of harmony and melody, a function of temporalization. And the musical composition of the *Search*, according to Proust, appears to be the same:

constantly changing blocks of duration, at varying speeds and free modifications, along a diagonal that forms the only unity of the work, the transversal of all the parts. The unity of the voyage is not in the vertical roads of the landscape, which are like harmonic cuts, nor is it in the melodic line of the route. It is in the diagonal, "from one window to another," that allows the succession of points of view and the movement of the point of view to be joined in a block of transformation or duration.[5]

The blocks of duration, however, because they go through high and low speeds, augmentations and reductions, appendices and deductions, are inseparable from the metric and chronometric relationships that define divisibilities, commensurabilities, proportionalities: the "pulse" is a smallest common multiple (or simple multiple) and the "tempo" is the inscription of a certain number of unities in a specific time. It is a *striated* space-time, a pulsed time, to the extent that the cuts can be determined, of a rational type (first aspect of the continuum) and the measures, regular *or not*, can be determined as sizes between cuts. The blocks of duration therefore follow a striated space-time where they trace their diagonals according to the speed of their pulsations and the variation of their measures. However, a *smooth* or non-pulsed space-time detaches itself in turn from the striated one. It only refers to chronometry in a global way: the cuts are indeterminate, of an irrational type, and the measures are replaced by distances and proximities that cannot be broken down and that express the density or rareness of what appears there (statistical distribution of events). A gauge of occupation replaces the gauge of speed.[6] That is where one occupies without counting instead of counting to occupy. Couldn't we reserve Boulez's term "bubbles of time" for this new, distinct figure of blocks of duration? Numbers do not disappear, but they become independent of metric and chronometric relationships; they become numerals, numbering numbers, nomadic or Mallarméan numbers, musical Nomos and no longer measure. And instead of dividing a closed space-time *according to* the elements that form a block, they distribute the elements contained in a bubble in open space-time. It is like the passage from one temporalization to another: no longer a Series of time, but an Order of time. Boulez's major distinction between striated and smooth is less a separation than a constant communication. The two space-times alternate and overlap, there is exchange between the two functions of temporalization, even if it is only in the sense that a homogenous division in a striated time gives the impression of a smooth time, while a very unequal distribution in a smooth time introduces *directions* that evoke striated time through densification or the accumulation of proximities. If we inventory all of the differences Proust describes between Vinteuil's sonata and his septet, there are those that distinguish a closed plane and an open space, a block and a bubble (the septet is bathed in a violet fog that makes a whole note appear as if "in an opal") and also those that associate the little phrase of the sonata with an indication of speed while the phrases of the septet refer to indications of occupation. More generally, each theme, each character in the *Search* is systematically disposed to a double exposure: one as a "box" from which all kinds of variations in speed and modification in quality can come depending on the period and the time (chronometry); the other as a nebula or multiplicity that only has degrees of density or rareness according to a statistical distribution (even the two "ways"—Méséglise and Guermantes—are presented as two statistical directions). Albertine is both at once, sometimes striated and sometimes smooth; sometimes a block of transformation, other times a nebula of diffusion, although according to two distinct temporalizations. The entire *Search* must be read as smooth and striated: a double reading following Boulez's distinction.

The theme of memory seems so secondary compared to these deeper motifs. Boulez can take up the "praise of amnesia" from Stravinsky or Désormière's statement "I abhor memory" without ceasing to be Proustian in his own way. For Proust, even involuntary memory occupies a very limited zone that art overflows in every direction and that only serves as a facilitator. The problem of art, the correlative problem of creation is the problem of *perception* and not memory: music is pure presence and calls for an extension of perception to the limits of the universe. Expanded perception is the aim of art (or philosophy, according to Bergson). Such a goal can only be reached if perception breaks with the identity to which memory binds it. Music has always had this object: individuations without identity that form "musical beings." Without a doubt, tonal language restored a principle of specific identity with the first degree octave or chord. But the system of blocks and bubbles leads to a general rejection of any principle of identity in the variations and distributions that define them.[7] The problem of perception then becomes stronger: how can one perceive individuals whose variations are constant and whose speeds cannot be analyzed, or even individuals that evade any measurement in a smooth setting?[8] Numerals or numbering numbers, avoiding both pulsation and metric relationships, do not appear as such in the sound phenomenon even though they create real phenomena, but precisely without identities. Is it possible that this imperceptible, that these holes in perception are filled by writing, and that the ear carries on through a reading eye that functions like a "memory"? Yet the problem takes another turn, for how can writing be *perceived* "without the obligation to understand it?" Boulez finds an answer in defining a third setting, a third space-time *adjacent* to the smooth and striated that is responsible for perceiving writing: the universe of the Fixed. This universe acts through surprising simplification, as in Wagner or in Webern's three sound figures, or by suspension like Berg's twelve strokes, or by unusual accentuation like in Beethoven or Webern again, presenting itself like a gesture brushing against the formal structure or an envelope isolating a group of constitutive elements. The relationship between the envelopes creates the richness of perception and keeps sensibility and memory alert.[9] In Vinteuil's little phrase, the high note held for two measures and "held like a curtain of sound to hide the mystery of its incubation," is a distinct example of the Fixed. As for the septet, Miss Vinteuil's friend needed fixed indications to *write* the work. That is the role of involuntary memory in Proust, to create envelopes of fixed.

This does not mean that the involuntary memory, or the fixed, reestablishes a principle of identity. Proust, like Joyce and Faulkner, is one of those who dismissed any principle of identity from literature. Even in repetition, the fixed is not defined by the identity of a repeated element but by a *quality common* to elements that would not be repeated without it (for example, the famous taste common to two moments, or in music a common pitch...). The fixed is not the Same and does not reveal an identity beneath variations. The contrary is true. It allows the *identification* of the variation, or individuation without identity. That is how it extends perception: it makes the variations perceptible in a striated setting and the distributions in a smooth setting. Instead of bringing difference to the Same, it allows the identification of difference as such. Thus, in Proust, taste as a quality common to two moments identifies Combray as always different from itself. In music as well as literature, the functional play of repetition and difference replaces the organic play of identity and variation. That is why the fixed imply no permanence but *make instantaneous* the variation or dissemination they force one to perceive. And the envelopes themselves constantly maintain a "moving relationship" between themselves in a single work or in a block, or a bubble.

Extending perception means making forces that are ordinarily imperceptible sensible, resonant (or visible). These forces are not necessarily time, of course, but they mix and combine with the forces of time. "Time is not usually visible...." We easily and sometimes painfully perceive things in time. We also perceive the form, units and relationships of chronometry, but not time as a *force*, time itself, "some time in its purest form." Using sound as the intermediary that makes time sensible, the Numbers of time perceptible, organizing the material to capture the forces of time and make them into sound: that is Messiaen's project. Boulez takes up his project under new conditions (particularly serial). But the musical conditions for Boulez echo the literary conditions of Proust in certain ways: giving sound to the mute forces of time. In developing the temporalization functions that operate in the sound material, the musician captures and makes sensible the forces of time. The forces of time and the functions of temporalization unite to form the Aspects of *implicated time*. For both Boulez and Proust, these aspects are multiple and are simply reduced to a "lost-found." There is lost time, which is not a negation but a full function of time. For Boulez, the pulverization of sound or its extinguishing is an affair of timbre, the *extinguishing of timbre*, in the sense that timbre is like love and repeats its end rather than its origin. Then there is "re-searched time," the *formation of blocks of duration*, their journey along the diagonal: they are not (harmonic) chords but veritable hand-to-hand fights, often rhythmic ones, sound or vocal embraces where one of the wrestlers subdues the other, and vice versa, like in the music of Vinteuil. That is the striated force of time. And then there is "re-gained" time; identified, but in the instant. It is the "gesture" of time or the *envelope of fixed*. Finally, "*utopian time*," as Boulez stated in homage to Messiaen: finding oneself again after penetrating the secret of the Numerals, haunting giant bubbles of time, confronting the smooth—discovering, following Proust's analyses, that human beings occupy "in time a place much more considerable than the all too limited place reserved for them in space." Or rather that comes to them when they count, "a place on the contrary prolonged without measure…"[10] In meeting Proust, Boulez creates a group of fundamental philosophical concepts that spring from his own works of music.

41

Preface to the American Edition of *Difference and Repetition*

1) There is a big difference between writing the history of philosophy, and writing philosophy. In the history of philosophy, you study the arrows or the tools of a great thinker, his or her quarry and prizes, the continents which he or she has discovered. In the other case, you make your own arrow, or you gather what seem to you the finest arrows, only to shoot them in other directions, even if the distance they travel is relatively short, rather than stellar. When you try to speak in your own name, you learn that the proper name designates only the results of your research, that is, the concepts which you discovered, provided you knew how to bring them to life and express them in the latent possibilities of language.

2) After writing books on Hume, Spinoza, Nietzsche, and Proust—their work inspired me with great enthusiasm—*Difference and Repetition* was the first attempt I made "to do philosophy." Everything I have done since then seems an extension of this book, even the books Guattari and I wrote together (at least from my point of view). It is hard to say just what it is that attracts someone to any particular problem. What was it about difference and repetition that fascinated me, why not something else? And

why did I couple them, rather than separate them? I was not dealing with new problems: they have been the constant preoccupation of the history of philosophy and contemporary philosophy in particular. Still, hadn't most philosophers subordinated difference to identity or the same—to the Similar, the Opposite, or the Analogous? They had introduced difference into the identity of the concept; they had put difference in the concept; they had even broken through to a conceptual difference—but not to a concept of difference.

3) Whenever we think difference, we tend to subordinate it to identity (from the point of view of the concept or the subject: for example, specific difference presupposes a genus as the concept of identity). We also tend to subordinate it to resemblance (from the point of view of perception), to opposition (from the point of view of predicates), and to the analogous (from the point of view of judgment). In other words, we never think difference in itself. Philosophy, in Aristotle's work, managed to develop an organic representation of difference, not to mention an orgiastic, infinite representation in the work of Leibniz and Hegel. But it had still yet to break through to difference in itself.

Repetition has perhaps fared no better. Though in a different way, we also tend to think of repetition in terms of the identical, the similar, the equal, or the opposite. In this case, we create difference without a concept: one thing is a repetition of another whenever they differ though they have the same concept. From then on, whatever arrives on the scene to vary the repetition seems at the same time to cover or hide it. Again, as with difference, a concept of repetition has eluded our grasp. But could it be that we adequately formulate a concept of repetition when we perceive that variation is not something extra added to repetition, only to conceal it, but rather its condition or constitutive element—interiority par excellence? Disguise belongs no more to repetition than displacement does to difference: a common transport, *diaphora*. Taking this to the limit, could we speak of a single power, whether of difference or of repetition, which would make itself felt only in the multiple and would determine multiplicities?

4) Every philosophy must develop its own way of talking about the sciences and the arts, just as it must establish alliances with them. This conquest is difficult, because philosophy cannot lay claim to the least superiority, and yet it can create and develop its own concepts only in relation to what these concepts are able to grasp of scientific functions and artistic constructions. A philosophical concept is not to be confused with a scientific function or an artistic construction, but it does have affinities with them, in a particular scientific field, or style of art. The scientific or artistic content of a philosophy can be rudimentary, since it is not philosophy's job to advance science or art, but philosophy cannot itself advance without forming properly philosophical concepts concerning a particular function or construction, however rudimentary. In other words, philosophy cannot be practiced independently of science and art. In this sense, I have tried to constitute a philosophical concept of differentiation, both as a mathematical function and as a biological function, all the while searching for a relation between them which could be articulated, but which did not appear at the level of their respective objects. Art, science, and philosophy seem to have mobile relations to one another, with each responding to the other, but each in terms which are proper to it.

5) Finally, it seemed that this book could break through to the powers of difference and repetition only by calling into question the image of thought which we had made for ourselves. What I mean is that method alone does not exclusively govern our thought, especially when there is a more or less explicit image of thought, tacit and presupposed, which determines our ends and means whenever we try to think. For example, we presuppose that thinking is possessed of a good nature, and the thinker, of good will (we "naturally" desire the truth). Recognition, or common sense, is the model we choose for ourselves whenever we use our faculties on an object which is presupposed the same. Error is the enemy to be defeated—the only enemy—and we presuppose that truth has to do with solutions, propositions capable of serving as answers. Such is the classic image of thought. As long as this image remains untouched by a critique, how will we bring thought to consider problems which surpass the propositional mode, to have such encounters as escape recognition, to confront enemies other than error, to reach into the heart of what necessitates thought, or wrests it from its usual torpor, its notorious bad faith? A new image of thought, or rather the liberation of thought from the images which imprison it, was what I was looking for already in Proust.[1] In *Difference and Repetition*, this project acquires its own autonomy and becomes the condition for the discovery of two concepts. Thus, of all the chapters, Chapter 3 now seems the most necessary and the most concrete. It provides an introduction to my subsequent books, including my work with Guattari, in which we claim a vegetable model for thought in the rhizome, as opposed to the model of the tree: not arborescent thought—rhizome-thought.

42

Preface to the American Edition of *Dialogues*

I have always felt like an empiricist, or a pluralist. What does this empiricism-pluralism equivalency mean? It derives from the two traits Whitehead used to define empiricism: 1) abstraction does not explain but must be explained, and 2) the search is not for an eternal or universal, but for the conditions under which something new is created (*creativeness*). It is evident that for so-called rationalist philosophers, abstraction is responsible for explanation, the abstract is realized in the concrete. They speak of abstractions such as the One, the Whole, the Subject, etc., and seek the processes through which these abstractions are embodied in a world made to conform to their requirements (this process can be Knowledge, Virtue, or History...)—even if it means experiencing a terrible crisis each time they realize that rational unity or totality turns into its contrary, or that the subject engenders monsters.

Empiricism starts with an entirely different assessment: analyzing states of things so as to bring out previously nonexistent concepts from them. The states of things are not unities or totalities but multiplicities. That does not simply mean that there are many states of things (where each state would be a whole) or that each state of things is multiple (which would only be an indication of its resistance to unification). The crucial point from an empirical point of view is the word "multiplicity." Multiplicity indicates a group of lines or dimensions that cannot be reduced to one another. Every "thing" is made up of them. A multiplicity certainly contains points of unification, centers of totalization, points of subjectivation, but these are factors that can prevent its growth and stop its lines. These factors are in the multiplicity they belong to, and not the reverse. In a multiplicity, the terms or elements are less important than what is "between," the *between*,[1] a group of relationships inseparable from one another. Every multiplicity grows from the middle like grass or a rhizome. We constantly oppose rhizomes and trees as two very different conceptions and even uses of thought. A line does not go from one point to another; it passes between the points, constantly bifurcating and diverging like a line from Pollock.

Bringing out the concepts that correspond to a multiplicity means tracing the lines that form it, determining the nature of these lines, and seeing how they overlap, connect, bifurcate, and avoid the points or not. These lines are veritable becomings distinguished from both unities and the history in which these unities develop. Multiplicities are made of becomings without history, individuations without subjects (the way a river, a climate, an event, a day, or an hour of the day are individualized...). A concept has no less existence in empiricism than in rationalism, but its uses are completely different and of another nature: the concept is a multiple-being instead of a one-being, all-being or being a subject. Empiricism is fundamentally connected to a logic, the logic of multiplicities (its relationships are only one aspect).

This book (1977) set out to indicate the existence and activity of multiplicities in very diverse domains. One day, Freud had the premonition that psychopaths felt and thought in multiplicities:

the skin is a group of pores; socks are a field of stitches, bones come from an ossuary... But he kept coming back to the calmer vision of a neurotic unconscious playing with eternal abstractions (and even Melanie Klein's partial objects hark back to a lost unity, a totality to come, a split subject). It is very difficult to think the multiple as such, as a substantive, in a way that does not need to refer to something other than itself: the indefinite article as particle, the proper name as individuation without subject, verbs in the infinitive as pure becoming, "a Hans to become horse" [*un Hans devenir cheval*]... It seemed to us that British and American literature had a great role in approaching these multiplicities: it is probably in this literature that the question "What is writing?" received the response closest to Life itself, both animal and plant life. It also seemed to us that science, math, and physics had no higher object, and that set theory was still in the early stages like the theory of spaces. It seemed to us that politics was involved as well, and that throughout a social field, rhizomes spread under arborescent apparatuses. This book is made up of just such an assortment of imagination about the formation of the unconscious as well as literary, scientific and political formations.

This book itself was "between" in many ways. It was between two books. *Anti-Oedipus*, which Guattari and I had finished, and *A Thousand Plateaus*, which we had begun, and that was our most ambitious, most inordinate, and least appreciated work. This book was therefore not only between two books, but between Guattari and myself as well. And since I wrote it with Claire Parnet, there was the occasion for a new between-line. The points—Félix, Claire Parnet, myself and many others—did not count and only served as temporary, transitory, fleeting points of subjectivation. What was important was the set of bifurcating, divergent, overlapping lines that formed this book as a multiplicity passing between the points, carrying them along without ever going from one to the other. As such, the initial project to have a two person interview with one person asking questions and the other answering no longer worked. The distributions had to include the increasing dimensions of multiplicity, following a becoming that could not be attributed to people, since no one could enter them without changing their nature. We might know all the more what writing is without knowing what came from one person or another or someone else altogether. The lines respond to each other like the subterranean tendrils of a rhizome as opposed to the unity of the tree and its binary logic. It was truly a subjectless book with no beginning or end, and no middle, like Miller said: "grass grows between…, it is an overflowing, a moral lesson."[2]

43

Preface for the Italian Edition of *A Thousand Plateaus*

For Giorgio Passerone

As the years pass, books grow old, or they experience a second youth. Some books bloat and swell, and some alter their appearance, showing their skeleton, or bringing new planes to the surface. Authors have no control over this objective destiny. But authors are entitled to reflect on the place that a particular book occupies in their project taken as a whole (subjective destiny), whereas the book at the moment of its composition was the whole project.

A Thousand Plateaus (1980) is the follow-up to *Anti-Oedipus* (1972). Objectively speaking, they have very different destinies. This probably has something to do with their contexts: *Anti-Oedipus* was written during a period of upheaval, in the wake of '68, whereas *A Thousand Plateaus* emerged in an environment of indifference, the calm we find ourselves in now. *A Thousand Plateaus* was the least well-received of all our books. And while it is still our favorite, we do not prefer it the way a mother prefers a problem child. *Anti-Oedipus* was a big success, but this success was accompanied by a more fundamental failure. The book tried to denounce the havoc that Oedipus, "mommy-daddy," had wrought in psychoanalysis, in psychiatry (including anti-psychiatry), in literary criticism, and in the general image of thought we take from it. Our dream was to put Oedipus to rest once and for all. But the job was too big for us. The reaction against '68 has demonstrated all too clearly just how intact the Oedipus family remains, to this day imposing its sniveling regime on psychoanalysis, literature, and thought. Indeed, Oedipus has become our albatross. But *A Thousand Plateaus*, despite its apparent failure, moved us forward, at least we felt that way. It allowed us to broach unknown territory, untouched by Oedipus, which *Anti-Oedipus* had seen on the horizon.

The three major claims of *Anti-Oedipus* were the following:

1) The unconscious functions like a factory and not like a theatre (a question of production, and not of representation);

2) Delirium, or the novel, is world-historical and not familial (delirium is about races, tribes, continents, cultures, social position, etc.);

3) Universal history indeed exists, but it is a history of contingency (the flows which are the object of History are canalized through primitive codes, the over-coding of the despot, and the decoding of capitalism which makes possible the conjunction of independent flows).

The ambition of *Anti-Oedipus* was Kantian in spirit. We attempted a kind of *Critique of Pure Reason* for the unconscious: hence the determination of those syntheses proper to the unconscious; the unfolding of history as the functioning of these syntheses; and the denunciation of Oedipus as the "inevitable illusion" falsifying all historical production.

The ambition of *A Thousand Plateaus*, however, is post-Kantian in spirit (though still resolutely anti-Hegelian). The project is "constructivist." It is a theory of multiplicities for themselves, wherever the multiple reaches the state of a substantive, whereas *Anti-Oedipus* still examined the multiple in syntheses and as conditioned by the unconscious. In *A Thousand Plateaus*, our commentary on the Wolf-Man ("one or several wolves") waves good-bye to psychoanalysis and tries to show how multiplicities cannot be reduced to the distinction between the conscious and the unconscious, nature and history, body and soul. Multiplicities are reality itself. They do not presuppose unity of any kind, do not add up to a totality, and do not refer to a subject. Subjectivations, totalizations, and unifications are in fact processes which are produced and appear in multiplicities. The main features of multiplicities are: their elements, which are *singularities*; their relations, which are *becomings*; their events, which are *haecceities* (in other words, subjectless individuations); their space-time, which is *smooth* spaces and times; their model of actualization, which is the *rhizome* (as opposed to the tree as model); their plane of composition, which is a *plateau* (continuous zones of intensity); and the vectors which traverse them, constituting *territories* and degrees of *deterritorialization*.

In this light, universal history assumes a much greater variety. The question in each case is: *Where* and *how* does each encounter come about? We no longer have to follow, as in *Anti-Oedipus*, the traditional succession of Savages, Barbarians, and Civilized Peoples. Now we come face to face with coexisting formations of every sort: primitive groups, which operate through series, through an evaluation of the "last" term, in a bizarre marginality; despotic communities, which on the contrary constitute groups subjected to processes of centralization (apparatuses of State); nomadic war-machines, which will be unable to lay hold of the State without the State in turn appropriating a war-machine which it did not originally possess; the processes of subjectivation at work in State and warrior apparatuses; the convergence of these processes effected in capitalism and its corresponding States; the modalities of revolutionary action; and the comparative factors, in each case, of earth, territory, and deterritorialization.

In *A Thousand Plateaus*, we see these three factors playing freely, that is, esthetically, in the *ritornello*: little territorial songs, or the songs that birds sing; the great song of the earth, when the earth cries out; the powerful harmony of the spheres, or the voice of the cosmos... That, in any case, is what this book would have liked to do—to assemble ritornellos, *lieder*, corresponding to each plateau. For us, philosophy is nothing but music, from the most humble melody to the grandest of songs, a sort of cosmic *sprechgesang*. The owl of Minerva (to borrow from Hegel) has its screeches and its songs. The principles in philosophy are screeches, around which concepts develop their songs.

44

What is the Creative Act?

I would also like to ask a few questions of my own. Ask you a few and ask myself a few. They would be of the type: What do you do exactly, when you do cinema? And what do I do when I do or hope to do philosophy?

I could ask the question a different way. What does it mean to have an idea in cinema? If someone does or wants to do cinema, what does it mean to have an idea? What happens when you say: "Hey, I have an idea?" Because, on the one hand, everyone knows that having an idea is a rare event, it is a kind of celebration, not very common. And then, on the other hand, having an idea is not something general. No one has an idea in general. An idea—like the one who has the idea—is already dedicated to a particular field. Sometimes it is an idea in painting, or an idea in a novel, or an idea in philosophy or an idea in science. And obviously the same person won't have all of those ideas. Ideas have to be treated like potentials already *engaged* in one mode of expression or another and inseparable from the mode of expression, such that I cannot say that I have an idea in general. Depending on the techniques I am familiar with, I can have an idea in a certain domain, an idea in cinema or an idea in philosophy.

I'll go back to the principle that I do philosophy and you do cinema. Once that is settled, it would be too easy to say that since philosophy is ready to think about anything, why couldn't it think about cinema? A stupid question. Philosophy is not made to think about anything. Treating philosophy as the power to "think about" seems to be giving it a great deal, but it in fact takes everything away from it. No one needs philosophy to think. The only people capable of thinking effectively about cinema are the filmmakers and film critics or those who love cinema. Those people don't need philosophy to think about film. The idea that mathematicians need philosophy to think about mathematics is comical. If philosophy had to be used to think about something, it would have no reason to exist. If philosophy exists, it is because it has its own content.

It's very simple: philosophy is a discipline that is just as inventive, just as creative as any other discipline, and it consists in creating or inventing concepts. Concepts do not exist ready-made in a kind of heaven waiting for some philosopher to come grab them. Concepts have to be produced. Of course, you can't just make them like that. You don't say one day, "Hey, I am going to invent this concept," no more than a painter says "Hey, I'm going to make a painting like this" or a filmmaker, "Hey, I'm going to make this film!" There has to be a necessity, in philosophy and elsewhere; otherwise there is nothing. A creator is not a preacher working for the fun of it. A creator only does what he or she absolutely needs to do. It remains to be said that this necessity—which is a very complex thing, if it exists—means that a philosopher (and here I at least know what they deal with) proposes to invent, to create concepts and not to get involved with thinking, even about cinema.

I say that I do philosophy, that I try to invent concepts. If I ask, those of you who do cinema, what do you do? You do not invent concepts—that is not your concern—but blocks of movement / duration. Someone who makes a block of movement / duration might be doing cinema. This has nothing to do with invoking a story or rejecting it. Everything has a story. Philosophy also tells stories. Stories with concepts. Cinema tells stories with blocks of movement / duration. Painting invents an entirely different type of block. They are not blocks of concepts or blocks of movement / duration, but blocks of lines / colors. Music invents another type of blocks that are just as specific. And alongside all of that, science is no less creative. I do not see much opposition between the sciences and the arts.

If I ask scientists what they do, they also invent. They do not discover—discovery exists but that is not how we describe scientific activity as such—they create as much as an artist. It is not complicated, a scientist is someone who invents or creates functions. They are the only ones who do that. A scientist as a scientist has nothing to do with concepts. That is even why—thankfully—there is philosophy. There is, however, one thing a scientist knows how to do: invent and create functions. What is a function? A function occurs when there is a regulated correspondence between at least two sets. The basic notion of science—and not since yesterday but for a very long time—is the notion of the set. A set has nothing to do with a concept. As soon as you put sets into regulated correlation, you obtain functions and you can say, "I am doing science."

Anyone can speak to anybody else, a filmmaker can speak to a person of science, a person of science can have something to say to a philosopher, and vice versa, only in terms of and according to their own creative activity. They would not speak about creation—creation is something very solitary—but I do have something to say to someone else in the name of my creation. If I lined up all the disciplines that define themselves through creative activity, I would say that they have a common limit. The limit common to all of these series of inventions—inventions of functions, inventions of blocks of duration / movement, inventions of concepts—is space-time. All of these disciplines communicate at the level of something that never emerges for its own sake, but is engaged in every creative discipline: the formation of space-times.

In Bresson's films, as we all know, there are seldom complete spaces. They are spaces we could call disconnected. For example, there is a corner, the corner of a cell. Then we see another corner or part of the wall. Everything takes place as if Bressonian space was made up of a series of little pieces with no predetermined connection. There are some great filmmakers who, on the contrary, use whole spaces. I am not saying it is easier to manage a whole space. But Bresson's space is a distinct type of space. It has certainly been used again in a very creative way by others who renewed it. But Bresson was one of the first to make space with little disconnected pieces, little pieces with no predetermined connection. And I would add: at the limit of all of these attempts at creation are space-times. Only space-times. Bresson's blocks of duration / movement will tend towards this type of space among others.

The question then becomes what connects these little pieces of visual space if their connection is not predetermined. The hand connects them. This is not theory or philosophy. It cannot be deduced like that. I say that Bresson's type of space gives cinematographic value to the hand in the image. The links between the little bits of Bressonian space—due to the very fact that they are bits, disconnected pieces of space—can only be done manually. This explains the exhaustion of hands in his films. Bresson's block of expanse / movement thus has the hand as the particular character of this creator, this space, the hand that comes directly from them. Only the hand can effectively make connections between one part of space and another. Bresson is certainly the greatest filmmaker to have reintroduced tactile values into film. Not only because he knows how to take excellent shots of hands. He knows how to take excellent images of hands because he needs them. A creator is not someone who works for pleasure. A creator only does what he or she absolutely needs to do.

Again, having an idea in cinema is not the same thing as having an idea somewhere else. There are, however, ideas in cinema that could also work in other disciplines, could be wonderful in a novel, for example. But they would not have the same appearance at all. And ideas in cinema can only be cinematographic. No matter. Even if there are ideas in cinema that could work in a novel, the ideas are already engaged in a cinematographic process that makes them destined in advance for cinema. This is a way of asking a question that interests me: What makes a filmmaker truly want to adapt a novel, for example? It seems obvious to me that the reason is that he or she has ideas in cinema that resonate with what the novel presents as novel-ideas. Sometimes powerful encounters can occur. The problem is not the filmmaker adapting an eminently mediocre novel. He or she might need the so-so novel, and it does not mean the film will not be brilliant; it would be interesting to look at that problem. My question is different: What happens when the novel is an excellent novel and an affinity is revealed through which someone has an idea *in cinema* that corresponds to the idea *in the novel*?

One of the most beautiful examples is Kurosawa. Why is he so familiar with Shakespeare and Dostoyevsky? Why does it take a man from Japan to be so familiar with Shakespeare and Dostoyevsky? I will give an answer that may concern philosophy as well. Something rather curious often happens to Dostoyevsky's characters, something that can come from a minor detail. They are in general very troubled. A character leaves, goes down into the street and says, "Tanya, the woman I love, has called for my help. I must hurry; she will die if I do not go to her." He goes downstairs and meets a friend or sees a dying dog in the street and he forgets, he completely forgets Tanya is waiting for him. He forgets. He starts talking, meets another acquaintance, goes to have tea at his home and suddenly says again, "Tanya is waiting for me. I must go." What does that mean? Dostoyevsky's characters are constantly caught up in emergencies, and while they are caught up in these life-and-death emergencies, they know that there is a more urgent question—but they do not know what it is. That is what stops them. Everything happens as if in the worst emergencies—"Can't wait, I've got to go"—they said to themselves: "No, there is something more urgent. I am not budging until I know what it is." It's the Idiot. It's the Idiot's formula: "You know, there is a deeper problem. I am not sure what it is. But leave me alone. Let everything rot… this more urgent problem must be found." Kurosawa did not learn that from Dostoyevsky. All of Kurosawa's characters are like that. This is a felicitous encounter. Kurosawa can adapt Dostoyevsky at least because he can say: "I share a concern with him, a shared problem, this problem." Kurosawa's characters are in impossible situations, but hold on! there is a more urgent problem. And they have to know what that problem is. *Ikiru* may be the film that goes the farthest in this sense. But all of his films go in this direction. *The Seven Samurai*, for example. Kurosawa's entire space depends on it, a necessarily oval space drenched in rain. In *The Seven Samurai*, the characters are caught up in an urgent situation—they have accepted to defend the village—and from the beginning of the film to the end, a more profound question gnaws away at them. The question is formulated at the end of the film by the leader of the samurai as they leave: "What is a samurai? What is a samurai, not in general, but at this time?" Someone who no longer serves a purpose. The rulers do not need them and the peasants will soon learn to defend themselves. Throughout the film, despite the urgency of the situation, the samurai are haunted by this question, one worthy of the Idiot: we samurai, what are we?

An idea in cinema is of this type once it is engaged in a cinematographic process. Then you can say, "I have an idea" even if you borrow it from Dostoyevsky.

An idea is very simple. It is not a concept; it is not philosophy. Even if one may be able to draw a concept from every idea. I am thinking of Minnelli, who had an extraordinary idea about dreams. It is a simple idea—it can be said—and it is engaged in a cinematographic process in Minnelli's work. Minnelli's big idea about dreams is that they most of all concern those who are not dreaming. The dream of those who are dreaming concerns those who are not dreaming. Why does it concern them? Because as soon as someone else dreams, there is danger. People's dreams are always all-consuming and threaten to devour us. What other people dream is very dangerous. Dreams are a terrifying will to power. Each of us is more or less a victim of other people's dreams. Even the most graceful young woman is a horrific ravager, not because of her soul, but because of her dreams. Beware of the dreams of others, because if you are caught in their dream, you are done for.

A cinematographic idea is, for example, the famous dissociation of seeing and speaking in relatively recent films, be it—taking the most well-known—Syberberg, the Straubs, or Marguerite Duras. What do they have in common, and how is it a particularly cinematographic idea to disconnect sight from sound? Why couldn't it be done in the theater? It could at least be done, but if it is done in the theater, barring any exception and if theater found the means to do it, one could say the theater borrowed it from film. This is not necessarily a bad thing, but it is such a cinematographic idea to disconnect sight from sound, seeing from speaking, that it would be an exemplary response to what an idea is in cinema.

A voice is speaking about something. Someone is talking about something. At the same time, we are shown something else. And finally, what they are talking about is *under* what we are shown. This third point is very important. You can see how theater cannot follow here. The theater could take on the first two propositions: someone is telling us something, and we are shown something else. But having what someone is telling us be at the same time *under* what we are shown—which is necessary, otherwise the first two propositions would make no sense and be of little interest. We could put it another way: the words rise into the air as the ground we see drops further down. Or as these words rise into the air, what they are talking about goes underground.

What is it if only cinema can do it? I am not saying it has to do it, just that it has done it two or three times. I can simply say that great filmmakers had this idea. This is a cinematographic idea. It is exceptional because it ensures a veritable transformation of elements at the level of cinema, a cycle that suddenly makes cinema resonate with the qualitative physics of the elements. It produces a kind of transformation, a vast circulation of elements in cinema starting with air, earth, water and fire. Everything I am saying does not eliminate its history. The history of cinema is still there, but what strikes us is why this history is so interesting, unless it is because it has all of this behind it and with it. In the cycle I have just quickly defined—the voice rising while what the voice is talking about drops under the ground—you may have recognized most of the Straubs' films, the great cycle of the elements in their work. We only see the deserted ground, but this deserted ground seems heavy with what lies underneath it. You might ask: How do we know what lies underneath it? That is precisely what the voice is telling us. As if the earth were buckling from what the voice is telling us; it is that which comes to take its place underground when ready. If the voice speaks to us of corpses, of the lineage of corpses which comes to take its place underground at that moment, then the slightest whisper of wind on the deserted land, on the empty space that you have before your eyes, the smallest hollow in this earth will all take on meaning.

I consider that having an idea, in any case, is not on the order of communication. This is the point I was aiming for. Everything we are talking about is irreducible to any communication. This is not a problem. What does it mean? Primarily, communication is the transmission and propagation of information. What is information? It is not very complicated, everyone knows what it is. Information is a set of imperatives, slogans, directions—order-words. When you are informed, you are told what you are supposed to believe. In other words, informing means circulating an order-word. Police declarations are appropriately called communiqués. Information is communicated to us, they tell us what we are supposed to be ready to, or have to, or be held to believe. And not even believe, but pretend like we believe. We are not asked to believe but to behave as if we did. That is information, communication. And outside these orders and their transmission, there is no information, no communication. This is the same thing as saying that information is exactly the system of control. It is obvious and it particularly concerns us all today.

It is true we are entering a society that could be called a control society. A thinker like Michel Foucault analyzed two types of societies relatively close to ours. He called one type *sovereign society* and the other *disciplinary society*. He had the typical passage from a sovereign to a disciplinary society coincide with Napoleon. Disciplinary society was defined—Foucault's analyses have remained famous, and rightly so—by the establishment of areas of confinement: prisons, schools, workshops, hospitals. Disciplinary societies needed them. His analysis gave rise to ambiguous interpretations for some readers because they thought it was his final word. Obviously not. Foucault never believed it and clearly said that disciplinary societies were not eternal. He clearly thought that we were entering a new type of society. There have been, of course, various remnants of disciplinary societies for years, but we already know we are in societies of a different type that should be called, using Burroughs' term—and Foucault had a very deep admiration for Burroughs—control societies. We are entering control societies that are defined very differently than disciplinary societies. Those who are concerned about our welfare no longer need, or will no longer need, places of confinement. The prisons, schools and hospitals are already places of permanent discussion. Wouldn't it be better to expand home visits by doctors? Yes, that is certainly the future. Workshops and factories are bursting at the seams. Wouldn't it be better to use more sub-contracting and working from home? Aren't there other ways to punish people than prison?

Control societies will no longer pass through places of confinement. Even the schools. We should closely watch the themes that develop over the next forty or fifty years. They will explain how wonderful it would be to pursue both school and a profession. It would be interesting to see what the identity of schools and professions will become with constant training, which is our future. It will no longer entail gathering children in a place of confinement. Control is not discipline. You do not confine people with a highway. But by making highways, you multiply the means of control. I am not saying this is the only aim of highways, but people can travel infinitely and "freely" without being confined while being perfectly controlled. That is our future.

Let's say that is what information is, the controlled system of the order-words used in a given society. What does the work of art have to do with it? Let's not talk about works of art, but let's at least say that there is counter-information. In Hitler's time, the Jews arriving from Germany who were the first to tell us about the concentration camps were performing counter-information. We must realize that counter-information was never enough to do anything. No counter-information ever bothered Hitler. Except in one case. What case? This is what's important. Counter-information only becomes really effective when it is—and it is by nature—or becomes an act of resistance. An act of resistance is not information or counter-information. Counter-information is only effective when it becomes an act of resistance.

What relationship is there between the work of art and communication? None at all. A work of art is not an instrument of communication. A work of art has nothing to do with communication. A work of art does not contain the least bit of information. In contrast, there is a fundamental affinity between a work of art and an act of resistance. It has something to do with information and communication as an act of resistance. What is this mysterious relationship between a work of art and an act of resistance when the men and women who resist neither have the time nor sometimes the culture necessary to have the slightest connection with art? I do not know. Malraux developed an admirable philosophical concept. He said something very simple about art. He said it was the only thing that resists death. Let's go back to the beginning: What does someone who does philosophy do? They invent concepts. I think this is the start of an admirable philosophical concept. Think about it… what resists death? You only have to look at a statuette from three thousand years before the Common Era to see that Malraux's response is a pretty good one. We could then say, not as well, from the point of view that concerns us, that art resists, even if it is not the only thing that resists. Whence the close relationship between an act of resistance and a work of art. Every act of resistance is not a work of art, even though, in a certain way, it is. Every work of art is not an act of resistance, and yet, in a certain way, it is.

Take the case of the Straubs, for example, when they operate the disconnection of voice and visual image. They approach it in the following way: the voice rises, it rises, it rises and what it is talking about passes under the naked, deserted ground that the visual image was showing us, a visual image that had nothing to do with the sound image. What is this speech act rising in the air while its object passes underground? Resistance. Act of resistance. And in all of the Straubs' works, the speech act is an act of resistance. From *Moses* to the last Kafka including—I am not citing them in order—*Not Reconciled* or Bach. Bach's speech act is that his music is an act of resistance, an active struggle against the separation of the profane and the sacred. This act of resistance in the music ends with a cry. Just as there is a cry in *Wozzeck*, there is a cry in Bach: "Out! Out! Get out! I don't want to see you!" When the Straubs place an emphasis on this cry, on Bach's cry, or the cry of the old schizophrenic women in *Not Reconciled*, it has to account for a double aspect. The act of resistance has two faces. It is human and it is also the act of art. Only the act of resistance resists death, either as a work of art or as human struggle.

What relationship is there between human struggle and a work of art? The closest and for me the most mysterious relationship of all. Exactly what Paul Klee meant when he said: "You know, the people are missing." The people are missing and at the same time, they are not missing. The people are missing means that the fundamental affinity between a work of art and a people that does not yet exist is not, will never be clear. There is no work of art that does not call on a people who does not yet exist.

45

What Voice Brings to the Text

What does a text, especially a philosophical one, expect from an actor's voice? A philosophical text can of course take the form of a dialogue: concepts then correspond to the characters that support them. Yet more profoundly, philosophy is the art of inventing concepts themselves, creating the new concepts we need to think our world and our life. From this point of view, concepts have speed and slowness, movements, dynamics that expand and contract throughout the text. They no longer correspond to characters, but are characters themselves, rhythmic characters. They fulfill each other or separate, clash or hug like wrestlers or lovers. The actor's voice traces these rhythms, these movements of the mind in space and time. The actor is the operator of the text: he or she operates a dramatization of the concept, the most precise, the most sober and the most linear. Almost Chinese lines, vocal lines.

The voice reveals that concepts are not abstract. Concepts cut up and combine the things corresponding to them in various and always new ways. They cannot be distinguished from a way of perceiving things: a concept forces us to see things differently. A philosophical concept of space would be nothing if it did not give us a new perception of space. And concepts are also inseparable from affects, from new manners of seeing, an entire "pathos," joy and anger, that form the feelings of thought as such. This philosophical trinity—concept-percept-affect—animates the text. It is up to the actor's voice to bring forth the new perceptions and new affects that surround the read and spoken concept.

When the actor's voice is the voice of Alain Cuny… It may be the most beautiful contribution to a theater of reading.

One dreams of Spinoza's *Ethics* read by Alain Cuny. A voice carried by a wind driving the waves of demonstrations. The powerful slowness of the rhythm is broken here and there by unprecedented precipitation. Waves, but also lines of fire. From them rise all the perceptions through which Spinoza lets us grasp the world, and all the affects to grasp the soul. An immense slowness capable of measuring all the speeds of thought.

46

Correspondence with Dionys Mascolo

Paris, April 23, 1988

Dear Dionys Mascolo,

Thank you sincerely for sending me *Autour d'un effort de mémoire* [On an Effort of Memory]. I have read and reread it. Ever since I read *Le Communisme*,[1] I have thought you are one of the authors who has renewed most intensely the relationship between thought and life. You are able to define limit-situations by their internal repercussions. Everything you write seems to me to be of great importance, the highest rigor, and a sentence like this one "such an upheaval of general sensibility can only lead to new dispositions of thinking…"[3] seems to contain a kind of secret in its purity. Let me express my admiration, and, if you accept it, my friendship.

Gilles Deleuze

April 30, 1988

Dear Gilles Deleuze,

Your letter arrived yesterday.

Beyond the praise it contained, of which I cannot believe myself worthy, and not wishing merely to thank you for the generosity you displayed, I must tell you how much your words touched me. A truly happy moment, as well as a wonderful surprise, to see oneself not only approved, taken at one's word, but in a way *found out* or, precisely, surprised. This occurred in regards to the sentence you quoted (the one concerning the "upheaval of general sensibility") a sentence that, you say, may hold a secret. This led me (of course!) to ask myself: What could this secret be? And I would like to tell you in a few words the response that came to me.

It seems to me that this apparent secret is none other (but then there is always the risk of wanting to pull it from the shadows) than the secret of thought that is suspicious of thinking. Which is not without it own concerns. A secret—if its concerns do not lead it to seek refuge in shame or affected humor as sometimes happens—that can always be justified in principle. A secret without secrets, or without wanting secrets in any case. And such that if it is recognized (or is found again in another person), it is enough to serve as the basis for any possible friendship. I hope my hypothesis in response to what I sensed was a question is not too reductive.

I send you my regards, in a comraderie of thought, and my thanks.

Dionys

August 6, 1988

Dear Dionys Mascolo,

I wrote to you, a few months ago already, because I admired *Autour d'un effet de mémoire* and because I sensed a "secret" rarely found in a text. Your answer was very kind and thoughtful: if there is a secret, it is the secret of a thought that is suspicious of thinking, thus a "concern" that, if found in another person, is the basis for friendship. And now I am writing to you again, not to bother you or ask for another answer, but rather [to continue] a kind of muted, latent conversation that letters do not interrupt, or even like a an interior monologue about a book that continues to haunt me. Couldn't we reverse the order? Friendship comes first for you. Obviously friendship would not be a more or less favorable external circumstance, but, while remaining the most concrete, it would be an internal condition of thought as such. Not speaking with your friend or remembering him or her, etc., but on the contrary going through trials with that person like aphasia and amnesia that are necessary for any thinking. I no longer remember which German poet wrote of the twilight hour when one should be wary "*even of a friend.*"[3] One would go that far, to wariness of a friend, and all of that would, with friendship, put the "distress" in thought in an essential way.

I think there are many ways, in the authors I admire, to introduce concrete categories and situations as the condition of pure thought. Kierkegaard uses the fiancée and engagement. For Klossowski (and maybe Sartre in a different way), it is the couple. Proust uses jealous love because it constitutes thought and is connected to signs. For you and Blanchot, it is friendship. This implies a complete reevaluation of "philosophy," since you are the only ones to take the word *philos* literally. Not that you go back to Plato. The Platonic sense of the word is already extremely complex and has never been fully explained. Yet one can easily sense that your meaning is altogether different. *Philos* may have been displaced from Athens to Jerusalem, but it was also enhanced during the Resistance, from the network, which are affects of thought no less than historical and political situations. There is a sizeable history of *Philos* in philosophy of which you are already a part or, through all sorts of bifurcations, the modern representative. It is at the heart of philosophy, in the concrete presupposition (where personal history and singular thinking combine). These are my reasons for returning to your text, and to reiterate my admiration, but with a concern for not disturbing your own research. Very sincerely yours, and forgive such a long letter.

Gilles Deleuze

Paris, September 28, 1988

Dear Gilles Deleuze,

I found your letter and your book when I returned. Thank you.

I am deeply touched by your consideration. Despite the confidence I have in your judgment, it has left me, to be frank, somewhat embarrassed, I admit. My perhaps misguided shame would have prevented me from responding if you had not already given me a certain freedom in speaking of a *monologue*.

What I was trying to say, in response to your first letter (your remarks led to this situation), was that if there were any wariness in a thought towards thinking itself, an emergence of confidence (which is too much, but at least the temptation to lower one's guard) can only come with the *sharing of thought.* This sharing of thought must also take place on the basis of the same distrust or a similar "distress" to form a friendship. (What does it matter if one "agrees" with someone on different points if that person has such intellectual assurance that he or she remains at an infinite distance of sensibility? Thus the all too easily obtained and empty agreements in the dialogues where Socrates administers the truth).

You suggest a reversal of the proposition, making friendship come first. Friendship would then put the "distress" in thought. Once again due to distrust, but this time distrust of friends. But then where would this friendship come from? That is the mystery for me. And I cannot imagine what *distrust* (an occasional disagreement, of course, on the contrary—and in an entirely different sense that excludes *malevolence*) is possible of a friend once he or she has been accepted in friendship.

I have called this *communism of thought* in the past. And I placed it under the auspices of Hölderlin, who may have only fled thought because he was unable to live it: "The life of the spirit between friends, the thoughts that form in the exchange of words, by writing or in person, are necessary to those who seek. Without that, we are by our own hands outside thought." (I would like to add that Mr. Blanchot did this translation and it was published anonymously in *Comité,* in October 1968).

To you, with complete and grateful friendship. Forgive the elementary aspects of this response.

Dionys Mascolo

P.S.

In the end, I should have limited myself to saying: but what if friendship was precisely the possibility of sharing thought, from and in a common distrust with regards to thought? And what if thought that distrusted itself was the search for this sharing between friends? Something that is already happy no doubt seeks something else that can scarcely be named. Daring to say it would be an obscure will, the need to approach an innocence of thought. To follow this "erasure of the traces of original sin," the only progress possible according to Baudelaire.

Of course I say this with a little laugh. Your questions have pushed me to avow some half-thoughts—like when you come to take the acts accomplished in a dream as your own. Forgive me.

October 6, 1988

Dear Dionys Mascolo,

Thank you for your very rich letter. My question was: How can a friend, without losing his or her singularity, be inscribed as a condition of thought? Your response is very lovely. And it is a question of what we call and experience as *philosophy*. Asking more questions would only hold you back, and you have already given me so much.

With my respect and friendship.

Gilles Deleuze

47

Stones

Europe owes its Jews an infinite debt that Europe has not even begun to pay. Instead, an innocent people is being made to pay—the Palestinians.

The Zionists have constructed the state of Israel out of the recent past of their genocide, that unforgettable European horror, but also out of the suffering of this other people, using the stones of this other people. Irgun was labeled a terrorist organization not only because they bombed English neighborhoods, but also because they destroyed villages, killing innocent people.

The Americans have made a multi-billion dollar Western out of the whole affair. We are to believe that the State of Israel has been established in an empty land which has been awaiting the return of the ancient Hebrews for centuries. The ghosts of a few Arabs that are around, keeping watch over the sleepy stones, came from somewhere else. The Palestinians—tossed aside, forgotten—have been called on to recognize the right of Israel to exist, while the Israelis have continued to deny the fact of the existence of a Palestinian people.

From the beginning, the Palestinian people have carried out, on their own, a war which continues to this day in defense of *their* land, *their* stones, *their* way of life. No one mentions this *first* war since it is so crucial to have people believe that the Palestinians are Arabs from somewhere else, and who can go back. Who will disentangle all these Jordans? Who will speak up and say that the ties between a Palestinian and another Arab may be strong, but no stronger than those between two nations of Europe? And what Palestinian can forget what they have suffered at the hands of their Arab neighbors, not to mention those of the Israelis? What is the crux of this new debt? The Palestinians, chased from their land, have settled where they can at least keep this land in sight, preserving their vision of it as the last contact with their hallucinatory being. The Israelis never could chase them away, never completely erase them, cover them in the oblivion of night.

The destruction of villages, houses dynamited, expulsions, assassinations—a history of horrors has started anew, once again on the backs of the innocent. They say the Israeli secret service is the envy of the world. But what sort of a democracy is it whose politics are indistinguishable from the actions of its secret service? "They're all named Abu," declares an Israeli official after the assassination of Abu Jihad.[1] Does he recall the hideous sound of those voices that said: "They're all named Levy…"?

How will Israel succeed—with its annexed lands, its occupied territories, with its settlers and its settlements, with its lunatic rabbis? Through occupation, infinite occupation: the stones raining down on them come from within, they come from the Palestinian people, to remind us that there is a place in the world, no matter how confined, where the debt has been reversed. The stones thrown from the hands of the Palestinians are *their* stones, the living stones of their country. A debt cannot be paid with one, two, three, seven, ten murders a day, and it cannot be paid with third-party agreements. The third-party is ultimately nowhere to be found, every death calls out to the living, and the Palestinians have become part of the soul of Israel. The Palestinians sound the depths of that soul and torment it with their piercing stones.

48

Postscript to the American Edition: *A Return to Bergson*

A "return to Bergson" does not only mean renewed admiration for a major philosopher, but a relaying or extension of his enterprise today, taking into account the changes in life and society along with the changes in science. Bergson himself esteemed he had made metaphysics a rigorous discipline that could be continued along new paths that constantly appeared in the world. I believe that a return to Bergson understood in this way rests on three primary characteristics.

1) **Intuition:** Bergson did not conceive of intuition as an ineffable call, sentimental participation, or identical experience—but as a veritable method. This method first aims to determine the conditions of problems, to denounce false problems or poorly designed questions and discover the variables through which a problem should be stated as a problem. The means used by intuition are, on the one hand, sectioning or distributing reality in a given domain according to lines of different natures, and on the other hand, intersecting lines taken from various domains that converge together. This complex linear operation which involves sectioning along the articulations and intersecting along the convergences leads to the good posing of a problem, so much so that the solution itself depends on it.

2) Science and Metaphysics: Bergson did not content himself with critiquing science as if it had stopped with space, solids and fixity. He thought that the Absolute had two "halves" that were science and metaphysics. Thought divides itself into two paths in a single stroke: one side towards matter, its bodies and its movements, and the other towards the mind, its qualities and its changes. Thus starting in Ancient Greece, just as physics related movement to privileged moments and positions, metaphysics constituted transcendent, eternal forms as the source of these positions. But so-called modern science begins, on the contrary, when movement is related to "any instant": it calls for a new metaphysics that only considers immanent and constantly varying durations. Duration became the metaphysical counterpart of modern science for Bergson. We know he wrote the book *Duration and Simultaneity* where he confronted Einstein's relativity. The misunderstanding surrounding this book stems from the fact that some thought Bergson was trying to refute or correct Einstein. He was only trying to give the theory of relativity the metaphysics it lacked using new aspects of duration. In his masterwork, *Matter and Memory*, Bergson draws the conditions for a new metaphysics of memory from a scientific conception of the brain to which he contributed much of his own research. For Bergson, science is never "reductionist." It always calls for a metaphysics without which it would remain abstract, deprived of meaning or intuition. Continuing Bergson today means for example developing a metaphysical image of thought that corresponds to the new lines, openings, leaps and dynamics discovered by molecular biologists of the brain: new connections and re-connections in thought.

3) Multiplicities: In *Time and Free Will*, Bergson defines duration as a multiplicity, a type of multiplicity. This is a unique word since he changes multiple from a mere adjective to a veritable noun. By doing so, he condemns as a false problem the traditional theme of the one and the multiple. The word's origin is physico-mathematical (Riemann). It is hard to believe that Bergson did not know both its scientific origin and the novelty of its metaphysical use. Bergson concentrates on a distinction between two main types of multiplicities, the first discrete and discontinuous and the second continuous; the former spatial and the latter temporal; the former actual and the latter virtual. This is a fundamental motif in his confrontation with Einstein. Here again, Bergson aims to give multiplicities the metaphysics that their scientific treatment demands. His establishment of a logic of multiplicities may be one of the least known aspects of his thought.

Finding Bergson implies following and pursuing his approach in these three directions. One will note that phenomenology also presented these three motifs: intuition as a method, philosophy as a rigorous science, and new logic as a theory of multiplicities. It is true that these notions are understood very differently in each of the two cases. Convergence is nonetheless possible, as can be seen in psychiatry where bergsonism inspired Minkowski's work (*Le Temps vécu*)[1] and in phenomenology with Binswanger (*Le Cas Suzanne Urban*)[2] for an exploration of space-times in psychosis. Bergsonism makes the pathology of duration possible. In an exemplary article on paramnesia (false recognition), Bergson calls on metaphysics to show how memory does not form *after* present perception but is strictly contemporaneous, since duration is divided in each instant into two simultaneous tendencies, one towards the future and the other towards the past.[3] He also calls on psychology to show how an error of adaptation can cause memory to occupy the present as such. Scientific hypothesis and metaphysical thesis constantly combine for Bergson to trace a complete experience.

49

What is a *Dispositif*?

Foucault's philosophy is often presented as an analysis of concrete "*dispositifs*" or apparatuses. But what is an apparatus? First of all, it is a skein, a multilinear whole. It is composed of lines of different natures. The lines in the apparatus do not encircle or surround systems that are each homogenous in themselves, the object, the subject, language, etc., but follow directions, trace processes that are always out of balance, that sometimes move closer together and sometimes farther away. Each line is broken, subject to *changes in direction*, bifurcating and forked, and subjected to *derivations*. Visible objects, articulable utterances, forces in use, subjects in position are like vectors or tensors. Thus the three main instances Foucault successively distinguishes—Knowledge, Power and Subjectivity—by no means have contours that are defined once and for all but are chains of variables that are torn from each other. Foucault always finds a new dimension or a new line in a crisis. Great thinkers are somewhat seismic; they do not evolve but proceed by crises or quakes. Thinking in terms of moving lines was Herman Melville's operation: fishing lines, diving lines, dangerous, even deadly lines. There are lines of sedimentation, Foucault says, but also lines of "fissure" and "fracture." Untangling the lines of an apparatus means, in each case, preparing a map, a cartography, a survey of unexplored lands—this is what he calls "field work." One has to be positioned on the lines themselves; and these lines do not merely compose an apparatus but pass through it and carry it north to south, east to west or diagonally.

The first two dimensions of an apparatus or the ones that Foucault first extracted are the curves of visibility and the curves of utterance. Because apparatuses are like Raymond Roussel's machines, which Foucault also analyzed; they are machines that make one see and talk. Visibility does not refer to a general light that would illuminate preexisting objects; it is made up of lines of light that form variable figures inseparable from an apparatus. Each apparatus has its regimen of light, the way it falls, softens and spreads, distributing the visible and the invisible, generating or eliminating an object, which cannot exist without it. This is not only true of painting but of architecture as well: the "prison apparatus" as an optical machine for seeing without being seen. If there is a historicity of apparatuses, it is the historicity of regimes of light but also of regimes of utterances. Utterances in turn refer to the lines of enunciation where the differential positions of the elements of an utterance are distributed. And the curves themselves are utterances because enunciations are curves that distribute variables and a science at a given moment, or a literary genre or a state of laws or a social movement are precisely defined by the regimes of utterances they engender. They are neither subjects nor objects but regimes that must be defined for the visible and the utterable with their derivations, transformations, mutations. In each apparatus, the lines cross thresholds that make them either aesthetic, scientific, political, etc.

Thirdly, an apparatus contains lines of force. One might say that they move from one single point to another on the previous lines. In a way, they "rectify" the previous curves, draw tangents, surround the paths from one line to another, operate a to-and-fro from seeing to speaking and vice versa, acting like arrows that constantly mix words and things without ceasing to carry out their battles. A line of forces is produced "in every relationship between one point and another" and moves through every place in an apparatus. Invisible and unspeakable, this line is closely combined with the others but can be untangled. Foucault pulls this line and finds its trajectory in Roussel, Brisset and the painters Magritte and Rebeyrolle. It is the "dimension of power" and power is the third dimension of space, interior to the apparatus and variable with the apparatuses. Like power, it is composed with knowledge.

And finally, Foucault discovered lines of subjectivation. This new dimension has already given rise to so much misunderstanding that it is hard to specify its conditions. More than any other, this discovery came from a crisis in Foucault's thought, as if he needed to rework the map of apparatuses, find a new orientation for them to prevent them from closing up behind impenetrable lines of force imposing definitive contours. Leibniz expressed in exemplary fashion this state of crisis that restarts thought when it seems that everything is almost resolved: you think you have reached shore but are cast back out to sea. And as for Foucault, he sensed that the apparatuses he analyzed could not be circumscribed by an enveloping line without other vectors passing above and below: "crossing the line," he said, like "going to the other side"?[1] This going beyond the line of force is what happens when it bends back, starts meandering, goes underground or rather when force, instead of entering into a linear relationship with another force, turns back on itself, acts on itself or affects itself.

This dimension of the Self is not a preexisting determination that can be found ready-made. Here again, a line of subjectivation is a process, a production of subjectivity in an apparatus: it must be made to the extent that the apparatus allows it or makes it possible. It is a line of flight. It escapes the previous lines; it escapes *from them*. The Self is not knowledge or power. It is a process of individuation that effects groups or people and eludes both established lines of force and constituted knowledge. It is a kind of surplus value. Not every apparatus necessarily has it.

Foucault designates the apparatus of the Athenian city-state as the first place of creation of a subjectivation: according to his original definition, the city-state invents a line of forces that moves through the *rivalry between free men*. From this line on which a free man can have command over others, a very different line separates itself according to which the one who commands free men must also be master of himself. These optional rules for self-mastery constitute a subjectivation, an autonomous subjectivation, even if it is later called on to furnish new knowledge and inspire new powers. One might wonder whether lines of subjectivation are the extreme edge of an apparatus and whether they trace the passage from one apparatus to another: in this sense, they would prepare "lines of fracture." And no more than other lines, lines of subjectivation have no general formula. Cruelly interrupted, Foucault's research was going to show that processes of subjectivation eventually took on other modes than the Greek mode, for example in Christian apparatuses, modern societies, etc. Couldn't we cite apparatuses where subjectivation no longer goes through aristocratic life or the aestheticized existence of free men but through the marginalized existence of the "excluded"? The sinologist Tokei explains how freed slaves in a way lost their social status and found themselves relegated to an isolated, plaintive, *elegiac* existence from which they had to draw new forms of power and knowledge. The study of the variations in the processes of subjectivation seems to be one of the tasks Foucault left those who came after him. I believe this research will be extremely fruitful and the current endeavors towards a history of private life only partially overlap it. Sometimes the ones subjectivized are the nobles, the ones who say "we the good…" according to Nietzsche, but under other conditions the excluded, the bad, the sinners, or the hermits, or monastic communities, or heretics are subjectivized: an entire typology of subjective formations in changing apparatuses. And with combinations to be untangled everywhere: productions of subjectivity escaping the powers and knowledge of one apparatus to reinvest themselves in another through other forms to be created.

Apparatuses are therefore composed of lines of visibility, utterance, lines of force, lines of subjectivation, lines of cracking, breaking and ruptures that all intertwine and mix together and where some augment the others or elicit others through variations and even mutations of the assemblage. Two important consequences ensue for a philosophy of apparatuses. The first is the repudiation of universals. A universal explains nothing; it, on the other hand, must be explained. All of the lines are lines of variation that do not even have constant coordinates. The One, the Whole, the True, the object, the subject are not universals but singular processes of unification, totalization, verification, objectification, subjectivation immanent to an apparatus. Each apparatus is therefore a multiplicity where certain processes in becoming are operative and are distinct from those operating in another apparatus. This is how Foucault's philosophy is a pragmatism, a functionalism, a positivism, a pluralism. Reason may cause the greatest problem because processes of rationalization can operate on segments or regions of all the lines discussed so far. Foucault pays homage to Nietzsche for a historicity of reason. And he notes all of the importance of epistemological research on the various forms of rationality in knowledge (Koyré, Bachelard, Canguilhem), of socio-political research into the modes of rationality in power (Max Weber). Maybe he kept the third line for himself, the study of the types of "reasonable" in potential subjects. But he refused essentially to identify these processes in a Reason *par excellence.* He rejected any restoration of universals of reflection, communication or consensus. In this sense, one could say that his relationship with the Frankfurt School and the successors to this school are a long series of misunderstandings for which he is not responsible. And no more than there are universals of a founding subject or exemplary Reason that would allow judgment of apparatuses, there are no universals of the disaster of reason being alienated or collapsing once and for all. As Foucault told Gérard Raulet, there is not one bifurcation of reason; it constantly bifurcates, there are as many bifurcations and branches as instaurations, as many collapses as constructions following the cuts carried out by the apparatuses and "there is no meaning to the statement that reason is a long story that is now over."[2] From this point of view, the objection raised with Foucault of knowing how to assess the relative value of an apparatus if no transcendental values can be called on a universal coordinates is a question that could lead us backward and lose its meaning itself. Should one say that all apparatuses are equal (nihilism)? Thinkers like Spinoza and Nietzsche showed long ago that modes of existence had to be weighed according to immanent criteria, according to their content in "possibilities," freedom, creativity with no call to transcendental values. Foucault even alluded to "aesthetic" criteria, understood as life criteria, that substitute an immanent evaluation for a transcendental judgment every time. When we read Foucault's last books, we must do our best to understand the program he is offering his readers. An intrinsic aesthetics of modes of existence as the final dimension of apparatuses?

The second result of a philosophy of apparatuses is a change in orientation, turning away from the Eternal to apprehend the new. The new is not supposed to designate fashion, but on the contrary the variable creativity for the apparatuses: in conformance with the question that began to appear in the 20th century of how the production of something new in the world is possible. It is true that Foucault explicitly rejected the "originality" of an utterance as a non-pertinent, negligible criterion. He only wanted to consider the "regularity" of utterances. But what he meant by regularity was the slope of the curve passing through the singular points or the differential values of the group of utterances (he also defined the relationship of forces as distributions of singularities in a social field). By rejecting the originality of utterances, he meant that the potential contradiction of two utterances is not enough to distinguish them or to indicate the newness of one in relation to the other. What counts is the newness of the regime of enunciation itself in that it can include contradictory utterances. For example, we could ask what regime of utterances appeared with the French Revolution or the Russian Revolution: the newness of the regime counts more than the originality of the utterance. Each apparatus is thus defined by its content of newness and creativity, which at the same time indicates its ability to change or even to break for the sake of a future apparatus unless, on the contrary, there is an increase of force to the hardest, most rigid and solid lines. Since they escape the dimensions of knowledge and power, lines of subjectivation seem particularly apt to trace paths of creation, which are constantly aborted but also taken up again and modified until the old apparatus breaks. Foucault's as yet unpublished studies on the various Christian processes will certainly open many directions in this regard. One should not believe, however, that the production of subjectivity is left only to religion; anti-religious struggles are also creative, just as the regimes of light, enunciation and domination move through very diverse domains. Modern subjectivations resemble the Greek subjectivations no more than Christian ones; the same is true of light, utterances and powers.

We belong to these apparatuses and act in them. The newness of an apparatus in relation to those preceding it is what we call its currency, our currency. The new is the current. The current is not what we are but rather what we become, what we are in the process of becoming, in other words the Other, our becoming-other. In every apparatus, we have to distinguish between what we are (what we already no longer are) and what we are becoming: *the part of history, the part of currentness.* History is the archive, the design of what we are and cease being while the current is the sketch of what we will become. Thus history or the archive is also what separates us from ourselves, while the current is the Other with which we already coincide. Some have thought that Foucault was painting the portrait of modern societies as disciplinary apparatuses in opposition to the old apparatuses of sovereignty. This is not the case: the disciplines Foucault described are the history of what we are slowly ceasing to be and our current apparatus is taking shape in attitudes of open and constant *control* that are very different from the recent closed disciplines. Foucault agrees with Burroughs who announced that our future would be more controlled than disciplined. The question is not which is worse. Because we also call on productions of subjectivity capable of resisting this new domination and that are very different from the ones used in the past against the disciplines. A new light, new utterances, new power, new forms of subjectivation? In every apparatus we must untangle the lines of the recent past from the lines of the near future: the archive from the current, the part of history and the part of becoming, *the part of analysis and the part of diagnosis*. If Foucault is a great philosopher, it is because he used history for something else: like Nietzsche said, to act against time and thus on time in favor, I hope, of a time to come. What Foucault saw as the current or the new was what Nietzsche called the untimely, the "non-current," the becoming that splits away from history, the diagnosis that relays analysis on different paths. Not predicting, but being attentive to the unknown knocking at the door. Nothing reveals this better than a fundamental passage from *The Archeology of Knowledge* (II, 5) that applies to all his work:

> Analysis of the archive therefore includes a privileged area: it is both close to us and different from our current time. It is the edge of time that surrounds our present, overlooks it and indicates its alterity; the archive is what, outside of us, delimits us. The description of the archive unfolds its possibilities (and the mastery of its possibilities) starting with discourses that have just stopped being ours; its threshold of existence begins with the break that separates us from what we can no longer say and what falls outside

> our discursive practices; it begins with the outside of our own language; its place is the distance from our own discursive practices. In this sense it can serve as our diagnosis. Not because it would allow us to draw a portrait of our distinctive traits and sketch out in advance the aspect we will have in the future. But it releases us from our continuities; it dissipates the temporal identity where we like to look at ourselves to avoid the ruptures of history; it breaks the thread of transcendental teleologies; and while anthropological thought would examine the being of humans or their subjectivity, it exposes the other, the outside. Diagnosis in this sense does not establish the recognition of our identity through the play of distinctions. It establishes that we are difference, that our reason is the difference between discourses, our history the difference between times, our self the difference between masks.

The different lines of an apparatus are divided into two groups: lines of stratification or sedimentation, lines of actualization or creativity. The final result of this method concerns Foucault's entire work. In most of his books, he determines a specific archive with extremely new historical means, the General Hospital in the 17th century, the clinic in the 18th, prison in the 19th, subjectivity in ancient Greece and then in Christianity. But that is only half of his task. Out of a sense of rigor, to avoid confusing things and trusting in his readers, he does not formulate the other half. He only formulates it explicitly in the interviews given alongside the publication of his major works: What are madness, prison, sexuality today? What new modes of subjectivation do we see appearing today that are certainly not Greek or Christian? This last question haunted Foucault until the end (we who are no longer Greek nor even Christian...). Foucault attached so much importance to his interviews in France and even more so abroad, not because he liked interviews, but because in them he traced lines of actualization that required another mode of expression than the assimilable lines in his major books. The interviews are diagnoses. It is like for Nietzsche, whose works are difficult to read without the *Nachlass* that is contemporary to each. Foucault's complete works, as Defert and Ewald imagine them, cannot separate the books that have left such an impression on us from the interviews that lead us toward a future, toward a becoming: strata and currentness.

50

Response to a Question on the Subject

A philosophical concept fulfills one or more *Functions* in fields of thought that are themselves defined by internal variables. There are also external variables (states of things, moments of history) in a complex relationship with the *internal variables* and the functions. This means that a concept is not created and does not disappear at whim, but to the extent that new functions in new fields dismiss it relatively. That is also why it is never very interesting to criticize a concept: it is better to construct new functions and discover new fields that make the concept useless or inadequate.

The concept of the subject does not escape these rules. For a long time, it fulfilled two functions. First, it was a universalizing function, in a field where the universal was no longer represented by objective essences but by noetic or linguistic acts. In this sense, Hume marked a decisive moment in the philosophy of the subject because he referred to acts that went beyond the given (what happens when I say "always" or "necessary"?). The corresponding field, instead of being the field of knowledge, then becomes the field of "belief" as the new basis of knowledge: under what conditions is a belief legitimate, with which I say *more* than what I am given? Second, the subject fulfills a function of individuation in a field where the individual can no longer be a thing or a soul, but a person, a living and lived person, speaking and spoken to (I-You). Are these two aspects of the subject, the universal I and the individual me, necessarily connected? Even when connected, don't they conflict with each other? And how can this conflict be resolved? All of these questions sustain what has been called the philosophy of the subject in Hume, and also in Kant. Kant confronts an I as the determination of time with a Me determinable in time. Husserl asks similar questions in the last of his *Cartesian Meditations.*

Can one assign new functions and variables capable of bringing change? Functions of singularization have invaded the field of knowledge thanks to new variables of space-time. Singularity should not be understood as something opposing the universal but any element that can be extended to the proximity of another such that it may obtain a connection: a singularity in the mathematical sense. Knowledge and even belief thus tend to be replaced by notions like "assemblage" or "arrangement" that indicate a discharge and distribution of singularities. Discharges like this, of the "toss of the dice" type, form a transcendental field without a subject. The multiple becomes the noun, multiplicity, and philosophy becomes the theory of multiplicities that refer to no subject as a pre-established unit. Truth and falsehood no longer count; the singular and the regular, the remarkable and the ordinary replace them. The function of singularity replaces the function of universality (in a new field that has no need for universals). One can even see it in law: the legal notions of "case" or "jurisprudence" dismiss the universal in favor of emissions of singularities and functions of extension. A conception of law as founded on jurisprudence can do without any "subject" of rights. Conversely, a philosophy without the subject presents a conception of law founded on jurisprudence.

Correlatively perhaps, types of individuation that are no longer personal have imposed themselves. Some wonder what makes up the individuality of an event: *a* life, *a* season, a wind, a battle, five o'clock in the evening... One could call these individuations that do not constitute a person or an I haeccities or ecceities. And the question arises as to whether we are not haeccities like that instead of an I. Anglo-American literature and philosophy are particularly interesting in this regard because they have often distinguished themselves by being incapable of finding an assignable meaning for the word "I" other than a grammatical fiction. Events raise very complex questions of composition and decomposition, speed and slowness, longitude and latitude, power and affect. Counter to any psychological or linguistic personalism, they lead to promoting a third person and even a "fourth" person singular, the non-person or *It*, in which we recognize ourselves and our community better that in the empty I-You exchanges. We believe that the notion of the subject has lost much of its interest *in favor of pre-individual singularities and non-personal individuations.* Yet it is not enough to oppose concepts to learn which is the best, we must oppose the fields of problems to which they respond to discover what forces make the problems change and require the formation of new concepts. Nothing of what the major philosophers have written on the subject has aged, but that is why, thanks to them, we have new problems to discover instead of trying to "return," which only shows our inability to follow them. The situation of philosophy here is not fundamentally distinct from those of science and the arts.

51

Preface to the American Edition of *The Time-Image*

A revolution took place in philosophy over several centuries from the Greeks to Kant: the subordination of time to movement was reversed. Time ceased to be the measure of normal movement; it increasingly appeared for itself and created paradoxical movements. Time out of joint: Hamlet's phrase means that time is no longer subordinate to movement, but movement is subordinate to time. It is possible that cinema underwent the same experience, the same reversal for itself under faster conditions. The movement-image of so-called "classic" cinema was replaced after the war by a direct time-image. This general idea obviously must be nuanced, corrected and adapted to concrete examples.

Why does the war mark the break? Because in post-war Europe, the number of situations to which we did not know how to respond multiplied in spaces we no longer knew how to describe. They were "ordinary" spaces, populated deserts, abandoned warehouses, empty lots, cities demolished or being rebuilt. In these ordinary spaces, a new race of characters, almost mutant characters, began to act. In fact they saw more than they acted, they were Seers. Take the great Rossellini trilogy, *Europa '51*, *Stromboli*, *Germany Year Zero*: a child in a devastated city, a stranger on an island, a bourgeois woman who starts to "see" around her. The situations could be extreme or on the contrary the most banal and common, or both simultaneously: what begins to fall apart or disqualify itself is the sensory-movement schema that formed the action-image in earlier cinema. And because of this lapse in the sensory-motor connection, Time, "a bit of pure time," rises to the surface of the screen. Time stops following movement; it appears as itself and elicits *false-moves*. This leads to the importance of *false-links* in modern cinema. Images are no longer connected by rational cuts and links but reconnect through false-links or irrational cuts. Even the body is no longer exactly the motor, the subject of movement and instrument of the action. It starts to reveal time, to bear witness to time through fatigue and waiting (Antonioni).

It would not be precise to say that the cinematographic image is in the present. What the image "represents" is in the present but not the image itself, since it is always distinct from what it represents, in cinema as in painting. The image itself is the system of relationships between its elements, or a set of time relationships of which the variable present is only one result. This is what Tarkovsky meant, I think, when he challenged the distinction between editing and the shot, defining cinema as the "pressure of time" in a shot.[1] Exclusive to the image, when it is a creative image, is to make sensible and visible relationships of time that cannot be seen in the represented object and cannot be reduced to the present. Take Welles' depth of field or one of Visconti's tracking shots: they go farther into time than into space. Sandra's car at the beginning of Visconti's film is already moving in time and Welles' characters occupy a giant place in time instead of moving around in space.

This means that the time-image has nothing to do with a flashback or even a memory. Memory is only a former present whereas the amnesiac characters of modern cinema plunge literally into the past or emerge from it to show what is hidden even from memory.

A flashback is only a signpost and when it is used by the major filmmakers, it only serves to present much more complex temporal structures (for example, "bifurcating" time in Mankiewicz: recapturing the moment when time could have taken another direction...). In any case, what I call a temporal structure of direct time-image clearly goes beyond a purely empirical, past-present-future succession of time. There are, for example, a coexistence of distinct durations or levels of duration, since a single event can take part in several levels: layers of the past coexist in non-chronological order. We can see it in Welles in his powerful intuition of the Earth and in Resnais with the characters that return from the land of the dead.

There are many other temporal structures as well. The object of this book is to bring out those that cinematographic images have been able to capture and reveal and that can echo the teachings of science, the revelations of other arts or what philosophy helps us understand, each in complete independence. When someone speaks of the death of cinema, it is a mistake because cinema is only at the beginning of its research: to make visible the relationships of time that can only appear in the creation of the image. Cinema has no need for television, whose image sadly remains only in the present unless it borrows from the art of cinema. The relationships and disjunctions between sight and sound, between the seen and the spoken, continue to feed this problem and give cinema new powers to capture time in the image (in very different ways for Pierre Perrault, Straub, Syberberg...). Yes, cinema, unless violently destroyed, has retained all the power of a beginning. Conversely, we should already be looking to pre-war cinema and even silent films for the work of a very pure time-image that always penetrated, held or enveloped the movement-image: a still life by Ozu as *an immutable form of time? I would like to thank Robert Galeta for the care he put into his translation of this adventure in movement and time.*

52

Rivette's Three Circles

A first circle appears (or a segment of one). Let's call it A, since it is first to appear, though it never ceases throughout the film. This circle is an old theater, which serves as a school where some young women are rehearsing the roles they will play (Marivaux, Corneille, Racine) under the direction of Constance (Bulle Ogier). The difficult thing here is for the girls to express authentic feeling—anger, love, despair—with words that are not their own, but those of an author. This is the first sense of play: *Roles.*

One of the girls, Cécile, has left a house in the suburbs to four other girls. She has gone to live elsewhere with the man she loves. The four girls will live together in the house, where they will experience the repercussions of their roles, as well as end-of the-day moods and personal postures, the effects of their private love affairs (to which they only allude), and their various attitudes toward one another. It is almost as if the girls had bounced off the wall of the theater to lead a life which they vaguely share in the house, where bits of their roles are carried over, but spread out in their own lives, with each girl minding her own business. You no longer have a succession of roles governed by a program, but rather a haphazard chain of attitudes and postures following several simultaneous stories that do not intersect. This is the second sense of play: the

Attitudes and *Postures* in their interconnected day-to-day lives. What ceaselessly inspires Rivette is both the group of four girls and their individuation: comic and tragic types, melancholy and sanguine types, graceful and clumsy types, and above all *Lunar and Solar* types. This is the second circle, B, inside the first, since it partly depends on the first, by receiving its effects. But circle B distributes these effects in its own way, moving away from the theater only to return to it endlessly.

The four girls are pursued by a man whose identity is unclear—a con-artist, a spy, a cop—looking for Cécile's lover (probably a criminal). What's it all about? Stolen IDs, stolen art, arms trafficking, a judiciary scandal? The man is looking for the keys to a locked chest. He tries to seduce each of them in turn, and succeeds with one. The three other girls will try to kill him: the first will try theatrically; the second, coldly; and the third, impulsively. The third girl will in fact beat him to death with a cane. These three scenes are Rivette's greatest moments: absolutely beautiful. This is the third sense of play: *Masks*, in a political or police conspiracy that goes beyond us, which no one can escape, a kind of global conspiracy. This is the third circle, C, which has a complex relationship to the other two. It prolongs the second circle and is intimately intertwined with it, since it increasingly polarizes the girls' attitudes, providing them with a common measure as it casts its spell on them. But it also spreads out over the whole theater, covering it, perhaps uniting all the disparate pieces of an infinite repertoire. Constance, the director, seems to be an essential element in the conspiracy from the beginning. (Is there not a blank period in her life spanning several years? Does she ever leave the theater, where she hides Cécile's naughty boy, who is probably Constance's lover?) And what about the girls themselves? One girl has an American boyfriend with the same name as the cop; the other girl has the same name as her mysteriously missing sister; and the Portuguese girl, Lucia, who is the epitome of the Lunar type, all of a sudden finds the keys and possesses a painting which is probably real... In short, the three circles are interwoven, acting on one another, progressing through one another, and organizing one another without ever losing their mystery.

We are all rehearsing parts of which we are as yet unaware (our roles). We slip into characters which we do not master (our attitudes and postures). We serve a conspiracy of which we are completely oblivious (our masks). This is Rivette's vision of the world, it is uniquely his own. Rivette needs theater for cinema to exist: the young girls' attitudes and postures constitute a theatricality of cinema which, measured against the theatricality of theater, contrasts with it and emerges as perfectly distinct from it. And if the political, judicial, and police conspiracies weighing on us are enough to show that the real world has become a bad movie, then it is cinema's job to give us a piece of reality, a piece of the world. Rivette's project—a cinema that opposes its theatricality to that of theater, its reality to that of the world, which has become unreal—rescues cinema from the theater and the conspiracies threatening to destroy it.

If the three circles communicate, they do so in places which are Rivette's own, like the back of the theater, or the house in the suburbs. These are places where Nature does not live, but has survived with a strange grace: the undeveloped parts of a suburb, a rural stretch of city street, or secluded corners and alleyways. Fashion magazines have managed to make perfect, frozen pictures of these places, but everyone forgot that these places came from Rivette, having been impregnated with his dream. In these places conspiracies are hatched, young girls live together, and schools are established. But it is also in these places that the dreamer can still seize the day and the night, the sun and the moon, like *a great external Circle governing the other circles*, dividing up their light and their shadow.

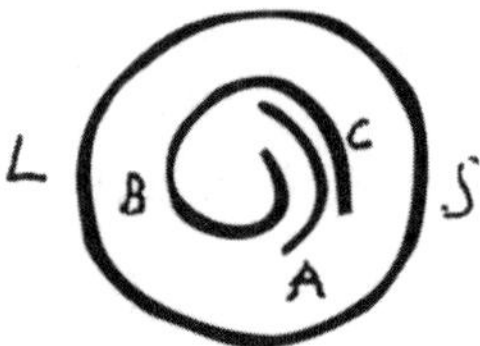

In a certain way, Rivette has never filmed anything else but light and its lunar (Lucia) and solar (Constance) transformations. Lucia and Constance are not persons, but forces. But this duality cannot be divided into good and evil. Hence Rivette ventures into those places where Nature has survived to verify the state in which the lunar and the solar subsist. Rivette's cinema has always been close to the poetry of Gérard Nerval, as though Rivette were possessed by him. Like Nerval, Rivette tours the remains of a hallucinatory Ile-de-France, tells the story of his own Daughters of Fire, and vaguely feels the conspiracy of an indeterminable madness approaching. It is not a question of influence. But this encounter makes Rivette one of the most inspired auteurs in cinema, and one of its great poets.

53

A Slippery Slope

LIBÉRATION: *Are you surprised by the scope of the debate surrounding the right to wear the Islamic veil in public school?*

Gilles Deleuze: The whole question of the veil, and the war raging at school over having a covered or uncovered head, has an irresistible absurdity to it. Not since Swift and the war fought between the partisans of cracking an egg from the larger end and their adversaries, have we seen such a motive for war. As usual, the spontaneous will of the young girls involved seems particularly reinforced by the pressure of parents who are anti-secular. We can't be sure that the young girls feel all that strongly about it. This is where it stops being funny.

Beyond the anecdotes, do you think the issue has potential consequences, do you think it merits serious consideration?

It's a matter of knowing just how far the Islamic associations want to take their demands. Will the second phase be to demand the right to Islamic prayer in the class room? And then will the third phase be to demand a reassessment of the literature taught in the class room, claiming that a text by Racine or Voltaire is an offense to Muslim dignity? So, it's important to find out just how far these

Islamic associations want to go, what exactly they reject or accept in secular public schools. Eventually, they should explicitly state their commitments on the matter. If it even needs to be said, there is a secular movement among the Arabs themselves. So there is no reason to believe that Arabs, or French citizens of Arab origin, have only religion at their disposal to construct an identity. Religions are worth much less than the nobility and the courage of the atheisms which they inspire.

You seem to see this issue as a religious assault on civil society.

Is this issue merely the first phase of a larger strategy? In the end, they could argue that since secular public schools cannot respect the rights of Muslims, the State must finance Koranic schools, just as it finances Christian schools. But I agree with those who oppose state financing of religious schools and who reject the reasons given in support of it, so I have no qualms about opposing any future financing of Koranic schools. An alliance among religious groups to impugn a hesitant secularism is not out of the question. Unless, of course, this is merely a skirmish over a veil.

54

Letter-Preface to Jean-Clet Martin

In reading your work, I am grateful for the care you have shown my own, and especially for the rigor and comprehension you bring to the task. I will try to provide answers to some of your remarks. Any difference between us is more often than not just a matter of words.

1. I believe in philosophy as system. The notion of system which I find unpleasant is one whose coordinates are the Identical, the Similar, and the Analogous. Leibniz was the first, I think, to identify system and philosophy. In the sense he gives the term, I am all in favor of it. Thus, questions that address "the death of philosophy" or "going beyond philosophy" have never inspired me. I consider myself a classic philosopher. For me, the system must not only be in perpetual heterogeneity, it must also be a *heterogenesis*, which as far as I can tell, has never been tried.

2. In this light, what you say about metaphor, or rather against metaphor, seems perfectly justified to me, and profound. I would only add something that does not in the least contradict what you say, but whose sense is somewhere in the neighborhood of your own: betrayal and double "appropriation" are operations which in

my view lay out a radical immanence. It is a layout of immanence—hence the essential relation to territory and *Earth*.

3. You have perfectly grasped the importance I assign to defining philosophy as the invention or the creation of concepts, in other words, as an activity that is neither reflective nor contemplative, but creative. I believe this has always been the case with philosophy, but I have not yet been able to express myself on the matter. This is why the next book I write will be a short text on the question: *What is philosophy?*

4. Similarly, you grasp the importance I assign to the notion of multiplicity: it is essential. As you say, multiplicity and singularity are intimately connected ("singularity" being at once different from "universal" and "individual"). "Rhizome" is the best term to designate multiplicities. On the other hand, it seems to me that I have totally abandoned the notion of simulacrum, which is all but worthless. *A Thousand Plateaus* is the book dedicated to multiplicities for themselves (becomings, lines, etc.).

5. Transcendental empiricism is meaningless indeed unless its conditions are specified. But the transcendental "field" must not be copied from the empirical, as in Kant. It must be explored on its own terms: "experienced" or "attempted" (but it is a very particular type of experience). This is the type of experience that enables the discovery of multiplicities, as well as an exercise of thought to which my third point refers.

6. Finally, I hope you will allow me one piece of advice: in the analysis of concepts, it is always better to begin with extremely

simple, concrete situations, not with philosophical antecedents, *not even with problems* as such (the one and the multiple, etc.). Take multiplicities, for example. You want to begin with questions such as what is a *pack*? (it is different from a lone animal), what is an *ossuary*? Or as you rightly ask: What is a *relic*? In the case of events: What is five o'clock in the evening? A possible critique of mimesis, for example, could be grasped in the concrete relationship between humans and animals. I have only one thing to tell you: stick to the concrete, and always return to it. Multiplicity, ritornello, sensation, etc., are all developed into pure concepts, but strictly speaking, they are inseparable from the passage from one concept to another. This is why we must avoid giving one term ascendancy over the others: every notion must drag in all the others, in its turn, and when the time is right [...]. The more gifted a philosopher is, I believe, the more he or she tends to leave the concrete behind, at least in the beginning. Resist this tendency, at least from time to time, just long enough to come back to perceptions, to affects, which will redouble your concepts.

Please forgive the immodesty of these remarks. I just wanted to be direct. I wish you all the best in your work.

55

Preface for the American Edition of *Empiricism and Subjectivity*

One sometimes dreams of a history of philosophy that would merely list the new concepts forged by a great philosopher, his or her most essential creative contribution. In Hume's case, one could say:

1) He imposed the concept of *belief* and used it to replace knowledge. He secularized belief by making knowledge a legitimate belief. He asked under what conditions a belief is legitimate and thereby started a theory of *probabilities*. The consequences are very important: if the act of thinking is belief, thought has to defend itself against *illusion* more than error. Illegitimate beliefs surround thought like a cloud of possibly inevitable illusions. Hume opens the way for Kant in this sense. And an entire art, all kinds of rules are needed to separate legitimate beliefs from the illusions accompanying them.

2) He gave *idea association* its true meaning, not as a theory of the human mind, but as a practice of cultural and *conventional* forms (conventional and not contractual). This is what the association of ideas is for Law, for Political Economy, for Aesthetics... There is the question, for example, of whether it is enough to shoot an arrow to a place to take possession of it or if one needs to touch it. The question involves the association between someone and some thing that would allow someone to own the thing.

3) He founded the first major logic of relation by showing that every *relationship* (not only "matters of fact" but relationships of ideas) was external to its terms. He thus developed an extremely diverse world of experience according to the principle of exteriority of relationships: atomic parts but with transitions, passages, "tendencies" that go from one to another. These tendencies produce *habits*. But isn't that the answer to the question: Who are we? We are habits, nothing but habits. The habit of saying Me... Maybe there is no more surprising response to the problem of the self.

One could continue this list; it is a testimony to Hume's genius.

56

Preface: A New Stylistics

This book originates in a reflection on both French and Italian literature. Its source is located somewhere on the border between the two countries, although its implications are far-reaching. Giorgio Passerone presents here not just a general treatise on style, but a study of certain procedures or operations in literature. These procedures and operations, with a little development, could very well migrate in changed form to other disciplines. But such a transformation is made much easier by Passerone's concentration on literature. The book is thus organized around two literary ideas. First, style is not a rhetorical phenomenon, but a syntactical production, a product of syntax and through syntax. One will therefore want to know how Passerone conceives of syntax, how his idea is different from Chomsky's idea. Second, following Proust's celebrated formulation, style is like a foreign language within the language. So one will also want to know how Passerone thinks about language, if Proust's statement is to be more than a simple metaphor, a mere rhetorical figure. On the contrary, one should take this idea literally.

In linguistics, a language at any particular moment is usually considered a homogeneous system, in or close to equilibrium. Passerone owes a greater debt to socio-linguistics, not because he invokes the action of external social factors, but because he treats each language as a heterogeneous group far from equilibrium and in perpetual bifurcation. Every language is a kind of Black or Chicano English. But we don't jump from language to language, the way bilingual or multilingual speakers do. Rather, there is always another language in every language ad infinitum. This is not a mixture, it is a heterogenesis. It is widely acknowledged that *free indirect discourse* (much richer in Italian, German, and Russian) is a unique syntactical form. It consists in slipping another expressing subject in a statement which already has an expressing subject. "I realized that she was about to leave. She would take every precaution to ensure that she was not followed…" The second "she" is a new expressing subject emerging in a statement that already has "I" as its expressing subject. It is almost as if every expressing subject contained others, each of which speaks a diverse language, the one in the other. Free indirect discourse led Bakhtin to his polyphonic or contrapuntal conception of language in the novel, and it also inspired Pasolini's reflection on poetry. But Passerone is not dabbling in theory: he goes directly to the great authors, from Dante to Gadda, to seize the procedure of free indirect discourse in practice. This procedure or operation can remain hidden in a language as uniform and centralized as French. However, it is coextensive with every language; it is the determinant element of syntax. Free indirect discourse carves out multiple languages that bifurcate from and resonate with one another. Even in French, Balzac splinters the language into as many languages as there are characters, types, and milieus. So much so that one might say: "There is no such thing as style." But this non-style is the grand style, the purest creation of style.

Linguists will object that, properly speaking, these are not languages. But we are always led back to the initial question: Is language a homogenous system, or a heterogeneous assemblage in perpetual disequilibrium? If the second hypothesis is right, a language cannot be broken down into its elements; it can be broken down into diverse languages ad infinitum; they are not foreign, style (or non-style) composes a foreign language in the language with them. Stylistics and pragmatics, which linguistics usually considers to be secondary determinations, now become primary factors in language. The same problem shows up elsewhere: linguistics examines constants and universals of language, elements and relations. But for Passerone and the theorists that inform his work, language has no constants, only variables. Style varies variables. Each style is a particular variation which must be concretely defined and understood. The profound and strange linguist Gustave Guillaume was the first to replace distinctive phonetic oppositions (constants) with the idea of differential morphemic positions: these are variable-points that run along a line or a determinable movement of thought. For example, the indefinite article 'a' is a variable that performs cuts or takes points of view on a movement of particularization. The definite article 'the' does the same sort of thing, this time for a movement of generalization. For verbs in general, Guillaume detected movements of incidence and decadence (and we could add "procadence"), with respect to which verb tenses are cuts, points of view, or differential positions. For example, Flaubert's use of the imperfect tense. Every verb undoubtedly contains dynamisms or special trajectories on which its tenses and modes set up positions and effect cuts. The variables thus traverse zones of variation which are finite or infinite, continuous or discontinuous, and which constitute style as a modulation of language.

Buffon's famous phrase, "style is the man himself," does not mean that style refers to the personality of the author. Buffon is an Arisotelian: style is the form actualized in linguistic material; it is a mold. But as Buffon's theory of organisms suggests, a mold has a paradoxical property. A mold does not just form the surface or outer layer; it informs the whole of whatever it forms ("an internal mold"). This is no mere mold, it is a modulation. In other words, it is a mold with a temporal transformation and an internal action. Using this notion of modulation, Passerone shows how a melodic conception of style develops: in the work of Rousseau, who sought to restore a monophonic practice of pure melody; but also in the Baroque, and later the Romantic eras, when polyphony and harmony, consonant and dissonant chords constitute an increasingly refined and autonomous modulation; and all the way down to the post-Romanticism of Nietzsche, perhaps the greatest philosopher-stylist. Here perhaps we have the secret of modulation: the way it traces a broken line in perpetual bifurcation, a rhythmic line, like a new dimension capable of engendering harmony and melody. These pages are Passarone's finest. Certainly, language brings something *before the eyes*, and what we *see* are figures of rhetoric. They are only the superficial effect of the polyphony of expressing subjects and the modulation of statements that constitute style. As Proust says, figures or metaphors are merely the grasping of different objects by and through "the necessary lenses of a beautiful style." Imagination relies heavily on syntax.

The variables of a language are like the positions or points of view on a movement of thought, a dynamism, a line. Each variable passes again and again through diverse positions on a line of particular modulation: hence the style composed of progression and repetition. Passerone analyzes three outstanding cases in French literature: the fold-line of Mallarmé, the unfolded line of Claudel, and the vibrating spiral-line of Artaud. Generally speaking, one can say that style *stretches* language, bringing into play genuine tensors headed toward the limit. This is because the line or movement of thought is, in each case, like the limit of every position of the variables being considered. This limit is not outside a particular language, nor language in general, but it is the outside of language itself. In the same way, when I say style is like a foreign language, it is none other than the language we speak—it is a foreign language *in* the language we speak. Stretched to its internal limit, toward this outside of language, language begins to stutter, to stammer, to scream, and to whisper. Again, but in another way, style appears as non-style and constitutes the madness of language, its delirium. Madelstan says: "A stuttering from birth weighs on me and many of my peers; we didn't learn how to talk, but how to babble, and it is only by lending an ear to the growing noise of the century, which like the foaming crest of a wave touched us, that we acquired a language of our own."[1] Is there a name for the line of this crest toward which the whole language is stretched in modulation? The closer language approaches it, the more "sober" style becomes—"non-style," as in Tolstoy or Beckett. The great writers do not appreciate compliments on their past or current work, because they know, and only they know, just how far they still are from what they desire, and what they seek. An "abstract line," says Céline, which has no contour or outline, but which can be found in any figure, provided the figure is unpacked, and the line extracted: "This famous line, which some find in nature, trees, flowers, Japanese mystery…"[2] Or else in a particular hour of the day (Lorca, Faulkner); or in an event that is about to happen, or is all the more expected for having already happened; or in a posture of the body, a movement in dance—the extension of language toward painting, toward music, but a music and a painting that are in language, that belong only to language.

Language as a heterogeneous group; free indirect discourse as coextensive with language; variables modulated and varied; the tensions or extensions that traverse a language; the abstract line as the outside or limit of language—I fear I may have made Passerone's book too abstract. It is for the reader to discover just how concrete the book is through the variable cases Passerone considers. It is indeed one of the newest, and one of the finest analyses of a difficult notion: style.

57

Preface: The Speeds of Time

Eric Alliez does not claim to explain conceptions of time or even analyze temporal structures. He writes of *conducts* of time. One might say that thought can only grasp time through several *speeds* that in fact form a conduct, as if one moved from one speed to another according to identifiable circumstances. Moreover, one moves from one conduct to another in various settings and at different periods that relate the time of history and the thought of time. In short, multiple conducts of time, each of which contains several speeds. In each conduct, some speeds become strange, deviant, almost pathological. But in the next conduct, they might become normal or find a new rhythm that was absent before. This introduction of profound rhythms into thought, in relation to things and societies, may be what inspired the work of Alliez. One has only to read, for example, the excellent pages analyzing the historical and noetic difference between Cosmos and Mundus.

Take a conduct of time as the number of the extensive movement of the world. It is obvious that speeds change depending on the mobile under consideration and the nature of the movement. The times will interlock between the original and the derived depending on the perfection of the mobile, the weight of its material, and the reducibility of its movement to circular compositions. There will also be a dislocation of times depending on whether the heavy materials encounter contingency or linear accident. An aberrant time may be undone to become more rectilinear, independent, abstracted from other speeds, and sometimes it may trip or fall. Hasn't meteorology introduced this time into things? And haven't money and "chrematistics" introduced this time into the community?

The world undoubtedly has a soul, and the soul is itself a world. But it takes a transformation of thought to define time as the integer of the intensive movement of the soul. It is a new conduct of time with different speeds. Original time refers to a synthesis performed by the soul that at every moment distinguishes present, past and future. This differentiation of time implies the dual movement of the soul leaning towards what comes after (procession) and turning back to what came before (conversion). The conduct is less the movement of a sphere than the tension of a spiral. One would say that time falls ideally, like light in a way (intensive quantity or zero distance from the moment), a fall that is constantly caught up in a return to the source. But the closer it comes to zero, the more the speed changes, the more the fall becomes real: a new aberrant time is formed where the spiral disappears in the foam, a time derived of distension that can no longer be converted.

Maybe we should reverse the order and start with the derivation to reach the original more closely by using a different conduct where the intensive becomes a kind of intentionality. This reintegrates aberration to the extent that sin founded a time of distension, diversion and redirection. The possibility of instituting an "intention" that returns to the original depends on new speeds that arrange the faculties of the soul and give them new rhythms: not only for memory, but for perception, imagination and understanding as well. What new aberration will ensue?

The history of philosophy is a spiritual voyage. The originality of Alliez's work is to mark the changes in conducts and speeds at each stage of the journey. The voyage has a provisional horizon: Kantian time. Not Kantian time as something predictable or as a goal, but more like a line that one can only see at first in fleeting bits and pieces revealing itself at the end. The pure line of time becomes independent.... Time shrugged off its dependency on any extensive movements, which is no longer the determination of an object but the description of space. We must precisely abstract from this space to discover time as a condition of action. Time equally does not depend on the intensive movement of the soul. On the contrary, the intensive production of a degree of consciousness in the moment depends on time. With Kant, time ceases to be original or derived to become the pure form of interiority that carves our selves, divides our selves at the expense of a vertiginous oscillation that forms time. The synthesis of time changes its meaning by establishing it as the unsurpassable aberration. "Time is out of joint": is this the rise of an urban, linear time that only refers to ordinary instants? Alliez never separates the processes of thought, things and societies (rural communities, commercial towns, empires, cities, states). Or things, societies and thoughts are caught up in processes without which conducts and speeds would remain arbitrary. The strength of his book is to discover and analyze these processes of extension, intensification, capitalization, subjectivation... that are the conditions of a history of time.

58

The Gulf War: a Despicable War

This war is despicable. Did the Americans really believe that they could carry out a quick and precise war with no innocent victims? Or did they use the UN as a screen to give themselves time to prepare and motivate public opinion for a war of extermination? Under the pretext of liberating Kuwait, then toppling Saddam Hussein (his regime and his army), the Americans are destroying a nation. Under the pretext of destroying strategic targets, they are killing civilians with mass bombardments; communications, bridges and roads are being destroyed far from the front; historical sites are menaced with destruction. The Pentagon is in command today. It is a branch of state terrorism testing its weapons. Concussion and fire bombs ignite the air and burn people deep in their shelters: they are chemical weapons ready for action.

Our government continues to contradict its own statements and is rushing deeper into a war that it had the power to oppose. Bush has thanked us as he would a faithful servant.

Our highest goal is to wage war well so we are given the right to participate in peace conferences.... Several journalists see themselves as soldiers for the United States and compete with enthusiastic and cynical declarations that no one asked of them. We have seen many people who do not want this war taken from them and who consider the hope of peace a disaster. The silence of most intellectuals is just as disturbing. Do they truly believe that UN approval legitimizes this war? Do they really buy the identification of Saddam Hussein with Hitler? Who believes in the newfound purity of Israel, which has suddenly discovered the merits of the UN, even while it considers any peace conference that would include the Palestinians the equivalent of the horrors of the Nazi's "final solution?" If this war is not stopped through efforts from which France is singularly absent, then not only is the servitude of the Middle East on the horizon, but so is the threat of American hegemony with no counterpart. If this war is not stopped, the complicity of Europe and, once again, a logic of socialist denial will weigh on the conscience of our own government.

59

We Invented the Ritornello

Didier Eribon: *Your definition of philosophy is rather offensive. Aren't you concerned about being criticized for maintaining, or restoring, the traditional privilege granted to philosophy?*

Gilles Deleuze: We can think of several less offensive definitions of philosophy: self-knowledge, wonder, reflection, right thinking... They are inoffensive because they're vague and don't define a definite occupation. We define philosophy as the creation of concepts. The burden is on us to show how science, for its part, works through functions instead of concepts. But philosophy gains no privilege from that. A concept is not superior to a function.

I asked you that question because you contrast philosophy with science and art, though not with the human sciences. The question of history, for example, is almost absent from your book.

We talk a lot about history. It's just that becoming is distinct from history. There are all sorts of correlations and echoes between them. Becoming begins in history and returns to it, but it is not of history. The opposite of history is not the eternal, but becoming. History examines certain functions according to which an event comes to pass. But in as much as the event surpasses its coming to pass, this is becoming as the substance of the concept. Becoming has always been the business of philosophy.

In the process of defining philosophy as the creation of concepts, you attack in particular the idea that philosophy is or should be "communication." Are you attacking Habermas and his theory of "communicative action"?

We're not attacking Habermas or anyone else. Habermas is not the only one who would like to index philosophy on communication. A kind of ethics of communication. Philosophy initially thought of itself as contemplation, and this idea gave us some splendid work, like Plotinus. Then it thought of itself as reflection, as in Kant's work. In both cases, however, a concept of contemplation or one of reflection had to be created. We're not so sure that communication has yet found a good concept, a truly critical concept. Neither "consensus" nor Rorty's "rules of democratic conversation" are enough to create a concept.

Contrary to this idea of communication, or the idea of philosophy as dialogue, you posit "the image of thought" which is then integrated into a much larger framework. This is what you call "geo-philosophy." Its chapter is at the heart of your book. It is at once a political philosophy and almost a philosophy of nature.

There are reasons why philosophy arises in the Greek city-states and continues in Western capitalist societies. But these reasons are contingent, and the principle of reason is one of contingent reason, not necessary reason. This is because these social formations are hotbeds of immanence, presenting themselves as a society of "friends" (competition, rivalry), and thus promoting opinion. These three fundamental traits only define the historical conditions of philosophy. Philosophy as becoming has a relation to them, but cannot be reduced to them. Its nature is other. It never stops questioning its own conditions. If the question of geo-philosophy is important, it is because thinking does not occur in the categories of subject and object, but in a variable relation to territory and to the earth.

In this "geophilosophy," you call out to the "revolutionary" philosopher and call on the necessity of "revolutions." This virtually revolutionary manifesto might seem paradoxical in the current climate.

The current political situation is very muddled. People tend to confuse the quest for freedom with the embrace of capitalism. It seems doubtful that the joys of capitalism are enough to liberate a people. The bloody failure of socialism is on everybody's lips, but no one sees capitalist globalization as a failure, in spite of the bloody inequalities that condition the market, and the populations who are excluded from it. The American Revolution failed long before the Soviet Revolution. Revolutionary situations and experiments are engendered by capitalism itself and show no signs of disappearing, unfortunately. Philosophy remains tied to a revolutionary becoming that has nothing to do with the history of revolutions.

One thing in particular struck me about your book: you say that the philosopher does not engage in discussion. His creative activity occurs only in isolation. This breaks radically with the traditional representations of the philosopher. Do you believe that the philosopher does not even engage in discussion with friends? What about readers?

It is already hard enough to understand what someone is trying to say. Discussion is just an exercise in narcissism where everyone takes turns showing off. Very quickly, you have no idea what is being discussed. But it is much more difficult to determine the problem to which a particular proposition responds. Now, if you understand the problem which someone has posed, you have no desire to discuss it: either you pose the same problem, or you decide to pose another problem and continue in that direction. How can you have a discussion without a common source of problems, but what is there to say when you share a common source of problems? You always get the solutions you deserve depending on the problems that have been posed. For indeterminate problems, discussion is just a waste of time. Conversation is something else entirely. We need conversation. But the lightest conversation is a great schizophrenic experiment happening between two individuals with common resources and a taste for ellipses and short-hand expressions. Conversation is full of long silences; it can give you ideas. But discussion has no place in the work of philosophy. The phrase "let's discuss it" is an act of terror.

In your estimation, what concepts have twentieth-century philosophers created?

Bergson uses the strange word "duration" because he doesn't want it to be confused with becoming. He creates a new concept. The same thing goes for memory, understood as the coexistence of sheets or layers of the past. Or the vital *élan*, which is his concept of differentiation. Heidegger creates a new concept of Being, whose two components are veiling and unveiling. Sometimes a concept requires a strange word, with crazy etymologies; and sometimes a contemporary word, but one with distant echoes. When Derrida writes "différance" with an 'a,' he is clearly proposing a new concept of difference. In his *Archeology of Knowledge*, Foucault creates a concept of utterance which is not to be confused with the concept of phrase, proposition, speech-act, etc. The primary feature of a concept is its novel redistribution of things.

And yourselves, do you think you have created any concepts?

How about the ritornello? We formulated a concept of the ritornello in philosophy.

60

For Félix

Right up until the end, my work with Félix was a source of discovery and joy. I do not wish to talk about the books we wrote together, but about the books he wrote on his own. I think they hold inexhaustible riches. They cover three domains and open paths of creation in each.

First, in the psychiatric domain, Félix introduced two main notions from the point of view of institutional analysis: group-subjects and (non-hierarchical) transversal relationships. As you can see, these notions are as political as they psychiatric. This is because madness as a psychotic reality is a power that immediately haunts the social and political arena: far from limiting itself to the father-mother of psychoanalysis, madness unmoors continents, races and tribes. It is both a pathological process to be treated and a factor of treatment to be politically determined.

Secondly, Félix may have been dreaming of a system composed of segments of science, philosophy, life-experience, art, etc.

Félix reached an unusual level that contained the possibility of scientific functions, philosophical concepts, life experiences and artistic creation. This possibility is homogenous while the possibles are heterogeneous. Thus the wonderful four-headed system in his *Cartographies*:[1] "Territories, flows, machines and universes." Finally, how could one not respond to his artistic analyses of Balthus and Fromanger, to his literary analyses, like the essential text on the role of the refrain in Proust (from the shouts of the shop keepers to the little phrase by Vinteuil), or to the poignant text on Genet and the *Prisoner of Love*?

Félix's work is waiting to be discovered or rediscovered. That is one of the best ways to keep Félix alive. Perhaps the most painful aspects of remembering a dead friend are the gestures and glances that still reach us, that still come to us long after he is gone. Félix's work gives new substance to these gestures and glances, like a new object capable of transmitting their power.

61

Immanence: a Life

What is a transcendental field? It can be distinguished from experience, to the extent that it does not refer to any object nor belong to any subject (empirical representation). It is thus given as pure a-subjective stream of consciousness, as pre-reflexive impersonal consciousness, or as the qualitative duration of consciousness without a self. One may find it odd that the transcendental be defined by such immediate givens, but transcendental empiricism is the term I will use to distinguish it from everything that makes up the world of subject and object. There is something raw and powerful in such a transcendental empiricism. It is certainly not the element of sensation (simple empiricism), because sensation merely cuts a slice in the continuous stream of absolute consciousness. Rather, it is the passage from one sensation to another, however close two sensations may be, but as becoming, as an increase or decrease in power (virtual quantity). Must the transcendental field then be defined by pure immediate consciousness with neither object nor self, as a movement which neither begins nor ends? (Even Spinoza's conception of this passage, or quantity of power, relies on consciousness).

But the relation of the transcendental field to consciousness is only conceptual. Consciousness becomes a fact only if a subject is produced simultaneously with its object, both outside the field, and both given as "transcendents." On the other hand, as long as consciousness traverses the transcendental field at an infinite speed everywhere diffused, consciousness can in no way be revealed.[1] In fact, consciousness expresses itself only by being reflected on a subject which refers it to its objects. This is why the transcendental field cannot be defined by the consciousness which is nonetheless coextensive with it, but which eludes revelation.

The transcendent is not the transcendental. Without a consciousness, the transcendental field could be defined as a pure plane of immanence, because it escapes all transcendence, both of the subject and of the object.[2] Absolute immanence is in itself: it is not in anything, nor can it be attributed *to* something; it does not depend on an object or belong to a subject. In Spinoza, immanence is not immanent *to* substance; on the contrary, substance and its modes are in immanence. Whenever immanence is attributed *to* subject and object, which themselves fall outside the plane, the subject being taken as universal, and the object as any object whatsoever, we witness a denaturing of the transcendental, which now merely presents a double of the empirical (this is what happens in Kant). And we witness a distortion of immanence, which is now contained in the transcendent. Immanence cannot be brought back to Some Thing as a unity superior to all things, nor to a Subject as an act that brings about a synthesis of things. Only when immanence is immanent to nothing except itself, can we speak of a plane of immanence. The transcendental field cannot be defined by consciousness any more than the plane of immanence can be defined by a Subject or an Object that is able to contain it.

We will say of pure immanence that it is A LIFE, and nothing more. It is not immanent to life, but the immanence that is in nothing else is itself a life. A life is the immanence of immanence, absolute immanence: it is complete power, complete beatitude. Fichte, to the extent that he overcomes the aporias of subject and object in his later philosophical works, presents the transcendental field as *a life*, which does not depend on a Being and is not subjected to an Act—an absolute immediate consciousness whose very activity does not refer to a being, but is ceaselessly grounded in a life.[3] The transcendental field thus becomes a genuine plane of immanence, reintroducing Spinozism into the most elemental operation of philosophy. Indeed, did not something similar happen to Maine de Biran in his "later philosophical project" (which was too exhausted to end well), when he discovered beneath the transcendence of effort *a life*, absolute and immanent? The transcendental field is defined by a plane of immanence, and the plane of immanence by a life.

What is immanence? A life... No one has described what a life is better than Charles Dickens, when he takes the indefinite article as an index of the transcendental. A scoundrel, a bad apple, held in contempt by everyone, is found on the point of death, and suddenly those charged with his care display an urgency, respect, and even love for the dying man's least sign of life. Everyone makes it his business to save him. As a result, the wicked man himself, in the depths of his coma, feels something soft and sweet penetrate his soul. But as he progresses back toward life, his benefactors turn cold, and he himself rediscovers his old vulgarity and meanness. Between his life and his death, there is a moment where *a life* is merely playing with death.[4] The life of the individual has given way to an impersonal and yet singular life, which foregrounds a pure event that has been liberated from the accidents of internal and external life, that is, from the subjectivity and the objectivity of what comes to pass: a "*homo tantum*" with whom everyone sympathizes and who attains a kind of beatitude; or an ecceity, which is no longer an individuation, but a singularization, a life of pure immanence, neutral, beyond good and evil, since only the subject that incarnated it in the midst of things made it good or bad. The life of such individuality is eclipsed by the singular immanent life of a man who no longer has a name, though he can be mistaken for no other. A singular essence, a life...

But a life should not have to be enclosed in the simple moment when individual life confronts universal death. *A life* is everywhere, in every moment which a living subject traverses and which is measured by the objects that have been experienced, an immanent life carrying along the events or singularities that are merely actualized in subjects and objects. This indefinite life does not itself have moments, however close they may be, but only between-times, between-moments. It does not arrive, it does not come after, but presents the immensity of an empty time where one sees the event to come and already past, in the absolute of an immediate consciousness. In his novels, Lernet-Holenia locates the event in an in-between time that can swallow up whole regiments. The singularities or the events which constitute *a life* coexist with the accidents of *the* life that corresponds to it, but they are not arranged and distributed in the same way. They relate to one another in a completely different way than individuals do. It even seems that a singular life can do without any individuality at all, even without any of the concomitants that individualize it. For example, infants all resemble one another and have hardly any individuality; but they do have singularities—a smile, a gesture, a grimace—such events are not subjective traits. Infants are traversed by an immanent life which is pure power, and even beatitude during moments of weakness or suffering. The indefinites of a life lose their indetermination to the extent that they occupy a plane of immanence, or what amounts to the same thing, to the extent that they constitute the elements of a transcendental field (individual life, however, remains inseparable from empirical determinations). The indefinite as such is not the mark of an empirical indetermination, but a determination of immanence or a transcendental determinability. The indefinite article is not the indetermination of the person without being the determination of the singular. The One (the 'a', the 'an') is not the transcendent which can contain even immanence, but the immanent contained in a transcendental field. 'A' or 'An' (one) is always the index of a multiplicity: an event, a singularity, a life… A transcendent can always be invoked which falls outside the plane of immanence, or which attributes the plane to itself. Nevertheless, all transcendence is constituted solely in the stream of immanent consciousness proper to the plane.[5] Transcendence is always a product of immanence.

A life contains only virtuals. It is composed of virtualities, events, singularities. What I am calling virtual is not something that lacks reality. Rather, the virtual becomes engaged in a process of actualization as it follows the plane which gives it its proper reality. The immanent event is actualized in a state of things and in a state of lived experience, and these states bring the event about. The plane of immanence itself is actualized in an Object and a Subject, to which it attributes itself. But, however separable an object and a subject may be from their actualization, the plane of immanence is itself virtual, in as much as the events that populate it are virtualities. Events or singularities impart to the plane their full virtuality, just as the plane of immanence gives virtual events their full reality. The event considered as non-actualized (indefinite) lacks nothing at all. It suffices to put the event in relation to its concomitants: a transcendental field, a plane of immanence, a life, a few singularities. A wound is incarnated or is actualized in a state of things and in lived experience. A wound itself, however, is a pure virtual on the plane of immanence which leads us to a life. My wound existed before me....[6] Not a transcendence of the wound as some higher actuality, but its immanence as a virtuality always within a milieu (a field or a plane). There is a big difference between the virtuals which define the immanence of the transcendental field, and the possible forms which actualize them and transform them into something transcendent.

Notes

1. Two Regimes of Madness

1. "On the Marionette Theater" in *Essays on Dolls* (London: Penguin/Syrens, 1994).

2. Bernard Schmitt, *Monnaie, salaries et profits* (Paris: PUF, 1996). Suzanne de Brunhoff, *L'Offre de monnaie (critique d'un concept)* (Paris: Maspero, 1971) and *Marx on Money* (New York: Urizen Books, 1976).

3. *On War* (Princeton: Princeton University Press, 1976), Book VIII, chapter 2.

4. In *Œuvres psychiatriques* (Paris: PUF, 1942) [new edition: Paris: Frénésie, 1987] 2 vol.

5. Cf. *The Metamorphosis, In the Penal Colony and Other Stories* (New York: Schocken Books, 1995).

2. Schizophrenia and Society

1. *The Empty Fortress* (New York: The Free Press, 1972).

2. Serge Leclaire, "La Réalité du désir" in *Sexualité humaine* (Paris: Aubier, 1970).

3. Antonin Artaud, in *84*, no. 5–6, 1948.

4. William S. Burroughs, *Naked Lunch* (New York: Grove Press, 2004).

5. Gisela Pankow, *L'homme et sa psychose* [Man and His Psychosis], coll. "La chair et l'esprit," IV,A (Paris: Aubier-Montaigne, 1969) 240.

6. Maud Mannoni, *Le Psychiatre, son fou et la psychanalyse* [The Psychoanalyst, His Madman and Psychoanalysis] (Paris: Seuil, 1970) 104.

7. Marcel Jaeger, "L'Underground de la folie" [The Madness Underground] in *Partisans*, February 1972.

3. Proust Round Table

1. For this question, Deleuze most often cites the work of Rémy Chauvin, *Entretien sur la sexualité* (Paris: Plon, 1969) p. 205.

5. Note for the Italian Edition of *The Logic of Sense*

1. The English of this quote is taken from Herbert Marshall's translation of Eisenstein's volume: *Nonindifferent Nature: Film and the Structure of Things* (Cambridge University Press, 1987), 244.

6. The Future of Linguistics

1. J.L. Dillard, *Black English* (New York: Random House, 1972).

7. Alain Roger's *Le Misogyne*

1. Gallimard, 1969.

2. See, in particular, *Visible et invisible* (Arcanes, 1953) and *Librement mécanique* (Minotaure, 1955).

8. Four Propositions on Psychoanalysis

1. French uses an infinitive where sometimes it makes more sense in English to use a present participle or gerund. Translators' note.

2. Robert Castel, *Le Psychanalysme* (Paris: Maspero, 1973).

3. David Cooper, *Death of the Family* (New York: Pantheon Books, 1971).

9. The Interpretation of Utterances

1. Cf. for example, Michèle Montrelay, *Recherches sur la féminité* in *Critiques.*

2. Bruno Bettleheim, *Symbolic Wounds: Puberty Rites and the Envious Male* (New York,: Collier Books, 1962).

3. These are the three errors found throughout the Freud's articles collected under the title *La Vie sexuelle*, Paris, PUF, 1969.

4. *Cinq psychanalyses*, Paris, PUF, 1954, p. 190.

5. *Ibid.*, p. 181.

6. *Ibid.*, p. 126.

7. Freud clearly has a premonition of what he is fighting against: he recognizes that the horse "represents the pleasure of movement" (p. 192) and that "Hans' imagination works under the sign of transportation" (p. 152). Freud makes maps, reproduces the topography, in other words he marks down the movements of deterritorialization and the libidinal lines of flight (like the house-street-warehouse map for Hans, p. 123–124; and the map for the Rat-Man, p. 237). But the program-drawing is immediately covered over by the fantasy-interpretation-reterritorialization system.

8. p. 107, 178, 182, 189.

9. Cf. among many other examples, the dialog between Hans and his father: "A little boy can think so.—That is not good, the father responds.—If he thinks it, it is still good enough for us to write it for the Professor."

10. Melanie Klein, *Narrative of a Child Analysis* (*The Writings of Melanie Klein*, vol. 4) (New York: The Free Press, 1984).

11. See the relevant passages on the school in Melanie Klein, *The Psychoanalysis of Children* (*The Writings of Melanie Klein*, vol. 2) (New York: The Free Press, 1984).

12. Melanie Klein substitutes the notion of organs without a body for the Organless Body due to her ignorance of the latter.

13. J. Hochmann et A. André, "Sur le 'Familiarisme,'" *Esprit,* Dec. 1972.

10. The Rise of the Social

1. For the formation of "bio-politics" or a power that proposes to control life, see Foucault, *The History of Sexuality,* vol. 1. (Vintage) And on the contract-tutelage relationship in this regard: Castel, *The Regulation of Madness: The Origins of Incarceration in France* (University of California Press).

2. IMP: Medical-Pedagogical Institute.

3. For example, in the case of delirium, civil or penal representatives accused psychiatry both of considering some people mad who "really" are not (President Schreber's case) and of not detecting in time those who are mad without seeming so (the cases of monomania or erotomania).

4. On the difference between norm and law, see Foucault, *History of Sexuality,* vol. 1

11. Desire and Pleasure

1. *D and P* for *Discipline and Punish* (New York: Pantheon Books, 1977).

2. *AK* for *The Archaeology of Knowledge* (New York: Pantheon Books, 1982).

3. *WK* for *The History of Sexuality: An Introduction* (*The Will to Knowledge*) (New York: Vintage, 1990).

4. "Interview with Lucette Finas" in *Michel Foucault: Power, Truth, Strategy* (Sydney: Feral Publications, 1979) p. 67–75. [Originally appeared as "Les Rapports de pouvoir passent à l'intérieur des corps", *La Quinzaine littéraire,* January 1–15, 1977.]

5. "The Political Function of the Intellectual" *Radical Philosophy* 17, Summer 1977, p. 12–14. [First appeared as "La Fonction politique de l'intellectuel" in *Politique Hebdo,* November 29–December 5, 1976].

6. Allusion to Deleuze, "Coldness and Cruelty" in *Masochism* (New York: Zone Books, 1991).

12. The Rich Jew

1. Interview with D. Schmidt, *Le Monde,* February 3, 1977.

13. On the New Philosophers (plus a More General Problem)

1. Bernard-Henri Levy, *Barbarism with a Human Face* (New York: Harper & Row, 1979).

2. Felix Guattari was one of the directors of CERFI (Centre d'Etudes de Recherche et de Formation Institutionelle / Study Center for Research and Institutional Preparation).

3. François Aubral and Xavier Delcourt, *Contre la nouvelle philosophie* (Gallimard, coll. 'Idées', 1977).

4. An allusion to the group that formed around the *Tel Quel* review, of which Philippe Sollers was one of the principle leaders.

14. Europe the Wrong Way

1. Andreas Baader and two other members of the "gang" killed themselves on October 18 in their cells under what some considered dubious circumstances.

2. Germany refused to extradite the criminal Kappler who returned to Germany after escaping Italy where he had been sentenced.

3. Hans Martin Schleyer was the president of German business leaders. He was kidnapped by members of the Red Army Fraction who demanded the liberation of ten members of their organization in exchange for his release. He was found dead on October 20.

17. Spoilers of Peace

1. This is an allusion to the major offensive begun a few weeks earlier by the Begin government in Southern Lebanon, in retaliation for a Palestinian commando raid to the north of Tel-Aviv which claimed several dozen lives. For the State of Israel, this offensive was the biggest ever in Lebanese territory, claiming hundreds of lives in the Palestinian camps and the Lebanese population, and provoking the exodus of tens of thousands of Lebanese civilians to the capitol. Despite its size, the Israeli offensive did not succeed in destroying the Palestinian military bases. The front remained open.

18. The Complaint and the Body

1. *Le Concept et la Violence* (Paris: 10/18, 1977); *Corps du vide et espace du séance* (Paris: Delarge, 1977).

20. Open Letter to Negri's Judges

1. The Reale law of 1975 introduced rules for exceptional cases into the Italian judiciary system. It notably introduced custody for an indeterminate period of time.

2. Piperno, then a member of the Autonomia Operaia (Workers' Autonomy), was arrested in Paris on September 18, 1978. Italian authorities requested his extradition for charges of "armed insurrection against the state."

3. Giulio Andreotti, frequent Prime Minister, was the leader of the Christian Democrats. Enrico Berlinguer was the general secretary of the Communist Party. He was one of the artisans of the "historic compromise" between the PCI and the Christian Democrats.

4. Reference to the Autonomia Operaia; Negri was one of its main leaders. It was a movement on the far left close to Marxism. Its theses took new forms of work and the struggle against work into account. See, for example, Deleuze-Guattari, *A Thousand Plateaus* (Minneapolis: University of Minnesota Press, 1987) p.469. Italian authorities and part of the Italian press saw the Red Brigades as the "armed wing" of Autonomia Operaia.

5. This accusation came from politicians on the left and the right following the "Call by French Intellectuals to Stop Repression in Italy" signed by Deleuze and Guattari in November 1977.

6. A vast international gathering in September 1977 against police repression in Italy. The new Italian left, most students and members of the Autonomia Operaia participated. (Guattari was present for the protests).

7. An anarchist thrown from the window of a Milan police station in December 1969. He was suspected of being linked to the deadly attack at the Piazza Fontant in Milan that took place a few days earlier (an attack by the neo-fascists with help from the Italian secret services that marked the beginning of the "strategy of tension.")

21. This Book Is Literal Proof of Innocence

1. Antonio Negri, *Marx Beyond Marx* (New York: Autonomedia, 1989).

2. "Special prison" is for white-collar criminals.

23. Painting Sets Writing Ablaze

1. David Sylvester, *Interviews with Francis Bacon: The Brutality of Fact* (New York: Thames & Hudson, 1988).

25. Preface to *The Savage Anomaly*

1. Eric Alliez, "Spinoza au-delà de Marx" [Spinoza Beyond Marx], *Critique*, Aug–Sept 1981, 411–412, p. 812–821, gives an excellent analysis of this antithesis.

26. The Indians of Palestine

1. Elias Sanbar, *Palestine 1948, l'expulsion* (Paris: Les Livres de la Revue d'Etudes Palestiniennes, 1983).

2. In *Revue des Etudes Palestiniennes*, 2, Winter 1982, p. 3–17.

3. Palestine was under a British military regime until 1921, when the League of Nations declared it a Trust Territory of Great Britain. The civil administration began in 1923 and lasted until May 15, 1948, when the British departed and the state of Israel was declared.

4. Ilan Halevi, *Question juive, la tribu, la loi, l'espace* (Paris: Editions de Minuit, 1981).

5. Boaz Evron, "Les interprétations de 'l'Holocaust:' Un danger pour le peuple juif," *Revue d'Etudes Palestiniennes*, no. 2, Winter 1982, 36–52.

31. Pacifism Today

1. The "double decision" is the simultaneous modernization and reinforcement of NATO's European installations (including the installation of Pershing missiles and ICBMs). This measure, adopted at the meeting of the member nations of NATO in 1979, was to be applied in April 1983 if negotiations with the Soviets should fail.

2. The interview was televised on 'Antenne 2' in the news journal "L'heure de vérité," November 16, 1983.

3. The Romanian government, concerned about its independence in foreign affairs, encouraged massive demonstrations that protested the installation of mid-range American nuclear missiles in Europe, as well as SS-20 Soviet missiles.

4. The November 24, 1961, resolution by the U.N. General Assembly concerns "the prohibition of nuclear and thermonuclear weapons."

5. This alludes to the initiative by Greek President Papandreou who started up "constructive" talks with Turkey, Bulgaria, Yugoslavia, and Romania to denuclearize the Balkans.

6. Edward Thompson is an English historian.

7. Cf. the note on the "double decision."

8. Schlesinger was Secretary of Defense in the Nixon administration.

9. Proektor is a Soviet military expert.

10. An allusion to the meeting of the European Council held in Athens on December 4–5, 1983, where no agreement was reached on budgetary questions or a common agricultural policy.

11. An allusion to André Glucksmann's book, *La Force du Vertige* (Paris: Grasset, 1983), which had appeared a few weeks earlier and dealt with these themes.

34. Michel Foucault's Main Concepts

1. *The History of Sexuality: The Use of Pleasure*, vol. 2 (New York: Vintage, 1990).

2. *Les Mots et les choses* (Paris: Gallimard, coll. 'Bibilothèques des sciences humaines,' 1966) 25, translated as *The Order of Things: An Archaeology of the Human Sciences* (New York: Random House, 1970).

3. *La Volonté de savoir* (Paris: Gallimard, coll. 'Bibliothèque des histoires,') 122, translated as *The History of Sexuality: An Introduction* (*The Will to Knowledge*) (New York: Vintage, 1990).

4. *Surveiller et punir* (Paris: Gallimard, coll. 'Bibliothèque des histoires,' 1975) 207, translated as *Discipline and Punish: The Birth of the Prison* (New York: Random House, 1977).

5. "Nietzsche, Genealogy, History" in *The Foucault Reader*, ed. P Rabinow (New York: Pantheon, 1984), pp. 76–100.

6. "The Thought of the Outside" in *Aesthetics, Method and Epistemology* (New York: The New Press, 1998).

7. The Nietzsche quote comes from *Daybreak*, § 130.

8. Tr. Note—*Une doublure* can refer to a double, replica, understudy, stand-in, stuntperson, or the lining of a piece of clothing.

9. *Histoire de la folie à l'âge classique* (Paris: Gallimard, 1972, reprint), p. 22, translated as *Madness and Civilization: A History of Insanity in the Age of Reason* (New York: Vintage, 1988).

10. *The Order of Things*, p. 322.

11. *The Use of Pleasure*, p. 76.

12. *Ibid.*, p..79.

35. Zones of Immanence

1. *La Philosophie de Nicolas de Cues* (Paris: Aubier, 1942).

2. *La Sagesse de Plotin* (Paris: Hachette, 1952).

3. Cf. "Approches de l'amitié" in *L'Existence* (Gallimard, 1946).

4. *Ainsi parlait Zarathoustra*, French trans by Maurice de Gandillac, in *Œuvres completes*, vol. VI (Paris: Gallimard, 1971).

36. He Was a Group Star

1. *La Naissance de l'histoire* (Paris: Editions de Minuit, 1961), new ed. 10/18, 1974.

2. *Les Années de démolition* (Paris: Ed. Hallier, 1975).

3. In *Questions, objections* (Paris: Denoël-Gonthier, 1979).

38. Foucault and Prison

1. The GIP (Groupe Information Prison) was created in February 1971 on the initiative of Daniel Defert and Michel Foucault. Their goal was to carry out "intolerance" surveys (secretly introduced into prisons by family members) to gather and reveal information on the living conditions of prisoners. By May, anonymous brochures were published detailing the survey results. For more on the history of the GIP, see the decisive *Groupe d'Information sur les Prisons, Archives d'une lutte 1970–1972* (Paris: Editions de l'IMEC, 2003).

2. QHS: Quartier Haute Sécurité [Maximum Security Area] used to isolate prisoners in cells under particularly inconvenient conditions.

3. George Jackson was an African-American militant held in San Quentin prison then in Soledad, where he was murdered in August 1971. Deleuze worked closely with members of the GIP on a special issue: *L'Assassinat de George Jackson* (Paris: Gallimard, coll. "L'Intolérable," 1971).

4. Serge Livrozet, *De la prison à la révolte* (Paris: Mercure de France, 1973).

39. The Brain Is The Screen

1. Michaux, *Les Grandes épreuves de l'esprit* (Paris: Gallimard, 1966) 33.

2. *Cahiers du cinéma*, no. 357, March 1984.

3. Tarkovsky, "De la figure cinématographique," *Positif*, no. 249, December 1981.

40. Occupy Without Counting: Boulez, Proust and Time

1. *Boulez on Music Today* (MT) (Cambridge: Harvard University Press, 1971). [Original French title: *Penser la musique aujourd'hui.*]

2. *Orientations: Collected Writings* (O) (Cambridge: Harvard University Press, 1986). [Original French title: *Points de repère.*] "Time Re-Searched."

3. On the diagonal and the block, see *Notes of an Apprenticeship* (NA) (New York: Random House, 1968) [Original French title: *Relevés d'apprenti*] in articles "Counterpoint" and "Webern." And MT: "I will have formed a block of duration and introduced a diagonal dimension that cannot combine with either the vertical or the horizontal." Also in O.

4. On Wagner, in O; on Webern in NA.

5. Cf. La Pléiade, I, p. 655. (the unity of the *Search* is always presented as a diagonal).

6. On cuts, striations and smoothness, see MT. It seems to me that both the distinction between irrational and rational cuts by Dedekind and the distinction between distances and sizes by Russell correspond to the difference between smooth and striated in Boulez.

7. MT: "in the serial system on the other hand, no function presents itself as identical from one series to another… an object composed of the same absolute elements can, through the evolution of their positioning, assume divergent functions."

8. MT: "when the cut is free to take place anywhere, the ear loses all orientation and any absolute knowledge of intervals, like the eye when it is forced to judge distances on an ideally smooth surface."

9. Cf. the essential article "The Musician's Writing: the Blind Man's Gaze?" in *Critique*, 408, May 1981. And on orientation in Wagner, O: "elements of fixation."

10. La Pléiade, III, p. 1048: Proust establishes an explicit distinction between this aspect of time and time regained, which is a different aspect. (On "utopia," Messiaen and Boulez, cf. O).

41. Preface to the American Edition of *Difference and Repetition*

1. *Proust et les signes* (Paris: PUF, 1970), translated as *Proust and Signs* (Minneapolis: University of Minnesota Press, 2004).

42. Preface to the American Edition of *Dialogues*

1. Tr. Note—In English in the original.

2. Henry Miller, *Hamlet Letters*, Vol. 1, with Michael Frankael (Santurce, Puerto Rico: Carrefour, 1939).

46. Correspondence with Dionys Mascolo

1. Dionys Mascolo, *Le Communisme* (Paris: Gallimard, 1953).

2. *Autour d'un effort de mémoire*, p. 20.

3. The poem in question is probably a poem by Eichendorff used in Schumann's Zwielicht lied (op. 39): "If you have a friend on earth, do not trust him in this hour; friendly might he seem in eye and mouth, yet he plans for war in deceitful peace." Deleuze and Guattari quote this lied in *A Thousand Plateaus* (Minneapolis: University of Minnesota Press, 1987), Chap. 11.

47. Stones

1. Close to Arafat, Abu Jihad was one of the founders of Fatah, a principal PLO deputy, and one of historical leaders of the Palestinian resistance. He played an important role as a political leader in the Intifada. He was assassinated in Tunis by Israeli special forces on April 16, 1989.

48. Postscript to the American Edition: *A Return to Bergson*

1. Eugène Minkowski, *Le Temps vécu* (Neuchâtel: Delachaux & Niestlé, 1968) [new ed PUF, 1995].

2. Ludwig Binswanger, *Le Cas Suzanne Urban* (Bruges: Desclée de Brower, 1957).

3. In *Mind-Energy: Lectures and Essays* (Westport, CT: Greenwood Press Reprint, 1977).

49. What is a Dispositif?

1. In "The Lives of Infamous Men," *Power: The Essential Works of Michel Foucault*, vol. 3 (New York: New Press, 2000).

2. In "Structuralism and Post-Structuralism" *Telos 55*, Spring 1983, p. 195–211.

51. Preface to the American Edition of *The Time-Image*

1. Tarkovsky, "De la figure cinématographique", *Positif*, 249, December 1981.

56. Preface: A New Stylistics

1. Mandelstam, *Le Bruit du temps* (Lausanne: L'Age d'Homme) 77.

2. In Marc Hanrez, *Céline* (Paris: Gallimard, 1969) 219.

60. For Félix

1. Félix Guattari, *Cartographies schizoanalytiques* (Paris: Galilée, 1989).

61. Immanence: a Life

1. Bergson, *Matter and Memory* (New York: Zone Books, 1988) 36: "as though we reflected back the light emanating from surfaces, a light which is self-propagating and does not need to be revealed."

2. Cf. Sartre, *La Transcendence de l'Ego* (Vrin): Sartre posits a subjectless transcendental field, which refers to an impersonal, absolute, immanent consciousness: with respect to this consciousness, the subject and the object are "transcendents." On James, cf. David Lapoujade's analysis, "Le Flux intensif de la conscience chez William James," *Philosophie*, no. 46, June 1995.

3. Cf. the second introduction to *Doctrine de la science*: "the intuition of pure activity which is nothing fixed, but is progress, not a being, but a life (p. 274, *Oeuvres choisies de philosophie première*, Vrin). On life according to Fichte, cf. *Initiation à la vie bienheureuse*, Aubier (and the commentary by Gueroult, p. 9).

4. Dickens, *Our Mutual Friend* (Oxford: Oxford University Press, 1989) III, ch. 3.

5. Even Husserl admits: "The being of the world is necessarily transcendent to consciousness, even in the originary evidence, and remains necessarily transcendent to it. But this does not change the fact that all transcendence is constituted solely in the life of consciousness, as inseparable linked to this life…." (Cartesian Meditations, Springer, 1999). This will be the starting point of Sartre's text.

6. Cf. Joë Bousquet, *Les Capitales* (Le Cercle du Livre).

Sources

1. Two Regimes of Madness
Translated by Hardwick Weston
Originally published in Armando Verdiglione, ed., *Psychanalyse et sémiotique* (Paris 10–18, 1975) 165–170. The talk was given in May 1974 during a conference in Milan organized by Armando Verdiglione. Deleuze's remarks immediately follow those of Guattari, whose talk was entitled "Sémiologies signifiantes et sémiologies asignifiantes." The discussion afterwards was not saved.

2. Schizophrenia and Society
Encylopaedia Universalis, vol. 14 (Paris: Encyclopaedia Universalis, 1975) 692–694. All references have been put in footnotes and completed.

3. Proust Round Table
Led by Serge Doubrovsky. Also present were: Roland Barthes, Gérard Genette, Jean Ricardou, Jean-Pierre Richard. *Cahiers Marcel Proust*, new series, 7, Paris, Gallimard, 1975, p. 87–116. The text was reviewed and edited by Jacques Bersani with the assent of the participants.

4. On the Vincennes Department of Psychoanalysis
With Jean-François Lyotard. In *Les Temps modernes*, 342, January, p. 862–863.

5. Note for the Italian Edition of *The Logic of Sense*
Originally published as "Nota dell'autore per l'edizione italiana" in Gilles Deleuze, *Logica del senso* (Milan Feltrinelli, 1976). Translated from the Italian by James Cascaito.

6. The Future of Linguistics
Preface to Henri Gobard, *L'Aliénation linguistique (analyse tétraglossique)* (Paris: Flammarion, 1976) 9–14. Linguist Henri Gobard was a teacher at Paris-VIII (Vincennes) in the English and Psychology departments.

7. Alain Roger's *Le Misogyne*

Originally appeared as "G. Deleuze fasciné par *Le Misogyne*" in *La Quinzaine littéraire*, no. 229, March 16–31, 1976, pp. 8–9. Alain Roger, *Le Misogyne* (Denoël, 1976). Born in 1936, Roger is a novelist and a philosopher who was a student in Orleans where Deleuze taught in the fifties. They always remained on friendly terms. This text was initially to serve as a preface for Roger's novel, but for technical reasons, editor Maurice Nadeau decided to print it in his literary review.

8. Four Propositions on Psychoanalysis

Deleuze-Guattari, *Psychanalyse et politique* (Alençon: Bibliothèque des mots perdus, 1977) 12–17. This and the following text were published together in a type-written brochure in part as a response to a pirated edition of the conference which Deleuze gave in Milan in 1973 (here in abridged form), and which appeared in *Psicanalisi e politica: Atti del convegno di studi tenuto a Milano l'8–9 maggio 1973*, ed. Armando Verdiglione (Milan: Feltrinelli, 1973) 7–11. Cf. "Five Propositions on Psychoanalysis" in *Desert Islands and Other Texts 1953–1974* (Semiotext(e), 2004), which derives from the Italian version.

9. The Interpretation of Utterances

With Félix Guattari, Claire Parnet, André Scala. In Deleuze-Guattari, *Psychanalyse et politique*, Alençon, Bibliothèque des mots perdus, 1977, p. 18–33. This text was published following the preceding one. It resulted from a seminar at the University of Vincennes. At the time, Claire Parnet and André Scala were students and friends of Deleuze. Some references have been completed.

10. The Rise of the Social

Postscript to Jacques Donzelot, *La Police des familles*, Paris, Editions de minuit, 1977, p. 213–220. [English translation: *The Policing of Families* (Baltimore: The Johns Hopkins University Press, 1997)].

11. Desire and Pleasure

Translated by Lysa Hochroth

Magazine littéraire, #325, October 1994, p. 59–65. The text was originally a letter addressed to Michel Foucault in 1977 after the publication of *La Volonté de savoir* [*The History of Sexuality*, vol. 1] (Paris: Gallimard, 1976). It is comprised of notes from A to H that Deleuze had François Ewald deliver to Foucault. According to Ewald's account that accompanied the notes, Deleuze wanted to extend the support of his friendship to Foucault, who was suffering a crisis during the publication of *The Will to Knowledge*. The notes are those of the *Magazine littéraire* with slight modifications

12. The Rich Jew

Originally published in *Le Monde*, February 18, 1976, p. 26, on Daniel Schmidt's film *L'Ombre des anges*. The Minister of Culture had prohibited the projection of several films in 1976, as well as Schmidt's film in 1977, and some fifty petitioners, including Deleuze, signed a declaration against "the irresponsibility of not analyzing the structure of a film" and "acts of violence which prohibit the viewing of a film."

13. On the New Philosophers (Plus a More General Problem)

On the New Philosophers (plus a More General Problem) An addition to *Minuit*, no. 24, May 1977. This text, dated June 5, 1977, was offered free of charge in bookstores where numerous polemical works, billed as "the new philosophy," were being distributed and sold.

14. Europe the Wrong Way

With Félix Guattari. *Le Monde*, November 2, 1977, p. 6. This article followed the request for the extradition of Klaus Croissant, lawyer for some members of the revolutionary terrorist group "Baader's group" (Red Army Fraction). Having taken refuge in France since July 10, Croissant was arrested in Paris on September 30. Rebmann, the prosecutor, accused him of "organizing the operational reserve of West German terrorism in his offices." His office was supposed to be "the place of residence for the preparation of attacks." Despite strong protests and marches in Germany, France and Italy, the Paris Court of Appeals pronounced in favor of extradition on November 16. Croissant was quickly extradited the next day.

15. Two Questions on Drugs

Editor's title: "Two Questions" in François Châtelet, Gilles Deleuze, Erik Genevois, Félix Guattari, Rudolf Ingold, Numa Musard, Claude Olivenstein, *...où il est question de la toxicomanie* [Where the Question is Drug Addiction] (Alençon: Bibliothèque des mots perdus, 1978).

16. Making Inaudible Forces Audible

Text distributed during a synthesis session at IRCAM in February 1978. The text here have been reworked.

17. Spoilers of Peace

First appeared in *Le Monde*, April 7, 1978.

18. The Complaint and the Body

First appeared in *Le Monde*, October 13, 1978, on the book by Pierre Fédida, *L'Absence* (Paris: Gallimard, 1978). Deleuze sat on the committee for Fédida's thesis, from which *L'Absence* resulted.

19. How Philosophy is Useful to Mathematicians or Musicians

A collective work published in collaboration with Jacqueline Brunet, Bernard Cassen, François Châtelet, Pierre Merlin, Madeleine Rebérioux: *Vincennes ou le désir d'apprendre*

[Vincennes or the Desire to Learn] (Paris: Editions Alain Moreau, 1979) 120–121. It was intended to defend the existence and the original project of the University of Vincennes, as the Minster of Education Edgar Faure had defined it. The existence of the university was threatened at the time by the government of Giscard d'Estaing, led by Alice Saunier-Seité with the active support of the mayor of Paris, Jacques Chirac.

20. Open Letter to Negri's Judges

"Lettera aperta ai giudici di Negri," *La Repubblica*, May 10, 1979, p. 1, 4.

Antonio Negri, an Italian philosopher born in 1933 and at the time a Political and Social Science professor at the University of Padua, fled to France to escape the attacks of the Italian magistrate. Invited by Louis Althusser to the Ecole normale supérieure, he presented a course on Marx's *Grundrisse* in 1977–78 (which led to the publication of *Marx Beyond Marx* (New York: Autonomedia, 1989)). During his stay in Paris, Negri notably became friends with Félix Guattari who, among others, kept Deleuze informed of the Italian political situation. Deleuze and Negri did not meet until 1987.

The "Aldo Moro Affair" began on March 16, 1978 with the kidnapping of the President of the Christian Democrats by the armed terrorist group the "Red Brigades." After a long confinement, Aldo Moro was killed on May 9, 1978. During the affair, the judge Galluci (a Christian Democrat) accused Negri of involvement on the basis of unfounded evidence. "Negri was arrested April 7, 1979, imprisoned, then taken to a "special prison" (the equivalent of the High Security sectors of French prisons). When Deleuze wrote this article, the trial had not yet started.

21. This Book is Literal Proof of Innocence

This article first appeared in *Le Matin de Paris*, December 13, 1979, p. 32. It is about Antonio Negri. See the introductory note for the preceding text.

22. Eight Years Later: 1980 Interview

This interview by Catherine Clément first appeared in L'Arc, no. 49 (1980) 99–102.

23. Painting Sets Writing Ablaze

An interview with Hervé Guibert for *Le Monde*, December 3, 1981, p. 15. It concerned the publication of *Francis Bacon: The Logic of Sensation* (Minneapolis: University of Minnesota Press, 2003, first published by Editions de La Différence, 1981).

24. *Manfred*: an Extraordinary Renewal

In Carmelo Bene, *Otello o la deficienza della donna* (Milan: Feltrinelli, 1981), p. 7–9.

The Italian version first appeared in the libretto accompanying the performance on October 1, 1981 at La Scala: *Manfred-Carmelo Bene* (Milan: Fonit Cetra, 1981). Italian translation by Jean-Paul Manganaro.

25. Preface to *The Savage Anomaly*

"Preface" in Toni Negri, *L'Anomalie sauvage: puissance et pouvoir chez Spinoza,* (Paris: PUF, 1982), p. 9–12. [*The Savage Anomaly: The Power of Spinoza's Metaphysics and Politics* (Minneapolis: University of Minnesota Press, 1991), trans. Michael Hardt].

For more on Toni Negri, see the presentation of text 18.

26. The Indians of Palestine

This interview with Elias Sanbar appeared in *Libération*, May 8–9 (1982): 20–21. Preceding this interview are a few words Deleuze wrote about the *Revue d'Etudes Palestiniennes*, created in October 1981, and whose objective was to analyze the factors responsible for the crisis in the Middle East: "For some time now we have been waiting for an Arab journal in French. We thought it would come from North Africa, but it turns out the Palestinians have done it first. Though clearly focused on Palestinian problems, this journal has two characteristics that should concern the Arab world as a whole. First, it contains in-depth socio-political analyses that display perfect self-control, in a cool-headed tone; second, it draws on a literary, historical and sociological "corpus" that is properly Arab, which is extremely rich and little known."

Elias Sanbar is a Palestinian writer born in 1947 and the editor-in-chief of the *Revue d'Etudes Palestiniennes*. He and Deleuze had been close friends since the late seventies.

27. Letter to Uno on Language

This letter is dated October 25, 1982. It was translated into Japanese by Kuniichi Uno, a student and translator of Deleuze, and published in *Gendai shisō* (The Journal of Contemporary Thought) Tokyo, Dec. (1982): 50–58.

28. Preface to the American Edition of *Nietzsche and Philosophy*

Editor's title. The type-written manuscript is entitled "Preface for the English Translation." Gilles Deleuze, *Nietzsche and Philosophy*, trans. Hugh Tomlinson (New York: Columbia University Press, 1983) ix–xiv.

29. Cinema-I, Premiere

Interview with Serge Daney, *Libération*, October 3, 1983, p. 30. For the publication of *Cinéma I—L'image-mouvement* (Paris: Editions de Minuit, 1983). [Published in English as *Cinema 1: The Movement-Image*, trans. by Hugh Tomlinson and Barbara Habberjam (The Athlone Press, 1986)].

30. Portrait of the Philosopher as a Moviegoer

This interview conducted by Hervé Guibert first appeared in *Le Monde*, October 6, 1983, p. 17, after the publication of *Cinéma I—L'image-mouvement* (Paris: Editions de Minuit, 1983). [Published in English as *Cinema 1: The Movement-Image*, trans. by Hugh Tomlinson and Barbara Habberjam (The Athlone Press, 1986)].

31. Pacifism Today

This discussion with Jean-Pierre Bamberger, recorded by Claire Parnet, was published in *Les Nouvelles Littéraires*, 15–21 December, 1983. Jean-Pierre Bamberger was a good friend of Deleuze. Having been trained in philosophy, he turned his attention to financial and economic problems from both a practical and a theoretical view, particularly problems related to the Third World such as the mutual commercial relations between these countries, e.g. Mozambique and Brazil.

This interview takes place just after the installation of the first Pershing missiles in Great Britain and West Germany in November 1982. NATO had decided in December 1979 to install these long-range missiles, aimed at strategic Soviet targets, in order to modernize and reinforce its European military installations against any Soviet aggression. This decision was presented as a strategic response to the deployment of Soviet SS-20 nuclear missiles in 1977.

At the same time, beginning in 1981, pacifist demonstrations were taking place in major European cities (Bonn, London, Madrid, Amsterdam, Paris) as well as in New York, protesting the renewal of the arms race.

32. May '68 Didn't Happen

Translated by Hardwick Weston

With Félix Guattari, *Les Nouvelles littéraires*, May 3–9, 1984, p. 75–76.

33. Letter to Uno: How Félix and I Worked Together

This letter is dated July 25, 1984. It was translated into Japanese by Kuniichi Uno and published in *Gendai shisō* (The Journal of Contemporary Thought) Tokyo, no. 9 (1984): 8–11.

34. Michel Foucault's Main Concepts

Written after the death of Foucault in 1984, this article appears to be a first version of what would later become *Foucault*. The type-written manuscript has editorial corrections, suggesting Deleuze's intention to publish it. The course Deleuze gave at Saint-Denis in 1985–1986, as well as the text he was working on at that time, finally discouraged him from publishing this article. The first few paragraphs show up in *Foucault*, though with substantial additions (cf. the chapter on strata, pp. 55–75). The rest of the article was left aside, except for a few passages here and there.

35. Zones of Immanence

Originally published in *L'Art des confins. Mélanges offerts à Maurice de Gandillac* (Paris: PUF, 1985) 79–81. Maurice de Gandillac was Deleuze's professor and eventually thesis director for his dissertation *Difference and Repetition*. Born in 1906, Gandillac was a professor at the Sorbonne from 1946–1977 and a specialist in Medieval thought, translating numerous philosophical texts from Latin and German. He was also the director of the International Cultural Center at Cerisy-la-Salle.

36. He Was a Group Star

Libération, December 27, 1985, p. 21–22.

The strong friendship between Deleuze and [François] Châtelet began when they were students at the Sorbonne. They formed a group including Jean-Pierre Bamberger, Michel Butor, Armand Gatti, Jacques Lanzmann, Michel Tournier, and Olivier Revault d'Allones among others. For more on this period, see the accounts by Michel Tournier, *Le vent Paraclet* (Paris: Gallimard, 1977) and François Châtelet, *Chronique des idées perdues*, (Paris: Stock, 1977). In 1969, Deleuze and Châtelet were reunited at the experimental branch of the University of Vincennes where Châtelet was chair of the Philosophy department.

37. Preface to the American Edition of *The Movement-Image*

Editor's title. This text was published with the title "Preface to the English Edition" in Gilles Deleuze, *Cinema 1- The Movement-Image*, trans. by Hugh Tomlinson and Barbara Habberjam (The Athlone Press, 1986).

38. Foucault and Prison

Editor's title. The text initially appeared with the title "The Intellectual and Politics: Foucault and the Prison," an interview by Paul Rabinow and Keith Gandal for *History of the Present*, 2, Spring 1986, p. 1–2, 20–21. Eng trans, Paul Rabinow. The version presented here was established from the transcription of the original recordings and sometimes differs from the [first] American presentation.

39. The Brain is the Screen

This text was first published in *Cahiers du cinéma* (no. 380, February 1986, 25–32). Revised by Deleuze, it derives from a round table discussion with Alain Bergala, Pascal Bonitzer, Marc Chevrie, Jean Narboni, Charles Tesson, and Serge Toubiana. The occasion was the release of Deleuze's *Cinema 2: The Time-Image* (Minneapolis: University of Minnesota Press, 1981).

40. Occupy Without Counting: Boulez, Proust and Time

Cf. Claude Samuel, editor, *Eclats/Boulez* (Paris: Centre Georges Pompidou, 1986), p.98–100.

41. Preface to the American Edition of *Difference and Repetition*

Editor's title. This text was published with the title "Preface to the English Edition" in Gilles Deleuze, *Difference and Repetition*, trans. Paul Patton (New York: Columbia University Press, 1994) ix–xiv. The typewritten manuscript is dated 1986.

42. Preface to the American Edition of *Dialogues*

Editor's title. First appeared as the "Preface to the English Language Edition" in Gilles Deleuze-Claire Parnet, *Dialogues* (New York: Columbia University Press, 1987), p. vii–x.

43. Preface to the Italian Edition of *A Thousand Plateaus*

Composed with Felix Guattari, this preface appeared in *Capitalismo e schizophrenia 2: Mille piani* (Roma: Bibliotheca bibliographia, 1987). Italian translation by Giorgio Passerone.

44. What is the Creative Act?

This text is the transcription of a filmed lecture given at the FEMIS film school on March 17, 1987 at the invitation of Jean Narboni. It was broadcast on FR3/Océaniques television on May 18, 1989. Charles Tesson, in consultation with Deleuze, made a partial transcription of the text that was published under the title "Avoir une idée en cinema" [To Have an Idea in Cinema] in a homage to the films of Jean-Marie Straub and Danièle Huillet (*Jean-Marie Straub, Danièle Huillet* (Aigremont: Editions Antigone, 1989), p. 63–77). The complete version of the lecture was published for the first time in *Trafic*, 27, Autumn 1998.

45. What Voice Brings to the Text

In *Théâtre National Populaire: Alain Cuny "Lire"* (Lyon: Théâtre National Populaire, November 1987).

46. Correspondence with Dionys Mascolo

"Correspondence Dionys Mascolo—Gilles Deleuze," Lignes, 33, March 1998, p. 222–226.

This brief exchange of letters followed the publication of Dionys Mascolo's (1916–1997) book, *Autour d'un effort de mémoire* (Paris: Maurice Nadeau, 1987). The work opens with a letter from Robert Antelme addressed to Mascolo, the first text he had the strength to write after his return from the Nazi camps.

47. Stones

The manuscript is dated June 1988. It was published in Arabic in the *Al-Karmel* review, no. 29, 1988, 27–28. Originally titled "De là où ils peuvent encore la voir" (From Where the Land Is Still Visible), this text was composed at the request of the editors of *Al-Karmel* just after the first Intifada in December 1987.

48. Postscript to the American Edition: *A Return to Bergson*

Editor's title. This text first appeared with the title "A Return to Bergson" in Gilles Deleuze, *Bergsonism* (New York: Zone Books, 1991), p. 115–118. Translated by Hugh Tomlinson. The type-written text, dated July 1988, bears the title "Postface pour *Le bergsonisme.*"

49. What is a Dispositif?

In *Michel Foucault philosophe. Rencontre internationale, Paris, 9, 10, 11 janvier 1988* (Paris: Le Seuil, 1989) p. 185–195. A partial version of this text first appeared in the

Magazine littéraire, 257, September 1988, p. 51–52. Living in seclusion since 1987, Deleuze's participation in this conference was his last public intervention. The record of the discussions—only presented in abbreviated form by the editor—is not included here.

50. Response to a Question on the Subject

The original typewritten text is dated February 1998. It first appeared in English in a translation by Julien Deleuze for the review *Topoï*, September 1988, p. 111–112 with the title "A philosophical concept..." before being retranslated for a French journal (the original text had at the time been lost).

51. Preface to the American Edition of *The Time-Image*

Editor's title. The manuscript is dated July 1988. First published as "Preface to the English Edition" in Gilles Deleuze, *Cinema 2: The Time-Image* (Minneapolis: University of Minnesota Press, 1989), p. xi–xii, translated by Hugh Tomlinson and Robert Galeta.

52. Rivette's Three Circles

The article originally appeared in *Cahiers du cinéma*, no. 416, Feb. 1989, 18–19. The film is Jacques Rivette's *La Bande des quatre* [The Gang of Four].

53. A Slippery Slope

Editor's title. "Gilles Deleuze craint l'engrenage" (Gilles Deleuze is wary of a slippery slope), *Libération*, October 26, 1989. The interviewer is Francis Zamponi. This article appeared after the debates, at the beginning of the school year, precipitated by the temporary suspension of young girls who refused to take off their "Islamic veil" during school hours.

54. Letter-Preface to Jean-Clet Martin

Editor's title. Orignally appeared as "Lettre-Préface de Gilles Deleuze" (Gille Deleuze's Letter-Preface) in Jean-Clet Martin, *Variations—La philosophie de Gilles Deleuze* (Paris: Payot & Rivages, 1993). The letter is dated June 13, 1990.

55. Preface to the American Edition of *Empiricism and Subjectivity*

Editor's title. First appeared, translated by Constantin V. Boundas, as "Preface to the English Language Edition" in Gilles Deleuze, *Empiricism and Subjectivity. An Essay on Hume's Theory of Human Nature* (New York: Columbia University Press, 1991), p. ix–x.

56. Preface: A New Stylistics

From Georgio Passerone, *La Linea astratta—Pragmatica dello stile* (Milano: Edizioni Angelo Guerini, 1991). The French manuscript, translated by Giorgio Passerone himself, is dated September 1990. Passerone, a young Italian researcher, took courses from

Deleuze at Vincennes and later Saint-Denis in the late seventies. Passerone was a friend of Deleuze and translated *A Thousand Plateaus* into Italian. *La Linea astratta* is taken essentially from the thesis which Passerone defended at Paris-VIII under the direction of Deleuze and René Scherer.

57. Preface: The Speeds of Time

Editor's title. "Preface" in Eric Alliez, *Les Temps capitaux, Récits de la conquête du temps* (Paris: Editions du Cerf, 1991). Translated into English as *Capital Times: Tales of the Conquest of Time* (Minneapolis: University of Minnesota Press, 1996). Born in 1957, Guattari's friend and Deleuze's student, Eric Alliez defended his doctoral dissertation at the University of Paris-VIII with Deleuze as his advisor. *Capital Times* reproduces the main points of his thesis.

58. The Gulf War: a Despicable War

With René Scherer in "La Guerre immonde," *Libération*, March 4, 1991, p. 11. They are referring to the first Gulf War launched by the United States against Iraq on January 16, 1991.

59. We Invented the Ritornello

Conducted by Didier Eribon, this interview with Deleuze and Guattari first appeared in *Le Nouvel Observateur*, September 1991, p. 109–110, for the publication of *Qu'est-ce que la philosophie?* (Paris: Editions de minuit, 1991), published in English as *What is Philosophy?*, trans. by Hugh Tomlinson and Graham Burchell (New York: Columbia University Press, 1994).

60. For Félix

Chimères, Winter 1992–93, p. 209–210. This text was composed after the death of Félix Guattari on August 29, 1992.

61. Immanence: a Life

Originally appeared in *Philosophie* no. 47 (1995): 3–7. This is the last text Deleuze published before he killed himself on November 4, 1995. The companion piece to this text appeared in the annex of the second edition of *Dialogues* (with Claire Parnet). Both belong to a project entitled "Ensembles and Multiplicities." Deleuze wanted to flesh out the concept of the virtual which he felt he had left relatively unexplored.

Index

Gilles Deleuze in Big Sur. © Jean Jacques Lebel

Other Semiotexte Titles by Gilles Deleuze

Nomadology: The War Machine (with Félix Guattari)

On The Line (with Félix Guattari)

Desert Islands and Other Texts 1953-1974